Links In Rebecca's Life, By Pansy...

Isabella Alden

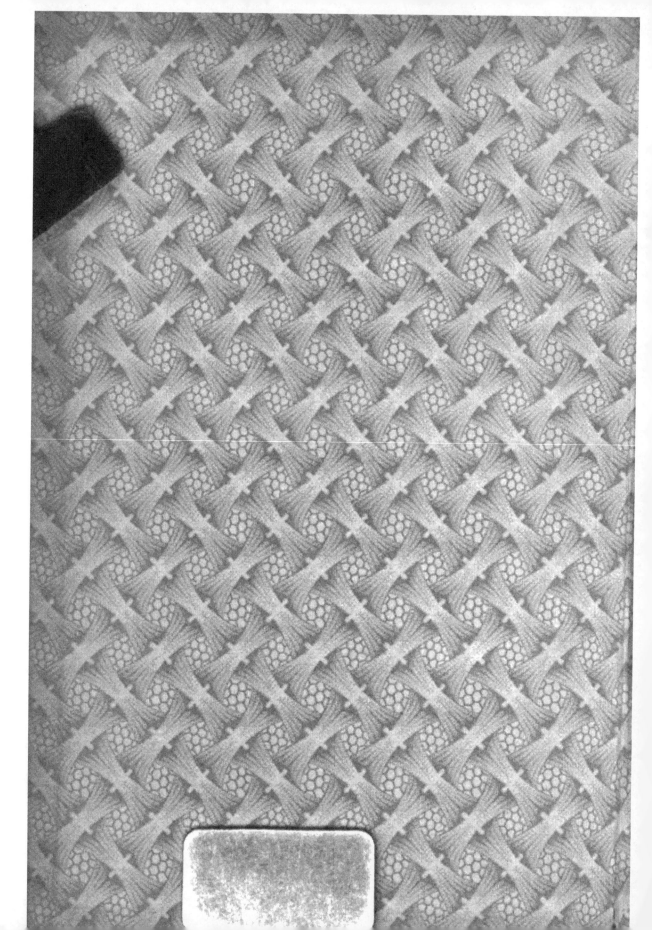

"Her eyes rested on these familiar words."   Page 10.

LINKS IN REBECCA'S LIFE.

BY

PANSY.

London:
HODDER AND STOUGHTON,
27, PATERNOSTER ROW.

MDCCCLXXXII.

Reprinted from American plates by special arrangement.

Hazell, Watson, and Viney, Printers, London and Aylesbury.

CONTENTS.

CHAPTER.   PAGE.

1.—How She Worked Out The Lesson   .   7

2.—Sparing Sallie   16

3.—A "Word in Season"   31

4.—Rebecca as a Witness   44

5.—New Found Relatives   58

6.—She Divides The Work   71

7.—Rebecca in The Temple   84

8.—Looking Ahead   101

9.—On a Visit   117

10.— "Breathing Out Threatenings"   .   .   145

11.—Rebecca Being Led   164

12.—Mrs. Frank Edwards at Home   .   .   .   184

13.—Halting Between Two Opinions   .   .   202

14.—Mrs. Frank Edwards Being Advised   .   218

v

15.—THE CLEANSING BLOOD 234

16.—MANAGING JONAH 250

17.—TRYING TO WORK IN LOVE 266

18.—PLANNING WORK 282

19.—SEEKING AN OPEN DOOR 298

20.—SHE FALLS IN WITH A NEW GOSPEL . . 314

21.—SHE HAS A CHANCE TO BE STRONG . . 330

22.—A CONSCIENCE NOT VOID OF OFFENSE . 345

23.—NEW VIEWS OF THINGS 364

24.—BEING "ALL THINGS TO ALL MEN" . . 377

25.—TWO WAYS OF DOING THINGS 391

26.—"PEACE ON EARTH, GOOD WILL TO MEN" 407

LINKS IN REBECCA'S LIFE.

CHAPTER I.

HOW SHE WORKED OUT THE LESSON.

SHE was in the parlor; the windows were open, and little whirls of snowflakes were dancing through the room every now and then. The process of sweeping was over, and now the dusting was going on. That means taking an old gray or brown rag and dashing upon the dust that had dared to settle, and sending it in dizzy whirls again through the room.

This work Rebecca was doing faithfully, with a three-cornered handkerchief tied over her frizzes.

a few of which peeped merrily out. As she dusted she sang little trills of music in a glad, happy voice. She felt very happy this morning; every snowflake fluttering down from heaven made her happier, for wouldn't each one help to improve the sleighing? She had a special interest in the sleighing. This was the evening for the fair and festival down at the school house in the "Hollow" — a fair and festival gotten up by the school boys and girls for the purpose of raising funds with which to purchase a school organ.

Now, Rebecca Harlow had not chick nor child belonging to her who had aught to do with the school at the Hollow. In point of fact, she was not supposed to care, except in a general, charitable sort of way, whether they had an organ at the Hollow or not; and yet her thoughts had been down there for two or three days, and her heart was there at this present moment.

Now let me explain: This young lady of eighteen lived a very busy life. She was the oldest daughter of a large family, where there was much to do and little money to do it with. The gala days that fell to her share were few

and far between, and when Frank Edwards said
to her one evening, as they walked home from
the lecture, "Let's go down to the Hollow next
week, Rebecca, and give them a lift," it was to
Rebecca just as if a little rainbow had whirled
down from heaven and dropped right at her feet.
Was not the Hollow seven miles away, over the
beautiful road, and was not the sleighing perfect, and the moonlight glowing? And she
hadn't had a sleigh-ride this winter. Oh, *she*
would give them a lift at the Hollow with all
her heart. To be sure she could not do much
besides look pretty and eat some oysters and admire the pretty things. But Frank Edwards
was capable of much better "lifting" than that
— his pocket-book was large and full, and his
heart was as large as his pocket-book and with
her at his side to admire and suggest, the "lifting" would be very helpful. Besides, there
were almost a hundred girls in town who were
quite well acquainted with Frank Edwards, and
who liked sleigh-riding and "lifting." Wasn't
it nice to be selected from all these as the one
to help? She smiled as she shook out the
brown rag at the side window and began again;

and her voice broke into a merry carol belonging to the Christmas just past. Then she carefully dusted the big Bible. There was a scrap of paper peeping untidily out at the edge, and she pulled at it. Who could so carelessly have left scraps of paper in that great, handsome Bible! She opened it to remove the offending bit and her eyes rested on these familiar words :

"Hath the Lord as great delight in burnt-offerings and sacrifices as in obeying the voice of the Lord ? "

Now, Rebecca Harlow was a Sunday-school teacher. She had studied this verse carefully among others in the lesson ; she had gone over it again in the teachers' meeting ; she meant to teach carefully the lesson involved in it to her bright little girls on Sabbath day.

Who shall say why, as she read it over now in haste, and without object, it suddenly made the smile on her face change to a grave and troubled look? Perhaps it was the town-clock striking just then in the old bell-tower that suggested the thought to her (it was the same bell that rang at evening) ; perhaps it was the Spirit of God that connected the thought with the verse ; who can tell ? This was the thought as it flashed upon her :

"To-night is prayer-meeting."

And this was the conversation that ensued between her heart and the mysterious being who so often stands up to controvert our inclinations :

"Well, the people at the Hollow have nothing to do with that."

"But the people who ought to be at the church to-night *have*."

"It is only once ; I'm almost never away from prayer-meeting, and besides it's a good cause. And besides it would be really too bad to have them lose Frank's donation. They say ever so many more would go to their Sunday afternoon meetings at the Hollow if they only had good music. They really need an organ."

"Hath the Lord as great delight in burnt-offerings and sacrifices as in obeying the voice of the Lord ? "

What a strange verse to keep repeating itself over and over in her mind !

"People have other duties besides going to prayer-meeting," said her petulant heart.

" As in obeying the voice of the Lord ? " said
the cool, quiet voice.

And she shut the big Bible with a slam and
went to her dusting, but she sang no more.

" I can't go, Frank ; I really can't. And if
you are half as sorry as I am why you feel pretty
sorry, that's all."

The sentence begun in earnestness ended in
an embarrassed little laugh. She had taken off
the three-cornered handkerchief and arranged
the frizzes, and she stood in neat and pretty
dress in the hall talking to Mr. Edwards.

" I was in hope you would get my message
earlier, in time to make other plans for the
evening. I never thought of your not being at
home. I do hope you will understand that it is
not because I don't want to go."

How clouded the gentleman's handsome face
was !

" What on *earth is* the matter, Rebecca ? " he
asked. " I didn't understand your note in the
least. What has happened ? There have been
prayer-meetings before, surely, and there will be
others. And, besides, you knew there *was* such
an institution, when you made the engagement."

What a fine glow there was on Rebecca's cheek !

" I don't know that I *can* explain," she began, hurriedly, " and I know how inconsistent I must seem to you. But really and truly I never thought about the meeting until this morning, when a verse in the Bible told me of it."

" A verse in the Bible told you there was to be a prayer-meeting to-night ! " he said, in great astonishment.

" Well, not that, quite, but it was about not following out our own plans when they come in contact with God's appointments, and — well, Frank, you know I *can not* quite make you understand how I look at such things, but I knew in an instant that I ought not to go."

There was no letting up of the frown on the handsome face before her, and his face was cold and dignified.

" Oh, well, of course I must not come in conflict with your 'ought nots,' but I do not pretend to understand them, and I find this one particularly disagreeable. I ought not to keep you standing in the cold. I will bid you good-evening."

What very handsome horses his were, and what a luxurious sleigh it was!

"He needn't have been quite such a bear," she said, as she watched the prancing horses with a queer swelling of her throat. "I wonder who he will take? Well, I can't help it. I know I have *done* right."

You ought to have been at the meeting that evening. There were a good many out, and someway the pastor's heart was very tender and hopeful. The blessed Spirit of God moved him to ask if there was not *one* present who would like to begin the new year on the Lord's side, and among several who arose in answer to the call was Rebecca's bright young brother, with his keen eyes and dangerous talents. Oh, to have missed that sight, and the sound of the trembling words he spoke! How could a hundred sleigh-rides have atoned for that?

Down on the seat before her went the frizzed head, and the brown eyes filled with thankful tears. As she stepped down from the outside steps a few minutes after a tall man was waiting for her.

"Didn't you go to the Hollow? And did you come to prayer-meeting ?"

Both questions expressed great surprise.

"I did *not* and I *did*," he answered, laughing a little.

"Did you think I would go *alone?* I came down to see if I could understand your 'ought nots.' I respect them, anyway, and I want you to try to make me understand them."

Then he put her into that handsome sleigh and tucked her among the robes.

CHAPTER II.

SPARING SALLIE.

THEY were not in a cave, and she had not the slightest temptation to kill Sallie; but, for all that, the motive for her actions had its root in the same soil that prompted David's patient endurance of his enemy.

It was not a party, but a little gathering of young men and maidens to enjoy the long winter evening together — not a dozen of them, all told; but they had been carefully selected, were just the ones who enjoyed spending an evening together, and their pleasure had been great. The special excuse for this particular gathering, if girls and boys need an excuse for their pleas-

16

ant evenings, had been to welcome a new comer into their set, little Kate Mills; she was spending the winter in town, and was the special property of this particular clique; so, at least, they considered her, and a sparkling bit of property they found her.

Frank Edwards was one of the dozen, of course; it would hardly have been so pleasant an evening to Rebecca, and, I may as well admit, to several others if he had been absent.

They had just come in from the dining-room, where some elegant refreshments had been served, and were standing in little groups having quiet talks that gave pleasant opportunity for a confidential word now and then, that sent pretty crimson flushes on fair cheeks, and made some hearts beat a trifle faster. These young things were just in the glow of life; they thought they understood its entire mystery, and that it was rose-color all the way through; and some of them were right; there is such a thing as rose-color lives; there is a sunlight so high and strong that the clouds of this world can not reach it.

Rebecca Harlow was at her best this evening; matters had gone pretty well with her during the past few weeks; petty annoyances that were given to fretting her had slipped smoothly past her, and on this evening she had been the life of the little circle. She caught a glimpse of herself now as she passed the mirror. Her eyes were sparkling and her cheeks were aglow with life and brightness. Also her new seal-brown dress was very becoming, and it was unmistakably set off by glowing carmine ribbons, in spite of the fact that Sallie Holland, who was a bit of an artist, said that seal-brown and carmine were very bad taste. Rebecca was by no means ill-natured enough to think that it was because · Sallie could wear neither of them. The fact was, she thought very little about it. Bad taste or good, her glass and her mother both told her that they were very becoming to her, and what more could a reasonable girl want? It was not any of these things that fixed her attention on the mirror as she passed it, but the fact that a stray snarl of hair had escaped from its imprisoning pin, and was hanging down upon her ruffles; it would be more poetical to call it a curl, but

the trouble is it was not a curl at all, but a little
frowzly brown snarl, that had blown in the wind
during her brisk walk from home, and had gradually drooped lower and lower until it now demanded attention, and she slipped into the room
opening from the parlor to repair this bit of
mischief. So, after all, it was the fault of that
mischievous snarl of hair that things snarled
themselves up as they did for the rest of
the evening. The hair was as smooth as
the present frowzly fashion would admit, and
Rebecca had shaken out her overskirt and was
preparing to emerge into the circle when she
heard her own name spoken, and in a voice that
rarely failed nowadays to arrest attention.

" Did I understand you to say that Miss Harlow corresponded with Mr. Mason ? "

It was Frank Edwards' voice, and it was dignified and astonished.

" Why, yes, of course; didn't you know it?
He was very attentive to her, I am sure, last
winter when he was here, and he is a capital
letter writer, Rebecca thinks."

She knew this voice, too. It was Sallie Holland who spoke, the pale-faced, blue-eyed girl

with a navy-blue suit on and navy-blue bows in her hair.

"I had an idea that Miss Rebecca was not the sort of young lady who held correspondence with young gentlemen of Mr. Mason's stamp."

Could that be Frank, speaking in such a haughty voice, and repeating her name so coldly! This was what Rebecca thought in her retreat behind the bedroom door. How her eyes blazed now! and her cheeks were like peonies. What *could* Sallie mean? Surely she could have no other object than to deceive. If she must needs talk about *her* affairs at all why couldn't she be truthful, and say that she wrote a merry reply to some nonsense addressed to her by Mr. Mason in her brother Ned's letter, and that that was the extent of their correspondence? *Had* she said that he was a capital letter writer? She remembered saying once that he was just the one to interest boys, and that Ned enjoyed his letters ever so much. *Was* that really the same thing that Sallie was telling? the envious creature! she said to herself there in the bedroom.

"It is just a miserable, low-lived jealousy, because Frank has been more attentive to me than he has to her! Now she is going to try to make him think that I actually write letters to Mr. Mason! I wonder if anything could be meaner than that! I don't know what Frank means about 'young gentlemen of Mr. Mason's stamp.' I don't know what kind of stamp Mr. Mason is, and I don't care, but I always supposed he was good enough for those who liked him, and Sallie Holland is one of them. Why doesn't she say that *she* receives letters from him every week? To think that the spiteful thing should try to make out that it is I who know so much about him! Oh, I'll be even with that girl! I won't endure such meanness as that!"

Fired by this determination, Miss Rebecca presently emerged from the little room, showing no traces of her recent excitement except that she looked prettier than ever, and so Frank Edwards thought as he watched her with a heavy sigh at his heart.

With the discrimination of young men on such occasions he began to fear that he had been mistaken in the bright, strong-hearted girl, and that she was nothing better than a flirt. "How could she be otherwise, and carry on a vigorous cor-

respondence with that fellow?" You will
please to observe that no one had told him there
was anything "vigorous" about it. But this
jumping at conclusions is a proceeding that
young people in his state of mind seem to consider themselves justified in doing. When he
came in her vicinity he answered her merry appeal to his opinion with the coldest and most
distant of answers, thereby deepening the red
on her cheek and making her eyes glow with
feeling.

It was plainly to be seen that he believed
every word that had been said to him; probably
he believed much more than had been said; it is
a way people have. The rest of that evening
was hard work to Rebecca. A good deal of the
time was spent in trying to decide how to right
herself in the eyes of her friend without appearing to take too much trouble to do so; though
why young ladies should meekly suffer under
false charges when a frank word from their
tongues would make everything straight is something that I do not understand; but I know the
fact, for I have often seen it done. She seated
herself beside the little new-comer, and quite

won that small lady's heart by her quiet, kindly
ways, and the silence and interest with which
she listened to certain long stories that the somewhat homesick young daughter was beguiled by
her kindness into telling. How could *she* know
that the preoccupied young lady heard not a
dozen words of all she was saying, but instead,
with sharpened head and brain, was listening to
a conversation between two people sitting opposite her. She was brought suddenly back to
the voice of her companion by hearing a familiar
name.

"Did you say Mr. Mason?" she asked with a
sudden eagerness. "Do you know him?"

The little creature laughed.

"Do I know him? Why, what a queer girl
you are! Haven't I been talking to you about
him for half an hour?"

"Have you?" said Rebecca, laughing, and
looking shamefaced. "I beg pardon; I did not
notice the name before. I met a Mr. Mason in
town last winter, but it is not likely he is the
same one of whom you are speaking."

"Yes, but he is the very one; and I had a
great desire to see you this evening, because I

have heard cousin Fred speak of you ; he is my cousin, you know, my own cousin, and we are as familiar as brother and sister. He has told me about you all. He doesn't know I am here ; he is away in Chicago this winter, and I came here suddenly and unexpectedly. He will enjoy my next letter I know, for I shall tell him about you all. It is my solemn duty, I suppose, to like that little blue and white Sallie Holland better than the rest, but I don't. I don't fancy her much. I think she is almost flirting with that dignified Mr. Edwards this evening. I mean to tell cousin Fred about it. If he really *does* care for her he better come and attend to her, I think. Do you suppose he does ? I never could quite make up my mind."

"Doesn't the fact of their correspondence give you any information ? " Rebecca asked, feeling guilty at the nature of the confidence that was being sought over other people's affairs, and yet feeling that she might as well try to be dignified to a little white kitten as to the creature beside her.

"Dear me, no ! " she said, promptly. " He corresponds with dozens of young ladies just for fun, you know ; or for friendship, I suppose that is the more proper term ; but I should think he would get all mixed up and not know what he was about, shouldn't you ? "

" Very likely," Rebecca said, in an absent-minded tone ; she was thinking. "So Mr. Mason is that sort of person, is he? I'm sure I never knew it before. I wonder if his correspondence with Sallie is ' just for fun ? ' "

Presently the conversation became more general. People changed their seats and lost their confidential air, and then as before Frank Edwards carefully avoided Rebecca's side. She grew silent and preoccupied, and as they were used to being led by her merriment the quiet was growing marked. At this point Sallie Holland roused to entertain the company.

" It is time somebody made a remark," she said, and Rebecca gave a nervous start and glanced toward the little stranger. To those who were accustomed to Mr. Mason's peculiar, aristocratic drawl, it was hardly possible to fail to recognize Sallie's tone as a capital caricature of his. She had a dangerous talent for mimicry, and the temptation to dish up other people's

foibles for the entertainment of present company
was generally too great for her to resist when
she once allowed herself to start. Where was
there one in all their acquaintance who had so
many whimsical eccentricities to turn into ridicule
as the absent but well-remembered Mr. Mason?
"But it isn't possible," argued Rebecca, " that
she can so far forget her friendship for him as to
make *him* the subject of her sarcasm?" Then
she gave a softly and wicked little laugh. It
was evident that Miss Sallie's friendship, however deep, was not proof against her love of fun.
The next quotation from some of Mr. Mason's
well-known words sent them all into bursts of
laughter — no, not all, Frank Edwards was as
gravely dignified as possible ; and Rebecca seeing this felt his keen glance at her, and understood that he feared *her* feelings were being hurt.
Evidently none but herself knew that the little
girlish creature over on the sofa was a confidential cousin of Mr. Mason, and that the bright
eyes had already understood that *her* cousin was
the subject of the hour. Don't you see how it
was ? The old story of Saul asleep in the cave
at the mercy of David. Rebecca had not studied

the lesson for the next Sabbath. She did not
know that the golden text was: " Recompense
to no man evil for evil." No matter, she knew
that the golden text of the Christian religion
was: "Whatsoever ye would that men should do
to you, do ye even so to them," and she knew
that her life *should* be guided by that rule ; but
she was awfully tempted. You see it was not a
question of *doing*, it was just of keeping still.
Perhaps Sallie would confine herself to little
harmless peculiarities that the person if he were
present could laugh over with them ; and if she
shouldn't, whose fault would it be but her own ?
What if she made a life-long enemy of the man
whom she really liked, with no· common liking,
whom could she blame but herself ? And had
she not said this evening what was utterly un-
true, and what was very hard indeed to bear ?
Now she had only to keep still and let this
wicked little sinner destroy herself, for she was
already trenching on what was dangerous ground,
and the color on the stranger's cheeks was growing pink ; but how was she to help it ? It
wouldn't do to shout out, " It would be well for
you to take care what you say ; there is a spy

in the camp." It surely was not her fault if
Sallie would destroy herself. A louder shout of
laughter called her back to the present moment,
and the golden text of her profession was sounding loudly in her ears. Sallie was in the midst
of a sentence, so sharp and keen, that Rebecca,
who knew what the end would be, felt that Mr.
Mason would be almost justified in never forgiving it. It must not be finished.

"Sallie," she said — "Sallie," and her voice
sounded queerly to herself, "let me interrupt
you. You are treading on Miss Mills' sash, and
besides I want help. This puzzle comes wrong
every single time, and if we are to have it this
evening it is quite time you taught me how to
get it out."

"I'll come in a minute, Rebecca dear. You
interrupted me in the very midst of a story."

But Rebecca was imperious: "I can't wait a
minute," she said, with the pretty air of positive-
ness that she knew how to assume. " You
promised that we should mystify this entire company ; and I'm determined to do it. See, where
does this sentence come in ? "

She had risen and advanced toward Sallie, and,

as she spoke, dropped a closely-written paper in her hand, which contained the game that had been gotten up for the evening, and pointed with her pencil to one sentence — " Miss Mills is Fred Mason's own cousin."

Sallie uttered an exclamation of dismay, and explained it quickly:

"No wonder you don't understand it. It is a mistake. Here, I'll correct it," and she wrote: " You horrid child ; why *didn't* you tell me before ? I didn't think you *could* be so mean."

And this is what Rebecca received for her pains ! Perhaps you remember that Saul, when he was confronted with David's kindness, lifted up his voice and wept, and made no mention of his disfigured robe.

The man over on the sofa, looking on with grave, keen eyes, saw through all the little subterfuge of course — men always do, you know — and said to himself, with a heavy sigh : " It was very well done, indeed. I thought her heart, if she had any, could stand no more of that. But what a monstrous mistake I have made ; and how is it possible that such a girl as Rebecca Harlow can care for such a fool as Fred Mason ? "

And then the miserable blunderer finished this miserable evening by going home in the darkness and the mist of a January thaw with Sallie Holland beside him, chattering like a magpie; and the gray-haired host himself saw the sore-hearted Rebecca to her house — a thing that had never happened to her before, since she went out of an evening without her mother.

Perhaps you think she sat down and cried as soon as ever she reached her room; but such was not her nature. She shut the door with a little bang, and said aloud: "I don't care! I did what was right at last; and the only thing I am ashamed of is that I was so long about it." And when she studies her Sunday-school lesson for next Sunday, as she is morally sure to do, her heart will be helped and strengthened by the Golden Text, with the official seal of the Master himself upon it: "Recompense to no man evil for evil."

CHAPTER III.

"WORD IN SEASON."

THEY were coming home from their choir rehearsal, Rebecca Harlow and John Milton. This young man had not often a chance for a walk and talk with Rebecca, for Frank Edwards was the tenor singer in the choir, and was apt to see that Rebecca was cared for; but John had sharp eyes, and had discovered that for some reason the two friends had taken to being dignifiedly polite to each other, and as he and Rebecca were almost brother and sister, being of the same age and having grown up next door to each other, he considered it his duty to see that she was comfortable, a duty he was very fond of doing. So they walked home together. Rebecca was not so bright as usual; something weighed heavily on her heart. The truth is, she had been hearing sad and ominous whispers about this gay young fellow by her side. People said he was getting into bad company, going more and more with a set of wild young scamps whose sole business in life seemed to be to get themselves and others into trouble. Now nobody was more likely to rush headlong into mischief than this same John. In the first place he had anything but a pleasant home. His father was there, and his mother, and a young lady sister, and they loved him with all their hearts. It is a sad thing, and a strange thing, but it is also a true thing, that it takes more than all these to make a pleasant home. John's father pored over his account books of an evening, doing work that he could not afford to keep a clerk to do; at least he thought he couldn't. Now if John had been a good boy, and done this work for his father, all would have been well; but, you see, he *wasn't* a good boy; and that is the first and sorest trouble with all the boys who go astray — they are not good. Then his

mother was an economical woman. She made
one light and one fire do for the entire family ;
and this light and fire were in her bedroom, because she liked a warm room to go to sleep in —
a most unhealthy thing to do, by the way, but
Mrs. Milton could not believe that. The bedroom was a pleasant enough room, and for the life
of her Mrs. Milton could not see what more a
person could want ; — but for all that, to an unreasonable young fellow like John, that bedroom
had its disadvantages. He had fallen entirely
out of the habit of bringing any of his compan-
ions home with him, because who wanted to poke
them into a chair at the foot or the side of the
bed ! Besides, they could not have talked, for
father was very nervous when he was adding
columns of accounts ; and besides all that, they
could not talk anyway, for Carrie, the sister,
was an invalid, young and yet faded, lying always on that lounge behind the stove, her eyes
shaded from the light, the smell of vinegar, or
camphor, or bay rum about her head, according
as they tried these several remedies for her relief.
John was by no means hard-hearted ; he often
felt a great pity swelling in his throat for Carrie,

almost seeming to choke him; he often tried to think of something to bring her. If he had only been one of those gentle, tender-fingered young men, whose soft touch could now and then have been as balm to her aching forehead, how glad he would have been! But to have tried to do anything for her comfort other than occasionally moving the light a trifle, or shutting the dampers when the heat became too fierce, would have been much like an elephant trying to make a lamb of himself; and, like all young men aglow with life and health, he hated the sickening, deadening smell of camphor and vinegar; so, according to his own ideas, there was nothing for it but to find his fun where he could. There was a handsome parlor, shut away in one of the further recesses of the Milton homestead; but, "what was the use of having it warmed and lighted on winter evenings when there was only John, and he almost never at home?" This was Mrs. Milton's question. Sometimes Rebecca Harlow perfectly ached to ask her to try it. So they took this walk home together, and it was for some moments a silent one. Suddenly Rebecca broke the quiet by saying, in a clear and unusually solemn tone:

"'He that pursueth evil, pursueth it to his own death.'"

"Does that cheering reflection have any reference to this present time or place?" queried John, a spice of mischief as well as wonder in his voice.

Rebecca laughed a little.

"I was just thinking aloud," she said. "That is our Golden Text for to-morrow's lesson, and it has been running in my mind all the evening."

"Remarkably 'golden,' I should say. To what class of people is it supposed to bring special comfort, the pursuers or their friends, after the prize is reached? Now a fellow would think that out of so big a book as the Bible something a little more golden could have been picked out for a hinge."

"I am not sure of that. Wouldn't you consider the light set to tell where a rock was, golden in its beams, especially if by its warning it succeeded in keeping you from shipwreck?"

"That is the way to put it, is it?" John said, good-humoredly. "Well, tell us about it. What old fellow made an example of himself for the benefit of the scape-graces of the present generation ? Those Bible scamps are the greatest in existence, anyhow. It fairly used to take my breath away when I was a youngster to see how sublimely wicked they could be ? Which are you studying up ? "

" Absalom."

" Absalom ? He was the fellow with the long hair, wasn't he ? And a handsome man he was, too. Oh, I know all about these stories ; mother used to do one for Carrie and me every Sunday evening."

" Then you remember all about his miserable death, I suppose ? It has made me almost sick studying about him to-day to think what splendid prospects he had, and what a father he had, so willing to forgive him and help him ; he might have been second to no one in the country, and he *would* just go straight to ruin."

Something in the tone or in the choice of words silenced the gay young fellow beside her, and set him to thinking. "It's an easy enough road to travel," he said to himself, thinking of that road to ruin. " And father thinks I am in one of the by-ways that lead straight to it. He is willing enough to help me out, too. I'll be

██████ if I don't think he was ahead of Absalom's father. If I remember the story right,
David was rather cross now and then. I wonder why I don't amount to somebody? I believe
I could, and my prospects are good enough. I
don't thank any one for better ones. 'Pursuing
evil!' That is a queer, stinging sort of idea.
Now most of us have a notion that it is pursuing
us, and that we want to get away from it and
can't. I wonder if it is a fellow's own fault
when he goes to the dogs? I wonder if Rebecca
is hitting at me? No, I don't believe she is;
she never hinted a word to make me think so;
she is just groaning over that worthless Absalom."

"The fools didn't all die with that long-haired
individual," he said aloud, and somewhat gruffly.

"No, and that is the saddest part of it." Rebecca spoke eagerly, and showed plainly that
some one besides Absalom was tugging at her
heart. "People *will not* be warned; they will
just go and throw everything away, just as Absalom did. I suppose he did it all for the sake
of ambition. I don't know whether, after all,
that don't indicate a trifle more character than

to do it for fun.   That is what people seem to
be after nowadays.   Anyway, so that the road
leads to the same end, I suppose it can't make
very much difference *why* we travel it."

"That is coming it pretty strong; and there
is more than Absalom in it, too."   This he *said*,
but, *mind you,* not aloud.   He left her to discover as best she might whether he had understood her anxiety, and only said, "Come in and
see Carrie as often as you can," when he left her
at her own door.   If she had stood there just a
minute she would have seen that he went on to
his own door and entered at once.   But even
then she would not have known that ten minutes
before such had not been his intention.   People
know very few of the things that are taking
place before their very eyes, after all.

It was between eight and nine the next evening when our friend John walked into Frank
Edwards' office, and seated himself without ceremony among the books.   Frank looked up with
a start of surprise.

"You here!" he said.   "Then you didn't go
after all?"

"So it seems."

"What possible inducement intervened at the last moment? I thought you were as sure to go as the night was to come. And I regretted it, too, more than I can tell you; for they are a meaner set than you have any idea of, I verily believe."

"Why didn't you give me a kindly bit of advice on the subject then? You were mum enough when I told you about it?"

Frank Edwards shrugged his handsome shoulders.

"I never give advice unless it is called for," he said tersely. "That is part of my profession, you know — to know when to hold my tongue as well as when to speak; especially, I don't speak when I meet a fellow who has common sense and two eyes, and should know what he is about as well as I possibly can."

"It is well that all people have not your degree of wisdom," John said, coldly. "In which case I should be half way on the road to Hopton Tavern by this time."

Mr. Edwards wheeled his office-chair around, and regarded his visitor curiously.

"If you have no objection to telling me about

it," he said, presently, "I should really like to
know who influenced you, because *I* shouldn't
have dared to do it. I should have expected
you to go twice as quickly."

"Thank you. I presume I should. It makes
a great deal of difference who does things, you
know. In this case it was a fellow called Absalom."

"Absalom!" Mr. Edwards eyed his visitor
critically. "I never heard of such a person.
Pray who and what is he?"

John laughed uproariously.

"Never heard of him! That's good. Speaks
well for your early education. Now mine wasn't
neglected to that degree. I know all about him,
and a vainer or meaner scamp never lived. I'll
be ▇▇▇ if I will be found 'pursuing' the
same course that he did, if it is for nothing but
for the sake of showing my contempt for the fellow. I say, Edwards, the Bible is a queer book;
did you know it? I could turn Spiritualist just
as well as not, I almost believe, if they would
give their attention to common sense now and
then. If ever a fellow was haunted I believe I
have been to-day. Turn which way I would,

and try to plan what I would, my plans all ran
in the wrong direction of course ; they have done
that for some time. In every single one of them
I have been brought up standing by that ▄▄▄
▄▄▄▄▄ sentence, 'He that pursueth evil, pursueth it to his own death.' Think of actually
pursuing evil ! There is a figure for you ; you
are always looking after startling metaphor.
You try that, and if it doesn't startle you when
you put it in the right place then I am no judge.
The long and short of the whole matter is, that
the words haunted me so that I could not go
down there to-night. I meant to, and I tried to.
I called myself a baby and a fool, and all sorts of
complimentary titles, but it was no use, I *couldn't*
get away from the miserable sentence, nor from
the feeling that I was engaged in just that pur-
suit ; and, someway, I don't feel exactly ready
for the conclusion to which it refers."

Frank Edwards was silent for some time
after this outburst. He was a good deal surprised and somewhat embarrassed ; he was a
nominal Christian ; he prided himself on his
high-toned moral character, as indeed he had
reason to do ; he had never been placed in a po-

sition before where he had not a word to say to
the wild and reckless young fellow before him.
Something in John's tones suggested a depth of
earnestness, and a decision being reached, if not
already reached, that would set a gulf between
them; with this strange feeling connected with
it all, that John would be on the safe side of it.
In that case, and according to all logical conclusions, where would *he* be? No wonder that
he had nothing to say. So he sat and stared in
silence at the coals, and occasionally at the face
before him, realizing for the first time that there
were lines of strength and power in the face
after all. Presently he asked in a somewhat
constrained and bewildered voice:

"What in the world has Absalom to do with
all this?"

John laughed.

"Ask Rebecca," he said, quickly. "She can
tell you all about him, and about a good many
other things. She is a dear little woman, with
more to her than there is to forty girls put together. She is as wise as an owl, too. Precious
few people would have the sense to put things as
she did last night. Any one can blaze out at a

fellow, and preach a sermon, and take him for the moral; but it takes a genius to drag Absalom in and make him bear all the blame."

Mr. Edwards arose suddenly and walked over to the window. Several thoughts stirred at his heart. One was that there was more in this matter of religion than he had ever supposed, if it had power to touch such a fellow as John Milton. Another was that there must be some mistake about the silly gossip that that silly Sallie Holland had poured into his ear, and that he would very soon take steps to get at the truth of matters; and *another* was that possibly he was fighting against and warding off what even *his* life needed to make it a success, in the highest sense of that word. To be sure, he was not "pursuing evil;" but then, if there was such a thing as a gulf, and if he were on one side of it, and Rebecca Harlow on the other — what then?

CHAPTER IV.

REBECCA AS A WITNESS.

A LEAF FROM HER JOURNAL DATED APRIL 5, 1876.

IT is 10 o'clock, and I am alone at last in my room. It has been a disappointing day, but nobody knows it but me, by which I I mean that my disappointments haven't been large enough for anybody to see or hear of, and those, someway, are the worst kind to bear. Last Sunday's lesson has been going around with me all this week. I have not had time to supplant it with the next Sunday's work yet. It was a very solemn lesson. I felt so sorry for the disciples to have to say good-by to the Lord, and see a cloud shadow him out of sight. Also, I felt sorry for myself. There are so many clouds,

44

and they come between Him and my soul so much. But the words that clung to me were His own: 'Ye shall be witnesses of me.' It is a positive promise, you see, and it came to me very sadly that I had done so little of the witnessing. I have thought about it ever since. There really seems to be nothing that I can do. I have just a little narrow round of life to go over every day, and look which way I will there seems almost nothing that I can do, or else I don't know how to do it.

"This morning, now, was one of my days for resolves. I have days when it seems to me I *must* do something and amount to something in the world. This morning I went around in my room saying to myself while I dressed: I am going to be on the alert all day. I am going to 'witness' for Him. There will surely be something to do, if I look and think of it all the time. I planned several things. I said, I will go and see Addie. Perhaps I can get her to give up going to that card party next week. I am more and more convinced that she can not ask Christ to bless her in trying to work for him while she is there. Then I will go to Old Auntie's and

read for her; perhaps she will let me sing a
hymn, and it shall be all about Jesus.   And so I
planned.   There were several other things that
I thought I might try to do, and the way seemed
bright and full of opportunities.   Well, I went
down stairs, and I found mother with a swelled
face and toothache, getting breakfast and planning to iron the clothes.   Of course that wouldn't
do.   I set about the breakfast at once, and
coaxed and scolded the clothes back into the
basket until the morning work should be done.
The rest of the day's story can be told in a short
space.   Before 10 o'clock mother was cuddled
in bed, with a hot brick at her feet and a hot
vinegar cloth at her face, and I had at least two
things to do at once.   There is never but half of
a one to do at a time when mother is there, but
when she leaves the kitchen the work multiplies
and grows perfectly bewildering and distracting,
until really I find myself at the end of the day
just overwhelmed with astonishment at what
mother lives through quietly every day of her
life.   I don't do things quietly.   Someway it
isn't my nature, and I can't acquire it.   Tom
wasn't at home to breakfast.   And when, at 9

o'clock, he looked in, he said: 'Mother is sick, isn't she? I see there is a whirlpool in the kitchen!' And this after I had been working two hours to make everything look right and natural. Well, it took all day long, the work did. A dozen accidents at least happened to delay me, and, though they were not my fault, they seemed to vex and tire me. Mother didn't get really better till toward night; then it was too late for any of my plans. There was nothing to be done but to wash up the tea dishes and go to prayer-meeting. I didn't even have time to run round for Sarah, to try to get her to go with me, which was another of my plans.

"There were a good many at prayer-meeting, and some that I did not expect. Frank Edwards was there, and John Milton was another. But the meeting dragged. Dr. Priestly did his best. He offered a real, earnest prayer, and he threw in little bits of talks all the way through, and sang often. But for all that, there were many of those dreadful pauses. All at once it rushed over me that the Lord had said, 'Ye shall be witnesses of me.' Here was a place to witness. But it is very hard for me to say anything in prayer-meeting.

In the first place, I am never quite certain that it is the right thing to do — so many people seem to think that women and girls ought to keep silence when they are in that room at a prayer-meeting. But I don't pretend to argue about it. I don't know enough to argue, though of course I couldn't help wondering whether the Lord Jesus would be displeased if I said right out, in one of those awful pauses, 'I love the Lord, and I want to serve him.' Wouldn't it look better than that dead silence? Then I applied the test to it that I found in an old book lately — tried to imagine myself saying, after I came home: 'Dear Lord, forgive me because I told the people in prayer-meeting to-night that I loved thee!' Of course, I couldn't do that, and I must say it sounded almost wicked even to think of doing such a thing. So what *was* right? There were other things in the way. I never heard Frank Edwards say very much about it, but I know he thinks it is not a 'woman's sphere' to say anything in public. That is the way he puts it, but he is inconsistent like the rest, for he admires Allie Barker's recitations ever so much, and says he would much rather

hear her read an essay than to hear any
college boy that ever was! And she speaks in
public, certainly. But then, it is at the Hall,
before a thousand people, and it is a school exhibition and not a prayer-meeting. I suppose
that makes the difference. Then there was Eva
Richards, right beside me. I knew what she
would say. She is good-natured, and not a bit
sarcastic, but she makes such cute speeches.
They are harder to bear than sharp ones would
be. They *are* sarcastic, too. But I mean they
have no sting in them — no intentional sting —
and therefore you cannot be angry with her, but
you dread her speeches, and hate to provoke
them. So there was I, in the midst of all these
objections, with the very first opportunity for
witnessing that I had had that day, and not
knowing what to do with it. Then I reflected:
What could I say? Nothing but what they all
knew. There wasn't one in the room but knew
that I professed to love Jesus. Why should I
tell them of it? But then we all knew that old
Deacon Willard had professed religion for forty
years, but someway it did us all good when he
arose and said: 'I'm serving Him yet, and I ex-

pect to serve Him for ten thousand years to
come.' So I thought it over, and wondered what
was right and what was wrong, and I wished
with all my heart that nobody had ever started
the question, but had taken things naturally,
just as we have done about other places where
we talk. And, presently I remembered how
anxious I had felt for Addie, and how much I
wanted to have her led to do what was right,
and I just forgot all about the argument and
asked the people to pray for a friend of mine
who was in temptation. That was every word I
said, and I can't see how any mortal could think
it was wrong. But some did, I dare say, and I
know Frank Edwards thought it was out of
taste.

" The next thing that came to me was a great
temptation. The Sociable of the Stone Street
Church was held this evening. I had not meant
to go, for it always did seem to me too much
like mixing things to go to prayer-meeting and
a party on the same evening, and especially if I
have been anxious about somebody. But I did
not expect Frank Edwards to ask me. He
hasn't asked me to go anywhere in weeks and

weeks. I wonder why he had to pick out to-night? He came to me just as he used to before he became so dignified, and said: 'Go over to the Stone Street Sociable with me to-night, will you?' And I had to say: 'I can't, Frank.' 'Why?' he said. 'Aren't you ready?' I looked down at myself and just wished that I could say 'no.' But I had on my brown dress, so there was nothing for it but to explain. 'I can't feel just like it now,' I said. 'You know there is a special interest in our church, and Dr. Priestly has just cautioned us against doing anything to dissipate any impression that may have been made. It seems to me that it will not be being cautious to go over there.' 'Oh,' he said, 'you have grown more rigid than you used to be.' And that was every word. I walked home with Mrs. Jones and the Deacon, and I suppose Frank went to the sociable and danced, for they are queer church sociables, not like ours.

"So this day is done, and nothing has been done by me. I feel like a great weary sigh of no more use than a puff of wind. Well, I must go to bed; it will come breakfast time just as soon as though I had had a happy day, and felt glad and hopeful."

EXTRACT FROM JOHN MILTON'S LETTER TO HIS FRIEND
HALBERT.

"DEAR HAL:

"I've gone and done it, and it's right that you
should know it. We have been spirits in mischief so long that I kind of want you to join me
in this new business. I have gone the whole
thing — signed the pledge and all. I'm not sure
but I shall go further. You want to know how
it came about? It was all of a sudden. You
remember the letter I wrote you about Absalom?
Well, I've thought of him considerably lately.
Somehow it don't feel good to be compared to
him. A fellow wants to amount to more than
that in the world. But the finishing up was the
other night. I went to prayer-meeting. I don't
deny but it was that fellow Absalom who was
the means of my going. Our little Rebecca was
there, and she spoke, too, and her voice sounded
as sweet as an angel's. You don't believe in it,
I s'pose, and you have very likely learned to
quote St. Paul, and talk a lot of stuff that he
would be ashamed of. I don't know anything
about it, and I don't care, only if it is wicked,
Satan makes awful poor use of it, for it makes

me go to thinking in spite of myself. But that
don't belong to the story. Only, as I tell you,
I had been thinking pretty steadily all the week,
and I kind of half made up my mind that I
would turn square around and have no more to
do with Absalom. The church dance—over at
the Stone Street, you know — was to come off
right after that meeting, and I was right behind
Rebecca, and what should I hear but Frank
Edwards asking her to go. Now, I happen to
know that Frank hasn't asked her to go there,
or anywhere else, for a good while, and I was
glad that he had got done acting like a simpleton, but it went against me to think of her going
to that affair. You see she had told about feeling very anxious for a friend who was in temptation, and says I to myself, I don't know about
such anxiety as can be swallowed up in a dancing party that would be wicked to go to at all
if it wasn't a church sociable. And says I to
myself, if she goes to that thing, it is all stuff to
talk about their being any different from other
folks, and I mean to just stop thinking about
them, and do as I like. And I can't deny that
I felt kind of relieved that I had shifted the re-

sponsibility to her shoulders, and got rid of it all.
And sure as I'm a sinner, Hal, *she didn't go!*
What do you think of that? And she told the
reason why, out and out. Not a bit of slipping
about it. And then, don't you see, I was sort
of committed, and I went on thinking about it,
till the short of it is I've turned about, and the
question is, Will you go along? I don't know
how to say these things in a nice way, but I
mean them just as much as though I did, and I
want you to go to thinking it up, and decide,
like a sensible fellow, as you are."

WHAT FRANK EDWARDS SAID TO HIMSELF AS HE
WALKED UP AND DOWN THE ROOM.

"There is a great deal in it. There is that in
it which I do not understand, because I do not
possess it. She is timid, naturally, and she
shrinks from going in a different line from others.
It was a downright conviction of duty that gave
her such a clear, sweet voice to-night, and such
an earnest sentence. I wonder who it is that is
in temptation? I could almost wish it were myself. One would like to have her pray for him.

How do I know but it is. I wonder if I *am* in temptation? I wonder if I am as strong as I think myself? If I am, then perhaps it is my duty to be praying for those who are in temptation. This praying is such a strange idea — a pleasant one, though — there must be much in it, for Rebecca certainly grows strong in doing what she thinks is her duty, and she certainly grows unlike many other girls. What a shock it would have been if she had gone over to that affair to-night! I like consistency, I must confess. If I professed certain things I would try to abide by them better than some do. Perhaps, in that case, it would be better for me to profess them, and set the example by abiding. I confess, too, that I was glad to have her speak so plainly and firmly as to her reasons, and not give any flimsy excuses about 'toilet' or 'engagements.' She has splendid courage, and she is naturally inclined to please people, too. It isn't pleasant for her to go counter to other people's views. I wish I had gone on with her to-night. I should if it hadn't been for appearing somewhat variable myself. I know one thing that I will do, I shall certainly go down there to-morrow

evening and set myself straight in regard to the
gossip that I have heard.   It is nonsense to suppose that she has anything in common with that
young Mason, except, perhaps, that she prays
for him.   I hope she does for me.   Anyway,
she made a splendid witness for her side to-
night.   I mean to look into this matter with real
seriousness; it is worthy of study.   If there is
in it what there seems, judging from her life, it
is worth having."

MOTHER HARLOW'S OPINIONS.

"Is Rebecca's light out, father?   Poor child!
She has had a real hard day.   She must be all
tuckered out.   I tried to not have her go to
meeting to-night, but she said it would rest her.
I hope it did.   Talk about 'doing good in the
world,' and 'woman's sphere,' and all that!   If
everybody did their duty as well as Rebecca
does it would be a real nice world.   I don't
know as she has any kind of a notion how much
she has made me think to-day, while I was
tucked up in bed and she peeking in every little
while to see if she couldn't do something for me.
I was thinking how different she used to be;

how impatient she was if things didn't go according to her notion, and how it seemed as though she *couldn't* do only just such things as she took a fancy to. But, dear me! nowadays, she can turn her hand to anything. Now, I didn't think that religion had much to do with what one had to be about every day, but our Rebecca's certainly has. She uses it to make things go nicer and happier all around. It makes a body feel as though they wanted such a help for themselves. And I don't know but you and I are about old enough to be thinking about it in real earnest. I know it would please Rebecca ever so much."

CHAPTER V.

NEW FOUND RELATIVES.

IT was society afternoon. Rebecca was there, and Addie, and Sallie Holland, and all the girls; to say nothing of the respectable company of married ladies who were there of course.

Among the young gentlemen John Mason and Robert Wells had made themselves useful all the afternoon in feeding the neat cook-stove in the kitchen, bringing water and spoons, and unloading certain baskets, besides doing a good deal of mischief in the spool-box and needle-case by way of pastime. Everybody knows what dreadful havoc young men make of such articles !

The day was beginning to wane; the gentlemen were gathering rapidly, and certain whiffs of delightful coffee every time the kitchen door was left ajar suggested that supper would be ready before long. John Milton had just seated himself with a basket of worsteds on the low pulpit-stool in front of Rebecca, and was supposed to be sorting worsteds under her care, when Frank Edwards made his appearance, and came, as if by instinct, to the little circle of which our Rebecca was the center.

"I thought this was a missionary society," John was just saying, when Frank took his seat among them. "What in the world do missionaries want of tidies and things?"

"To be sure," said Rebecca sympathetically, "they haven't any chairs; and, besides, what business have they to be tidy?"

Which answer was like a match to Sallie Holland, she being apparently all ready to be touched off.

"Now, Rebecca Harlow, don't let John think such a silly thing as that we are making these fancy articles to send to the missionaries! John, you simpleton, don't you know that there are

people in the world who *buy* 'tidies and things,'
and give money for them — which is exactly the
article that the missionaries are after?"

"Rebecca," broke in one of the Martel girls,
'*did* you hear that missionary letter read? And
did you ever hear anything so ridiculous? Girls,
she sent for a black dress and a black velvet
hat!"

"Who did?"

"Why, that missionary's wife out in Kansas,
or somewhere, I don't know where. Such in-
sufferable impudence!"

"I know it," Rebecca said. "She ought to
have wanted a sky-blue dress made out of my
mother's old window curtains; and as for a hat,
why, Sallie, your last year's run-about would
have been just the thing!"

"She won't get it!" Sallie said, with spirit,
"nor anything else of mine. I'm as interested
in missions as any one, but when it comes to dic-
tating what sort of a dress shall be given them
I think it is time to stop."

Miss Marsh, the school-teacher, was sewing
away over in the corner, but she leaned forward
a little now and took part in the talk.

"Miss Sallie, that isn't *quite* what she wrote. I saw the letter. She said she always wore black hats, and if any of the ladies had an old black velvet that they were done with, she could fix it over for herself."

"Well, what is the difference?" asked Miss Sallie, energetically twitching her worsted until it broke. "*She* always wears black hats! Indeed! What if she couldn't get one to wear? She might be thankful for a green one *I* think. I don't believe in beggars being choosers."

Then Addie Wheeler took up the subject.

"Girls, I am going as a missionary, and I want a blue silk dress trimmed with thread lace, and a black velvet cloak — silk velvet, remember. John, you start a subscription paper for me this evening — that's a good boy."

Then the very spirit of absurdity seemed to settle over that entire clique in the corner. The nonsensical things which they said would fill a small book. It was all about home missionaries and their supposed needs, and the boxes that should be filled for them. There *are* times when girls can act like simpletons. This was one of them. These young ladies, representing a church society, descended to the business of raking together all the thread-bare and unauthentic stories that they had ever heard about home missionaries and their wives and children. You would have supposed to listen to them that these people were a peculiar and unfortunate race, set apart from the civilized world; and that the boxes sent to them were sent because they were objects of charity, instead of being sent to eke out a support which the Church as much owes to those self-sacrificing ones as she owes to her own pastors their salaries. Are they not doing the work together? Those at home doing it with money, and those on the field doing it with brain, and heart, and life.

Some of the wilder of these Christian (?) young ladies even lowered themselves by burlesquing certain defects of speech and sight which had happened to be the misfortune of one whom they had met, without once seeming to realize that the squint and the stammer were defects which belonged to her as a woman, and not in any sense having to do with her position as a home missionary.

Rebecca, conscious of looking remarkably well

in her new spring suit of self colored plaid, and possibly conscious that she was considered by some of the company the most brilliant one of their set, and, anxious to sustain the reputation, joined in with glee, not actually *saying* anything so very absurd, but adding little brilliant touches to many of the sentences, that convulsed the listeners with laughter. Not all of them, though. The gay group became presently aware that there was one exception. Little Mrs. Fenton sat quietly by, neither joining in the rush of words nor the merriment. The lady deserves a word of introduction. She was a new-comer in their circle, and a person of consequence in society, inasmuch as she was at once daughter of a much-honored senator and the wife of young Chester Fenton, the lawyer, who was already whispered of as the coming judge. Also, it may not have detracted from her importance that both senator and lawyer were unmistakably of the wealthy, cultured class; in short, they belonged undeniably to that set of beings who are unhesitatingly spoken of as "the first, the very first families." Also, she was a young and beautiful bride. Why shouldn't she have distinction?

She had joined this particular corner of the society early in the afternoon, and very bright and sparkling had they found her. Perhaps her sudden silence was the more noticeable on that account.

Rebecca, with an uncomfortable sense that possibly Mrs. Fenton might think her new acquaintance very wild and unlady-like, and moved by a courteous desire to include her in conversation, said in a sweet and winning voice:

"Are *you* interested in home missionaries, Mrs. Fenton?"

The answer was quick and decided:

"Indeed I am, Miss Harlow. I have both brothers and sisters engaged in that work."

Then, indeed, if you are a student of human nature, would you have been interested in noting the various changes and expressions of feeling on each astonished face. Sons and daughters of Senator Wilcox engaged in home missionary work! They knew his was a large family, and a religious family; but home missionaries! this certainly *was* news. How utterly mortified, and embarrassed, and chagrined the circle felt. Amid all the hilarity of the preceding half hour there

had been those who had thrown in sentences
that were spoken in earnest, and understood as
the decided sentiments of their hearts.

"I don't believe in sending boxes to missionaries, anyway," Nettie had said. "They are
quite as well off as we are I dare say; I know I
wish *I* had as many nice things as they get."

And Sallie Holland had chimed in: "I don't
believe in all these stories of suffering that we
hear. All the home missionaries that I have
ever seen looked as well off as other people for
all I could see."

It is a curious fact that these who had spoken
in earnest now felt more chagrin than the gay
ones, who had said senseless things as they happened to occur to them. All of them, however,
were sufficiently dismayed, and such a sudden silence fell upon their corner that people on the
other side began to look around to see what had
happened. John Milton was the first to recover
his speech.

"Upon my word, Mrs. Fenton," he said, with
a curious mixture of fun and earnestness on his
handsome face, "we none of us mean anything
that we have said here to-night, to be sure, but I

don't know as that is any apology for what we have been talking about. We are pretty sure of one thing, that we wouldn't have said anything that would seem to ridicule each other's friends for the world; but I am afraid that is what we have been doing."

Rebecca's sweet voice, tremulous with embarrassment, took up his sentence: "We are afraid we have hurt your feelings, Mrs. Fenton, and we would not have done it for the world."

Mrs. Fenton turned toward her a face aglow with feeling. "I know you wouldn't," she said, emphatically, "and yet I don't deny that I am just a little bit hurt, for my brothers and sisters who are working on those far-away fields are *very* dear to me. Yet, of course, I should not feel it any more than you; if I have been rightly informed, you also have relatives engaged in that work."

"No, indeed!" Rebecca said, her face glowing. "I have no friends there, and I know very little about their life. If I had I could not have been betrayed into the folly that I have been guilty of this evening."

Mrs. Fenton's voice was very clear, but re- markably tender, as she said :

"Don't you recollect our 'Elder Brother' said, 'Whosoever shall do the will of my Father which is in heaven, the same is my brother and sis- ter?' If they are *His* brothers and sisters then are they not ours, if we belong to his family, and you know we do not like to see our kindred sub- jects of ridicule, even though they may some- times be guilty of bad taste in dress, and have among them those who have physical infirmi- ties."

I shall not try to tell you of the sense of relief that stole over the group, not unmingled with a feeling of vexation that the elegant lady had frightened them so throughly. So much less terrible was this form of relationship than the actual ties of blood! Thus many of them looked upon the matter. Not so with Rebecca. She was overwhelmed with a sense of shame and grief. Brothers and sisters! truly hers accord- ing to Christ's rule. Had she then esteemed his infinite condescension to her so lightly as to turn into ridicule those whom he had claimed and honored! What if she did it unthinkingly?

Would she have ridiculed her own sister? Nay. Would she for the world have said aught even in fun disparaging to the sister of Mrs. Fenton when that lady was present to hear, and was not Christ present? 'The same is my brother and sister.' Had she really been speaking lightly of the kindred of Jesus Christ? Mrs. Fenton was watching her closely, and presently she said in a low tone, so low that it reached the ears of only a few of the circle:

"Isn't your golden text for next Sabbath the one which so reminds us of our intimate union with one another, if we really are the Lord's? 'We, being many, are one body in Christ, and every one members one of another.' Isn't that it? Shall we who belong to that body have aught to say against the different members of that body? Don't you think it is a subject that we, as Christians, need to think much of? Aside from the missionary field, right here at home in our own churches, do we not constantly forget that we are 'members one of another?'"

"I have never realized it," Rebecca said; "I have done more than simply forget it, I have ignored it. Mrs. Fenton, I thank you for the lesson; it has been sharp," and she smiled a little, "but I think I will not forget it."

"No, indeed," murmured others of the group, for Rebecca's voice had been distinct. "We shall not be likely to forget."

"We all need to learn charity about such matters, that is a fact," said Addie, and Sallie Holland said, "Oh, of course, we ought not to make fun of Christian people."

Then the circle separated, drifting in opposite directions, some to repeat to intimate friends the account of Mrs. Fenton's sharp thrust, and to close it with, "I don't think she was very polite to try to catch us in that way, do you?" And yet they were '*members* one of another!' and yet any one of them would have been shocked to speak thus of another's sister according to blood!

It was, perhaps, two hours afterward that John Milton and Frank Edwards came in contact again.

"See here, Frank," said John, "do you see the difference between that girl and the rest of the girls?" his eyes as he spoke indicating Rebecca. "She was just as wild as any of us this

afternoon, but she got a new idea from that
sharp Mrs. Fenton, and she is acting upon it.
You watch her awhile and you'll see. She has
had that poor little Miss Snyder in tow all the
evening. Nobody speaks to *her* ever, hardly.
You see she works in Mrs. Jonson's kitchen;
that is reason enough for some, and the rest of
us never thought of it. But she is a member of
the church, and Rebecca has discovered this afternoon that she is a sister. She won't forget it
again. Oh, I tell you, that girl is one in a
thousand! You just watch her awhile and
you'll see what I mean."

"I have seen her all the time," said Frank
Edwards, with decision.

John eyed him closely. "Look here, Frank,"
he said at last, "are you engaged to see Rebecca
safely home to night, or may I look out for
her?" She is my sister, you know."

Frank smiled a curious smile. "She will have
no occasion for your brotherly services to-night,
my dear boy. Thank you all the same for your
kind intentions."

'CHAPTER VI.

SHE DIVIDES THE WORK.

IN Mrs. Harlow's parlor June roses blossomed in every vase, on every table and window seat.

Rebecca, in her summer toilet — made by taking the skirt of the brown dress that had done duty all winter and adding a white overskirt and basque — looked as fresh and summery as the roses themselves. It was still early twilight, and the halo of the sunset was yet in the sky, its tints lighting up her brown hair and making a pretty picture of her. Something like that Frank Edwards thought as he leaned back

in the comfortable, old-fashioned rocker that
Rebecca always contrived to smuggle in from
the sitting-room on evenings when she expected
him.   Their quiet was interrupted by the ringing of the door-bell.

"I hope and trust that isn't a caller," Frank
said, and he shrugged his shoulders and looked
so frowning that John Milton, who was being
let in by the little sister, paused in the half open
door-way and wondered whether he would not
be one too many in that pretty room.   Rebecca
sprang forward:

"Oh, John, come in. I am so glad it is you.
I have been thinking of you all the afternoon.
I've been looking ahead and I have found just
the place where you will fit in."

"I hope it is in this chair, then," John said,
taking a seat across from Rebecca. "That is
just where I want to fit."

"It is a more useful place than that. Really
and truly, I want you for work. Have you
looked ahead in the lessons any for this month?"

"It is as much as *I* can do to remember to
look ahead enough to see where the lesson for
the day is on Sabbath morning. There is little

hope of my getting in advance of that." This from Frank, who leaned back in his chair and looked as lazy as his words. In justice to him be it explained that he was not by any means of that nature, but had plenty of energy at command.

"Well, now," said Rebecca, "*I* have been looking ahead, and I want you, John."

"I'm awful glad of that," John said, significantly, and he and Frank laughed, while Rebecca hurried on. "Toward the end of the month there is a lesson about 'Dividing the Work,' choosing some to preach, and some to attend to the business matters and look after the poor. They chose seven men to do that sort of thing. It made me think of you right away, and I have a plan."

Both gentlemen were ready with questions.

"Why are you doing so far ahead?" Frank Edward's asked. "It is only the *first* of June now. Why don't you wait till you get 'toward the last' before you study about it?"

"What in the world have the men who were selected to look after the poor to do with me?

I hope you are not going to make a deacon of me?" This from John.

"Oh, I like to look at the whole month, to see if I can run a chain through it to link the lessons together." This from Rebecca to Frank. Then to John ; "Why, John, it made me think of your talk the other night about never being able to do things. The work has to be divided, you see; and I know your part, and you are dreadfully needed there."

"Where is it?" asked John, looking around, as if for his hat. "If there is a place on the face of this globe where I seem to be *needed* I have the curiosity to go and look at it right away ; for I'll be hanged if I ever seemed to find such a place yet!"

"Oh, you know that is nonsense! Well, it is our library. The way that is managed is enough to drive one distracted — children running back and forth, and thinking all the time about their books and grumbling. They elect new librarians next Sunday, and you must go in there and set your systematic brain at work."

That was the very beginning of it all. Of course John said he couldn't do it. He knew

nothing about that sort of thing, and of course
he was talked and laughed out of that. They
spent half the evening in a discussion, some of
it earnest, and some of it very funny. The end
of it was that John was elected the very next
Sabbath. No, that was not the end. It was a
little place right in the middle. The end came
just two weeks afterward, and John and Rebecca discussed that while they were waiting for
Frank to get his horses one evening after prayer-
meeting.

"John," Rebecca said, "I have half a mind
not to stand here with you. I'm real vexed
and disappointed. How ugly it was in you to
go and resign on the very second Sabbath after
getting elected. I didn't think you would shirk
like that, when we needed your help so much,
too."

"Well, now," said John, planting his stout
form in the doorway, and looking aggrieved, "I
call that pretty hard on a fellow, before you have
heard his side of the question! There are two
sides to everything, Rebecca — even a Sunday-
school library. I'll be hanged if I don't think
there are twenty-five sides to that!"

"John, you promised that you would try not to use slang phrases any more."

"I do *try;* but how is a fellow to help it when you pitch into him so without any mercy? What would you think of yourself if I told you it was from an honest sense of duty that I resigned that place as librarian?"

"A sense of duty!" repeated puzzled Rebecca. "Why, I am afraid I should say that you had a very mistaken 'sense' about you. How was it, John? I had an idea you would go in there and work a complete revolution in the system."

"It couldn't be done," said John, confidently. Besides, there was no need of doing it. The *system* is good enough. It is new consciences that they need."

"Consciences!" echoed Rebecca again. "I didn't think *conscience* had anything to do with giving out library books!"

"That's precisely what they, every one of 'em, think," John said, laughing. "And there is where we quarreled. I think it has. I say when there are honest laws an honest man is bound to try to live up to them. Now the laws of that library are strict enough. It says no scholar shall take more than one book at a time, and no scholar shall draw a book until he has brought back the one charged to him, and no scholar shall get a book without bringing his card. Now the way they ride over all those rules would make you laugh if it didn't make you mad. It came pretty near making *me* mad. What's the use in being dishonest about a Sunday-school library?"

"Why," asked Rebecca, "how is it managed?"

"Managed! It isn't managed at all. The scholars rush in there, pell-mell, any time it happens. They got around me like bees: 'Say, John, I want two books to-day, one for Jim and one for Joe,' or somebody else. I don't know what their excuses were. And others forgot all about their cards: 'Didn't see the use of cards anyhow; often left them at home and got books all the same.' And it's true. Half that library is lying round loose in people's houses, and the school are grumbling because there are not books enough to go around."

"Why didn't you work a reform?" Rebecca spoke with an interested, not to say sympathetic voice, and in a decidedly more respectful tone than she had before. She began to see that there were difficulties even in the way of managing a Sunday-school library.

"Couldn't do it. I tried to straighten out matters, and that is what made the row — I beg your pardon, the uproar — no, the dis — Well, the uncomfortable state of things between us. You see I was only second fiddle — second librarian, I mean — and that played the mischief. The first librarian had let each boy and girl take home as many books at a time as they could lug or happened to want. You never saw the like of it all, Rebecca. They get books, marked to them, and then they exchange with each other, and bring back a book that isn't charged to them at all. That is all against the rules, of course. But why should the scholars keep rules when the officers don't? Then some of them don't like selections that have been made for them, and they pounce in on you when you are trying to clear up and make their own selections. Oh, we had a lovely time! I said I wouldn't allow such goings on; that I had been elected to office and given a code of laws to abide by, and I meant to obey them; and that

made the librarian mad. He said he had managed this thing hitherto without advice from me,
and he thought he knew almost as much about
the rules as one who had just come in. Then I
asked him to be kind enough to read his rules
over to me, that I might see wherein they
differed from my copy, and so get this thing
straightened out. Well, that made him madder;
and the boys and girls were grumbling: 'Never
had had any trouble before'—'Who cared what
the rules were?' And the end of it all was, I
resigned, partly to keep the peace, and partly because I won't pretend to be going by rule and
square and be all the time doing nothing but
breaking rules! I'd just as soon undertake to
keep my father's books and swindle him out of
half the profits. It's the principle of the thing,
after all, Rebecca; it isn't the fuss—though
you hinted pretty plainly that you thought it
was. But what kind of education is that for
boys and girls. I hold that the management of
the Sunday-school library ought to be part of
their education. And who wants to have a set
growing up around us being taught that law,
and rule, and system are of no consequence;

that library books can be stolen, or lost, or injured, and nothing said because they are Sunday-
school books? I say the fellows who are learning such ways in the Sunday-school will go to
practicing them in stores and shops one of these
days and get brought up standing by the laws of
the land. Pretty result that will be from a religious education."

"John," said Rebecca, heartiness in every
fiber of her voice, "I am sorry I said what I did
to you. You are right. This is a serious business. I never thought of it before. There are
so many important things that one never seems
to get around to think about until they are
pushed before one's eyes by some one who is
sharper. I am sorry I accused you of shirking.
I knew it wasn't in you."

"That's all right," John said; "let it go for
some time when I *do* need a rub. There's plenty
of times." But his handsome face glowed. He
was glad to have Rebecca understand that he
meant right.

"Since you spoke about that Sunday-school
lesson," he began again, speaking in a more subdued tone, "I looked into it a little myself.

Not that I thought I was equal to one of the deacons, you know; but this was *work*, real church work, and if it was worth doing at all it was worth doing well. So I thought I would see if there were any rules in that lesson to help me. The very first direction I found was, 'Look ye out among you seven men of *honest report.*' 'Well,' says I, 'I've got to be *honest*, it seems, and not only that, but I must be of honest *report.* I must look out for my p's and q's if common report as to what I say and do is to be thought about.' So I started out on the honest tack, and this is where it brought me! Not that I am quarreling with honesty — I believe in it more than ever I did — but sometimes you have to haul in sails and slip into harbor when the gale is too much for you. Talk about 'reports!' you should have heard the reports that circulated about me! You would have thought that I was engaged in sending everything to wreck and ruin instead of trying to make things smooth."

Rebecca laughed, but there were almost tears in her eyes. John was such an intense and tempestuous fellow. What tornadoes he would have to brave in his attempt to make things smooth !

"You should have looked further in that lesson," she said, trying to speak gayly. "You would have discovered that even Stephen had to endure the setting up of false witnesses against him."

By that time the horses were at the door. Frank and Rebecca were going to have a nice little moonlight ride. John lifted Rebecca into the carriage and lifted his hat to them both. Rebecca bent forward; she had a last word to say :

"Mind, I don't say that you did *just exactly* right, my good deacon. I believe Stephen would have stuck to that library through 'evil and good report.' If ever reform was needed it seems to be there. Perhaps you will see your way clear to go back to it. In the meantime I slandered you, and I am *not* disappointed in you, not a bit. John, I am proud of you, and I always want to be."

John stood still, watching the horses as they danced away.

" It's something, anyhow," he said, meditative-
ly, " to have people care whether a fellow tries
to do something or not. I guess perhaps I was
a simpleton for drawing off so suddenly from
that muddle. Next time I'll try to stand fire.
I wonder if there isn't some way to get a new
lot of books in ? Then, maybe, I could get them
to listen to common sense."

So, on the whole, the end of that matter was
not even yet. Who can tell when it *will* end ?

CHAPTER VII.

REBECCA IN THE TEMPLE.

IT was prayer-meeting night — a lovely summer moonlight evening. As she went along the familiar walk Rebecca's heart warmed at the thought of the gathering for prayer.

"There will surely be many out to-night," she said. "It is so lovely that they cannot help coming. I think we will have a good meeting."

But they *did* help coming, ever so many of them; and after Rebecca had been in her seat fifteen minutes she ceased to wonder so much at it. By that time she had nearly lost the amount of energy necessary to the moving to and fro of

84

her palm-leaf fan, and a horrible sleepiness was stealing over her.

"What *can* be the matter with me?" she thought at last. "I certainly am not so very tired; at least I wasn't when I came in here. I feel now like dropping from the seat."

Whereupon she began to look about her to see if other people were any wider awake than herself. John Milton wasn't sleepy; sleep and he seemed to be antagonistic at all times; his keen black eyes never looked as though they had time to close and shut out from him all the interesting and funny things that were constantly happening. So he looked not sleepy but restless; that sort of restlessness which a man has not the least idea how to control; so he fidgetted, he sat erect, and he leaned on his elbow; he crossed his limbs and he swung one foot; in short, he tried every possible position that could be conceived of as consistent with a seat in church. The rest of the people seemed to be in various stages of unrest or dullness. Frank Edwards was not there at all.

"It's so warm," Rebecca said within herself, feeling that some apology was necessary for

them all.   But then it was no warmer at church
than at home.   Yes it was, too.   Who had
thought of being so overpowered with the heat
during the day?   "There is no air at all," she
said, with a sudden flash of understanding, looking about on the carefully-closed windows; "at
least it's the air of last week and week before,
cooked over again in to-day's sun.   That is just
the trouble.   The room needs ventilation."

Her thoughts once fixed on the room it was
difficult to call them off again, especially since,
with her propensity for looking ahead, she had
that morning taken a dip into the Sunday-school
lessons for July, and discovered much about the
glory and the beauty of the house which it was
in the heart of Solomon to build for the Lord.
How strangely the wonderful magnificence of
that ancient temple contrasted with the present
room, dedicated to the same worship!   She went
back to that ancient building, with its pillars,
and posts, and arches, and doors of gold; with
its golden angels keeping solemn watch over the
holy place, where no man save one dared enter;
with its blue, and purple, and crimson vail hiding
from common gaze the sacred spot where alone

Jehovah chose to grant his presence. How wonderful it was! How blessed it was to think that that vail was "rent in twain from top to bottom," and that every Wednesday evening, week after week and year after year, he invited his children to meet him in the temple, without sacrifice other than of the heart! Yet where were the people? She looked about her; seats plenty of them, but empty. A church-membership of one hundred and seventy, and seventeen of them at the prayer-meeting! She was very much startled to find that this was the actual number present. All this, by some strange process of reasoning, brought her back to the want of fresh air in the room.

"People like to breathe," she said, indignantly, "and air, at least, is free. I wonder if those miserable windows are nailed down, that they are so tightly closed on such a night as this? I mean to find out."

She looked around. John Milton was still fidgeting; he had just folded his arms and drawn himself erect, as if he had said to himself sternly:

"Now sit still; don't you move hand or foot

again at your peril until the benediction is pronounced."

But he leaned forward at Rebecca's very slight inclination of the head, and was ready to obey her whispered message:

"Can't you rescue us from utter extinction by opening one of the windows? They are not nailed, are they?"

He went with alacrity to see. Had he been able to see results he might not have been so prompt.

In the first place, the sash was swollen so that it required the bracing of his strong knee against the wall, and the very decided pressure of his firm lips, to make any impression at all. It is wonderful what a fondness those church sashes have for puffing themselves out, so it requires a young giant to manage them. Then *you* know just how, when they get ready to go, they do it as if, were they human, they would say, "Well, if you are *determined* I shall go, I'll do it with such a jerk that you won't forget it. There! take that!" John Milton took the sudden jerk with what composure he could, and struggled with the spring to fasten the irate window, those little black-headed springs that seem to be inventions of Satan, if he troubles himself with such matters. John pushed the sash up, and drew it down, and pushed it up again, all the time with a disagreeable racket among the catches; a racket was all they could make — they were evidently powerless to hold the sash. Poor John, with his face growing red, looked about him for a book. Was there ever a book near enough for you to reach when you were holding a window-sash? Nothing to be seen that was available. But the unseen forces that work in such a depraved way about all these trifles had chosen the wrong man to play with. There came that look of quiet will on John's face that said as plainly as words, "Now you are to be put up, and you are to *stay* up; and if it takes an hour, why it will have to take an hour, that's all."

He let the sash down with a little bang; he took a jack-knife from one pocket and a stick from the other, and while the minister read a hymn he deliberately whittled a peg to take the place of the black-headed imp; and then, having fitted it with quiet triumph into its place, he walked composedly back to his seat. His boots sqeaked, of course. Several people had been pretty thoroughly awakened; but as to the air being materially improved, it would take more than one window in the southeast corner of the room to do that. And who would ever have the face to suggest the opening of another one ?

The next thing that occurred was the coming of a drop of kerosene plump on Rebecca's little freckled nose ! Now kerosene, under the most favorable circumstances, is only to be tolerated as a necessary evil; but when it comes as far as the nose it is simply unendurable. Rebecca started as if a tiny bullet had touched her, and rubbed the poor nose vigorously, and moved spitefully away from the lamp-post, and became aware of another annoyance, namely, that every exasperating lamp in the earthly " temple " was doing what it could to poison the air. Most people know to their sorrow what lamps *can* do in that line. Rebecca stared up at them. Were they turned too high or too low ? Not too high certainly; for it was with difficulty that the people, bending forward toward their near-

est post, could see to blunder through the hymn.
Still, the chimneys were smoky with long thick
lines of smoke. Some time or other those wicks
must have been raised too high. Rebecca made
a mental resolve to investigate, the moment the
meeting closed. Then she went back to that
glorious temple again. There was a contrast
certainly between those times and these ; and in
some respects the contrast was *not* favorable.
The worshipers in that gorgeous temple were
not offended with bad kerosene oil. "That thine
eyes may be open toward this house night and
day," had been King Solomon's petition for the
temple that he had built. God answered his
prayer. Was not the petition far-reaching?
Did not the eye of God look down through the
ages and see every temple dedicated to his service, and promise to have each in his peculiar
care? Was he surely looking down on theirs?
Was he pleased with lamps that poisoned the
air, and choked the lungs, and made it impossible
to think of anything except that the "temple"
was an exceedingly uncomfortable, not to say
disagreeable, place? Could such service as that
be such as the great King delighted to have?

Rebecca Harlow was so constituted that her thoughts never simply wandered back and forth through her brain without producing results of any sort. With her to think was at least to attempt the accomplishment of something. Blessed, are those people who are so made that thinking must be followed by doing.

Her "doing" resulted in the gathering together of a company in unusual attire for the sanctuary. Half a dozen girls and less than that number of boys invaded the chapel one afternoon, not, apparently, for the purpose of worship; and yet, if service is worship, they were the true worshipers. Rebecca contrived to look remarkably well in a dark calico dress and bib apron, with a dainty little sweeping cap covering her hair. She was armed with the great key that gave them entrance, and no sooner was she inside than she dropped the roll she was carrying and pushed her sleeves above her elbows.

"Now for work," she said. "I meant it should be earlier; we'll never get around in time for evening meeting with all that we have to do. Charlie Thorn, how many pails of hot water can you carry at once from Mrs. Wheeler's? She promised to have the great boiler on. Girls, you all want windows to wash instead of lamps — I know you do by your looks. But I am willing. I got so enraged at those lamps last Wednesday evening that I shall just enjoy a fight with every one of them. Harry and Lewis, you are going to look out for the springs, aren't you? And as for you, John Milton, I've made up my mind that you shall daub your fingers in kerosene all this afternoon."

"All right," said John. "Fingers before noses for that business I say, any day, But you've brought a duster along I see. Now my mother always sweeps before she dusts, or trims lamps either, for that matter?"

This hint met with bursts of applause, and brooms were speedily borrowed, and the business of transformation commenced.

"It's a shame that this church can't raise money enough to have a regular sexton," shouted Rebecca, as she emerged from a cloud of dust.

"How can we expect to have things in decent order when we depend upon one poor man, who doesn't know how to do it, and hasn't any time to do it in, and gets nothing for it at that? John, let you and I be sexton after this."

"Agreed," said John. "I'll light the lamps, and you may make the fires and ring the bells."

"John shall open the windows," said Sallie Holland, shaking her black curls at him.

"Make the pegs so they will never come out then, do," called out Lewis Miller, as he dug away at the stubborn bit of wood that John had fitted, in his desperation, the last time he was in the chapel.

Of course these foolish young people managed to extract more fun out of this afternoon of work than the same number of staid middle-aged people could get up in a week, even though they set themselves at making the attempt. In the course of time the sweeping and dusting were accomplished, and Rebecca and John began at the lamps.

"These need new wicks," said Rebecca. "Dear me! no wonder they smoke! Why the wicks have been in here since last year some time! Why, John, these screws won't turn at all. The lamps all need new burners."

"And then they need smashing," growled

John, twitching savagely at one of them, and getting oily fingers thereby. "I'm willing to be put in chief manager of that job any time you choose. What abominations in the name of lamps! What kind of trustees are there in this church to stand such nuisances as these?"

"Trustees!" laughed Sallie Holland. "Hear the innocent boy! Any one might know that he is very 'new' in church matters. Who ever heard of trustees bothering their brains about lamps and windows, and things of that sort? Their business is to stand on the street corners, with their hands in their pockets, and wonder how the church debt is to be paid, and whether it isn't going to be necessary to get a cheaper minister."

This same Sallie was sometimes more truthful than wise in her remarks. Despite all the talking, the business of the afternoon went on swiftly.

"Look at that," said Rebecca, holding up a chimney; "doesn't it shine? I wonder if Solomon took as much pride in his angels as I do in these clean chimneys?"

John turned around in the seat where he was

perched, leaned both elbows on his knees, spread his oily fingers out, and regarded his companion in wild wonder.

"Do you mean old Solomon Evans, or who? And what had he to do with angels?"

Rebecca laughed till she shook the soapy water over on the carpet.

"I mean an older and wiser man than Solomon Evans. I was thinking of the temple, and how wonderfully it was decorated, and how Solomon must have enjoyed it all; and then I thought, after all, there could not have been such a sense of need about it as even in these little things that we are doing. They didn't actually *need* all that magnificence to worship God; but I think we do actually need clean lamps and things."

"There is no doubt about that; and I shall need new fingers. It can't be that these will ever be clean enough to use again. What a way you have of going back to the Bible days, haven't you? Do you remember Absalom, and the lecture you read me over his shoulders? Well, it's a grand idea; but I don't see how you do it. They always seem to me like mysterious beings, made out of different stuff from just dust. In fact, I can't make it seem as if they ever *were* at all. How did you get the notion of looking up all such things, and sort of hinging them on to the present times ? "

" Why, I don't know," Rebecca said, laughing. "I didn't know I 'hinged' them on any differently from others. Of course, they 'belong,' just as much as Washington, or Lincoln, or any of those. It is only going a little further back. What is the use of reading about them if they can't fit into our lives somewhere ? Now I am just as much obliged to Solomon as I can be; for if I had not been reading about him and his grand temple I should never have thought about washing these lamp chimneys." Then, after a minute, she said in a lower voice: " Isn't it nice, John, to think that even in such little homely duties as these one is actually serving the King ? "

John came down then from his perch, and looked at her in silent surprise for a little, before he spoke:

" Do you actually think that cleaning lamps and fixing windows, and all that, has anything to do with serving God ? "

"Why not? Suppose we do it so his house will be an inviting place, and so those whom we desire to see here will love to come; and suppose the added comfort does induce some to be present, haven't we served him in one of his own appointed ways?"

Still John stared.

"But then," he said, "see here — where will your logic lead you? If it is service to do such things, why then it is *neglect of service* not to do them. Don't you see?"

"I see," she said, looking up at him with bright eyes; "this is the inevitable conclusion to be reached. Now, remember, to one who sees his duty and does it not, to him it is sin."

"Whew!" said John, and he climbed back and continued his vigorous rubbing of the chandelier. Presently he looked around again.

"See here, I've got a question for you that never bothered the head of Solomon, I'll venture. Every one of these lamps needs a new burner, as you remarked; and, as I amended it, it is truer still they every one need smashing and replacing with better ones. They will burn very well to-night because we will adjust the wick to exactly the right level; but they will turn down and they *won't* turn up, and the tendency of mankind, especially of sextons, is to turn lamp-wicks down whenever they can get a chance; so, by next Wednesday night there will be a smoke-house here as usual."

"No, there won't," said Rebecca, and she shut her lips together in that firm way which means that a question is settled.

"How are you going to help it? It is one of those things that need a fund; and you know a fund is what never was, and never will be, discovered in this church. The trustees and deacons have been looking for it ever since I was born, and I don't know how much longer. The fact is, these things, though they look small enough in themselves, mount up, and they need not only work but money. Now in these dull times I can give an hour or two as well not, but money is an article that is uncommonly scarce with me most of the time; and I know a good many who are in the same state. In fact, if you think of it you will see that Frank Edwards seems to be the only one who has plenty of it; and it hardly stands to reason that he should be

called upon to furnish the entire running expenses
of this institution.   He does about twice his share
now.   Always provided he *had* a share.   It isn't
his Church, you know, as he belongs to the grand
Park Place Church up town.   He seems, however,
constantly drawn by certain unseen forces to this
little mission chapel."

"Of course, we don't want him to do it all,"
Rebecca said, with a satisfied smile.   The liberality of that gentleman was one of the things
that was very pleasant to this young lady to remember.   "We are going to do this thing without one speck of help from him.   I don't see quite
how yet, of course; I haven't had time.   But
there is a way.   There is always a way, if you
are only willing to hunt it up.   That is what I
mean to do.   A fund is the very thing that we
want next, and we are to have one."

"When you find it," said John, "I hope you
will let me see it."   And then he announced the
chandelier to be in running order.

Rebecca went on polishing her chimneys and
looking thoughtful; she had already started out
to hunt up that fund.

CHAPTER VIII.

LOOKING AHEAD.

IT was not quite September yet, but she had an eager desire to see what the September lessons were to bring. On the very threshold of them she paused, and her face took a grave and troubled look. Such an array of solemn questions as greeted her!

"Who hath woe?"

"Who hath sorrow?"

"Who hath contentions?"

And so on through the long list of evils. How truly could she say "Amen" to the inspired answer! Beyond a question the inspired one was right in his conclusion, and every dweller on this sin stricken earth could add his testimony. Yet Rebecca was not one of those whom intemperance had touched closely; that did not explain the troubled look. She sat by the open window, and it was a leisure evening with John Milton, so instead of walking *by* the house, as he had intended, he walked *in.*

" What's up ? " he asked her. " I've seen you look more comfortable than you do now."

Instead of answering his question she did as Rebecca Harlow was very apt to do, jumped at once to her subject of thought.

" John, why don't you and I join the church temperance society ? "

" Pooh ! " said John, and leaned contentedly back in his chair.

Now that word is certainly not an argument, and yet it is very provoking sometimes to see what an unanswerable sentence it becomes. It irritated Rebecca.

" If that is all you have to say on the subject," she said, coldly, " of course your opinion is worth very little."

"I might say a volume if it wasn't too warm, and there was any sort of use in it ? "

" In what, your volume or the society ? "

" Both. More especially just now the society. See here, Rebecca, what mortal use would there be in *my* going to that meeting ? If I were a person of consequence you might talk; or if I were a drunkard, by turning around and joining them, I could do some good; but, you see, I never was an out-and-out gutter drunkard, though I was traveling that road, but I hadn't got far enough to be interesting to some people ; but I've signed the pledge and I keep it, and every one that knows me knows that I am a temperance fellow; and as for doing anything at that meeting to interest anybody I haven't got brains enough for it, so what earthly use is there in my going to it? I'll tell you what it is, I'm glad you've waked up to remember that there *is* such a thing as a temperance meeting. I've wondered that you didn't. There is only a piece of one. It is just half alive, hardly that; but it can be brought to life. You get Frank Edwards to join you, and you both go in for it, and see what a dust you can raise."

" Frank Edwards ! " repeated Rebecca, with a sudden sinking of enthusiasm, without attempting to reason about it, and without ever having exchanged a word with him on that subject. She knew to an absolute certainty that the gentleman in question would not go to the temperance society. "Every one knows that he is a strictly temperate man, John. What difference does it make whether he goes or not?"

"Of course they know it; and they know that he doesn't sign the pledge, and won't sign it. If he's been asked once to do so he has been asked seventy-five times; and there isn't an old drunkard in town, nor a young one either, that doesn't know it and chuckle over it. Frank is a bright light, you see, a model young man, and they know it, and it's too blamed mean that he should be on the wrong side. I beg your pardon, I mean it's extremely unfortunate."

Rebecca's cheeks were in a fine glow.

"I presume Frank would join if he could see it in that light," she said.

"Oh, I've no doubt of it; but the trouble is he *won't* see it in that light, as I said, and for the flimsiest of all reasons that ever were invented. How a fellow of common sense can make up his mind to submit to talking like a fool I can't comprehend."

" Halloo! " see here; we are having an argument and we want your help. Come in a minute." This last sentence was called out of the window by John Milton. Then he drew in his head and said: " There is the man himself. He's coming in. Now you ask him for his reasons and see what you think of them."

Whether Rebecca would have chosen so public a manner in which to have held an argument with her friend is doubtful; but Frank Edwards crossed the street with alacrity and entered the little parlor.

" Are you two quarreling? " he said, as he looked curiously at Rebecca's cheeks. "And did you think it advisable to have me step in between you and keep the peace ? "

" No, we are not quarreling," John said ; "and as for stepping in between us, you did that long ago. The fact is, Rebecca here is pitching into me for not going to that temperance meeting, and being an out-and-out temperance man. I tell her I am, and I referred her to you."

" What temperance meeting is that? " Mr.

Edwards said, with wide opening eyes. "Is there to be a lecture? I hadn't heard of it."

"Why, no, Frank," Rebecca said, in vexation, while John laughed mischievously, "we were talking about the church temperance organization. You surely know all about that; it is connected with our own church."

"Oh, that baby performance you mean; I had forgotten its existence. Well, what is the point for me to decide?"

"The point is, why don't you belong to it?" This from John.

"I might give several reasons if I should set out. One of them probably would be 'total indifference.'"

"Give *me* a better one." Rebecca said it gently and winningly.

"Do you really want to enter into the merits of the question on this warm evening?" he said. "Well, then, one difficulty in the way is that in order to be enrolled as a member one has to sign the total abstinence pledge, and I don't believe in that sort of thing."

"Bah!" said John, with emphasis; and it annoyed Frank, even as his other remark of the same nature had annoyed Rebecca, and curiously enough he made a similar reply.

"Is that supposed to be an argument, my dear fellow?"

"Yes," said John, "an unanswerable one. It is my way of saying that it is an incontestable fact that a brilliant young lawyer, and banker, and the like, will now and then talk very much as if he were an idiot."

"Very well," Frank said, with unfailing composure; "you have stated your premises, now prove them."

"But, Frank, you don't mean that you do not believe in any one signing the pledge?"

"Yes, my dear Rebecca, I *do* mean just that. I hold that no one has a right to make a solemn promise that he will or will *not* do a thing, when he does not know whether he will or will not. It is calling God to witness to the truth of what may possibly turn out to be a lie; besides, the very fact that a man has pledged himself *not* to do a thing increases ten-fold his desire to do it. That is the inevitable law of human nature, and he can't get away from it."

Here John Milton leaned back in his arm-chair and laughed a long, low chuckle, peculiarly exasperating. "Ha! ha! ha! ho! ho!" it ended with.

"Now of all the notions a smart fellow ever put forth I call that the oddest. I know what will be *my* duty. I shall warn all the ladies of my acquaintance never to sign the marriage pledge with you, 'cause you know you can't be sure whether you will continue to 'love and cherish until death do you part'; you might take a notion to go to drinking, and throw her out of the window some cold night; and, besides, the minute you had pledged you feel a desire *not* to do it. This is the inevitable law of human nature, you know, and you can't get away from it."

Be it recorded to Frank Edwards' honor, that at this revelation of his absurd self he had the grace to laugh; nevertheless he said:

"But that is not a parallel case, you know."

"Oh, yes," John said, "of course I know it. Was there ever a fellow caught in an argument when there *was* a parallel case? There's more than one thing you can't do with your peculiar views. I hope I may never be so unlucky as to hold a note of yours, with an 'I promise to pay' on it! Only think of your having an awful desire come over you *never* to pay it the minute you had put your name to it; and then, you know, there's your written agreement with the bank, and the deed of that office; and — oh, my! there's no end to them. I say you are not a safe man to have in society, Frank!"

"You are disposed to be witty to-night," Frank said, and he said it stiffly. There really seemed to be nothing else for him to say. Rebecca came to the rescue.

"Of course, Frank doesn't mean that *all* promises are wrong."

"Oh, it is a rule that applies only to temperance pledges. I understand. But of all queer things that is the queerest. When I promise not to steal it is all right; but when I promise not to drink rum it is all wrong."

"I have no special inclination to do the one or the other," Frank said, still speaking stiffly. "I don't need a pledge to help me."

"But you are principled against helping those poor fellows who are inclined that way."

"None but idiots are helped by the temperance pledge."

Frank was growing angry, and was, of course, less careful to be reasonable. John, on the contrary, was in perfect humor.

"Suppose I grant, for the sake of the argument, that you are correct," he said, quietly. "Is there any moral or divine law against helping idiots to be as decent members of society as the circumstances will permit? Besides, after all, I am not quite willing to grant the argument. I don't amount to much, I know, but I'll be hanged if I'm quite willing to own myself an idiot; and *I* certainly was helped by the pledge. I don't know how long it would have stood me without the grace of God to back it; but I know that if it hadn't helped me to get sober I would not have been very likely to have been converted. A drunken man is not exactly in the state of mind to *be* converted."

Mr. Frank Edwards rose abruptly.

"You are too sharp for me to-night," he said, trying to speak pleasantly. "I didn't know I was to hear a lecture on temperance. I will recommend you to the lecture committee for the coming winter if you so desire. In the meantime I believe you are mistaking your vocation. You should study law, or, rather, practice it; I am not sure that you need a course of study. I was on my way to call on Dr. Dennis when you arrested me, and I think, with your permission, I will go. By the way, Rebecca, don't you allow yourself to be drawn off your balance by the eloquence of this young man. There are some honest people yet in the world who are not so afraid of their morality that they have had to pledge themselves not to steal."

"I have pledged myself," Rebecca answered, in a low, firm tone. "I have pledged my life to be loyal to the ten commands, of which 'Thou shalt not steal' is one. I am not ashamed to be bound by a pledge. I believe in them. It is not John who says, 'Let him who thinketh he standeth, take heed lest he fall.' I'm going to join that temperance society, Frank. I wonder that I haven't done it before. It is the lesson for the first Sunday in September that made me think of it. You read that over and see if it doesn't incline you to help the cause in any way that you can."

"It won't be in that way, though." And now Mr. Edwards' cheek glowed a little, and he was evidently annoyed.

"But, Frank, what harm can it do, even if it does no good?"

"Why it disposes people to drink, don't you know," put in John. "It is a law of human nature, an inevitable one. Just think, Rebecca, of the awful desire that will rush over you to drink a glass of brandy the minute you have put your name to that paper."

Mr. Edwards turned upon him sharply.

"Are you so foolish, John, as not to know that I have stated a simple axiom, as plain as that two and two make four, and not to be overcome by ridicule?"

"I don't believe it in its present application," Rebecca said, firmly. "Why, Frank, when you asked me not to go on that sleigh-ride last winter and I said I wouldn't, I hadn't the slightest inclination to go, because I had promised you *not;* although before that I had looked forward to it with pleasure."

It cost an effort to refer, before a third person, to the sacred familiarity of friendship existing between them, and it brought a deep flush over Rebecca's face. John respected it. He turned his head away, and resisted manfully the temptation to make a funny application. As for Frank he had no answer ready save the threadbare one:

"That is hardly a parallel case. We will talk together privately of this matter, Rebecca. Just now I really *must* go."

"John," said Rebecca, the minute the door closed after him, "You and I will go to that society from this time forth, and do what we can to sustain it. Shall we?"

"Amen," said John, heartily. "But then you won't. Frank is as obstinate as a mule about it. I can't think what is the matter with him. It is some old grudge that he has against the idea of a promise, and he whisks all his prejudices over on the pledge without ever seeing how inconsistent he is, nor how much harm he is doing. Other promises can be made by the score, and no one is more rigid and honorable about keeping them than he; and yet he sticks to this folly. I can't understand him. But he'll talk you over, and get you to promise to have nothing to do with it. It isn't wrong to get *you* to make promises, you'll find; and then he will be as sure of your keeping your word as I shall, in spite of all the axioms in the universe."

"John," said Rebecca, and she got out of her chair and came over to him, "I see plainly enough that I can't teach that Sunday-school lesson to my boys as I want to teach it unless I have the moral force of the pledge on my side. I'm going to join that society; I'm going to attend its meetings, and do all that I can for it. I pledge myself to *you now* to do so; and when I take a pledge I mean it. Now mind, *I promise.*"

"Amen," said John, again, not in jest, but solemnly; and as he went home he said to himself: "She's a brick; she'll do it, and several other things before she gets through. Hurrah for the temperance society! Brighter days are dawning. What a fool Frank is!"

As for that gentleman he worked hard at some bank accounts until ten o'clock, interrupted twice by somewhat curious incidents. First came a paper, commencing, "We, the undersigned, do," etc. It was a petition in reference to some town taxation, and Mr. Edwards gave it

the most careless glance through, merely to satis-
fy himself that he knew all about it, and then
signed his name without hesitation. The next
was a subscription list for a family that were
burned out the night before. " I haven't the
money convenient," he said, " but I will hand it
over to you to-morrow," and he signed his name
for twenty-five dollars, and strangely enough
it never once entered his logical brain that he
had taken two pledges that he felt bound in
honor to keep. As he fumbled for his night-
key half an hour afterward he was an acci-
dental listener to a conversation between one of
the young clerks in the store next door and an
older friend. To his horror the young clerk was
partially intoxicated.

" I don't believe in pledges," he was saying,
in a thick, and altogether disgusting voice. " A
fellow doesn't want to sign away his right to do
as he likes; it's a free country ; besides, it's
wicked to promise what you don't know whether
you will do or not. How am I going to know
that I never'll drink another drop of whisky ?
I think it's more than likely that I will. It's
wrong to make such promises. The principle

underlying the total abstinence pledge is wrong,
and shows a want of knowledge of human nature that is unpardonable in *would be* leaders.
I heard Lord Edwards say so this very morning,
and if he doesn't know who does? Tell me
that?" And with a disgusting hiccough the
young man swaggered off.

"Confound the fellow!" Frank Edwards said,
as he recognized his very words spoken that
morning to one of the temperance fanatics. That
was all he said. But it is a pity that John Milton hadn't been there to tap him on the shoulder
and say:

"Do you consider that an argument, my dear
fellow?"

CHAPTER IX.

ON A VISIT.

DATE: the Centennial year, 1876. Time: a sunny Sabbath morning in October. Miss Almina Wardwell came late, and lingered long at the breakfast table.

"I don't think I shall get to church this morning," she said, toying over her coffee. "It is distressingly late; we really ought to try to have breakfast earlier. Still, I don't care to go to church. If I get around in time for Sunday school it is as much as I expect to do. Do you want to go?"

The last sentence was addressed to her guest, our friend Rebecca, who, being her cousin, was

117

making her a visit, and taking observations on various things.

" Why, I don't know," she said, rather at a loss how to answer so singular a question. "I am in the habit of going to church on Sabbath morning; but, it isn't a necessity, I suppose."

" Oh, go by all means if you won't find it too fatiguing. Some of us always go. But, really, my class exhausts me so that it is as much as I am equal to. I have the primary class, you know. Little wrigglers! They are never still for five seconds. I am going to get rid of them just as soon as I can. I have been trying for a month to get somebody to take my place. I don't believe in primary classes, anyway. I think there ought to be six or eight classes made out of mine. It would be a good deal easier."

After this talk Rebecca was seized with a desire to visit the infant class, and thither she betook herself after morning service. Miss Almina was there, looking fresh and lovely in a new blue and white striped summer silk, covered over with rows of pleats and puffs, and a fairy of a hat where lilies of the valleys nestled and smiled, and almost perfumed the room so real were they. Every slightest detail about Miss Almina was perfect. The toilet was one that might be called elaborate, and was arranged evidently with a careful artist eye; the requisite three shades of color glimmered in subdued beauty from hat to necktie. Rebecca's simple country eyes took in the whole at one glance, and was charmed; and at the same time she was aware that the floor was carpetless and dusty, and Miss Almina was meeting with trouble and discomfiture in the effort to keep the elegant blue and white trail from doing untimely sweeping. Another annoyance beset her. Some little children came with love offerings, but they were dandelions, and very moist at that; and the delicate four-buttoned kids, lavendar, of a bluish tinge, soiled at a touch. What in the world should she do with them? "Yes, they are very nice," she said; "lay them on the table, dear. Absurd little snip! she is always bringing me some wet weeds; but that is the way when one teaches babies!" The last part of this sentence was addressed to Rebecca, but the baby heard every word. What wonder that her lip quivered in such a way that Rebecca longed to kiss it?

Miss Almina presently seated herself with much care as to the gathering up of her train, and fanned herself in an exhausted manner. She *was* exhausted. She had frizzed her hair, and combed the frizzes out, and frizzed it again, until her arms ached.

"I have had a horrid time," she whispered to Rebecca, while the opening hymn was being sung; "my new bonnet would not set well. I tried my hair low, and I tried it high, and I tried it with a comb. Four times I took every pin out, and put them back again. I am just tired out. What a horrid tune that is they are singing! Miss Hart always flats. She thinks she is a good singer, too. Only see what queer faces Dr. Nellis makes when he sings! Isn't it comical?"

"Who is Dr. Nellis?" Rebecca ventured to whisper.

"Why, he is our pastor! Haven't you heard his name before? How queer."

And Miss Almina stopped whispering, for Dr. Nellis was praying. After the prayer the folding doors between the main room and her own were closed, and Miss Wardwell was alone with her class of forty little restless immortals. Just there arose one of her grievous mistakes. She called them restless "*mortals.*" That solemn first syllable that invested them with eternity slipped out of her thoughts.

"Where is your lesson?" Rebecca asked, as Miss Almina tugged at her glove, after vainly trying to write the name of a new scholar with it on.

"I'm sure I don't know. I haven't had time to look. It is the next in the International course. The lesson paper will tell you. Dr. Nellis insists on using the International Lessons for this class. That is one of his hobbies; a perfectly absurd one! What do those little tots know about Peter, and all those? Do look where the lesson is, and tell me. I have some new scholars to look after. I shall complain of Miss Mills if they send another one into my class; I have more now than I want."

"But how are you ever going to teach the lesson if you haven't studied it?" asked Rebecca, appalled at the magnitude of such an undertaking.

Miss Almina looked amazed.

"Why, dear me!" she said, "one doesn't have to study the lesson for such little mites as these, you know. I shall find *something* to say."

Meantime, she seemed to have forgotten that the "little mites" had ears, and were listening eagerly to the talk—some of them; others of them were comparing the beauty of their new summer hats, and whispering as to the beauty of their sashes, and the number of buttons on their boots. That was not to be wondered at, for Miss Almina, as she drew off her glove, said:

" These gloves are not going to wear worth a cent; I have to pull them on and off so often. But those little mortals are always taking hold of my hand, and their hands are not over clean. Don't you think it wears out gloves dreadfully to take them off so much?"

Then the business of the hour actually commenced, Miss Almina turning to it with a sigh and a loudly whispered, "I really must attend to this class. Dr. Nellis will be popping in here the next thing I know. I wish he were not so att ntive to the lambs of his flock. He's a real nuisance."

"Children, what shall we sing to-day?"

"Please, Miss Wardwell, can't we sing, 'I am so glad that Jesus loves me?'"

"What! that old thing, child! Why, you want to sing that all the time. I am perfectly sick of that hymn, I wish Mr. Bliss had been asleep when he wrote it. The children are always wanting to scream it out, and they make the horridest discord. Some of them have really no more ear for music than so many kittens, and these are the ones who are sure to sing the loudest." This, of course, was a side explanation to her guest. Then to the class: "Choose something else, children, for to-day; my nerves are not equal to 'Jesus loves me.'"

A dozen voices answered her. Each had a choice; or, if they hadn't, they thought up one hastily to embrace the opportunity to use their little tongues.

"Oh, dear me!" said the teacher, "what a din. Children, you really *must not* make such a noise; it is impolite to all speak at once. I'll select a hymn myself. You have made such a commotion about it I can't allow you to tell this time.   We'll sing, 'I'm but a traveler here.' We haven't sung that in a good while."

So forty little voices, belonging to forty little flutterers, gay with white robes, and sashes, and flowers, and looking as merry as so many humming-birds, piped out, " Earth is a desert drear, heaven is my home."   Let us hope with all our hearts that each of the forty darlings will find at last that heaven is indeed their home ; but as for " earth " being a " desert drear " to them at present, that is all nonsense.   I doubt if the beautiful earth ought to be that to any human being.   But if the forty babies had not remained in blissful ignorance of the meaning of the words they would have sounded like a caricature on life.   Directly the hymn was concluded the spirit of parade came over Miss Almina.

" We will not take time to repeat the Lord's Prayer this morning," she said ; " you all know it so well there is no need of saying it every Sunday."   Think of there being no need to pray because we all know the prayer so well !   " You may rise and recite the Bible alphabet for Miss Harlow ; I know she will like to hear you."

They recited it well; but Rebecca could not help wondering if they understood the hard words, and also what was the connection of ideas:

"A is for Advocate, Absalom, Adam. B is for Bethlehem, Benjamin, Boaz."

"They recite it nicely. Have you explained it to them? Do you think they attach any meaning to the words?" This she said when the pretty show that had been given for *her benefit* was concluded.

"Bless your heart, no," said the amused Almina. "They recite it just as parrots would. Why, they are nothing but babies. Do see how the sun fades this shade of lavender! Horrid, isn't it? Hush, children! Don't you know it is naughty to whisper in Sunday-school? How many times I have told you you ought to be very quiet. Susie Marks, what *are* you talking about? That little tongue of yours is always busy."

"Well, Miss Wardwell, she says her sash is widest, and I *know* it isn't, for I just measured the ends; and she won't believe me."

"Well, it's very naughty to talk about clothes

in Sunday-school. I'm astonished at you. That isn't being good children. Now we must have a lesson. Oh, first, have any of you a verse to recite?"

"I have," piped a dozen little voices. They liked to recite verses; that rested their dear little tongues. So the verses were heard.

What a pity, thought the practical visitor, since they are really fond of saying verses, that Almina didn't pick one out of the lesson and give it to them all to learn. Then they would have known something about it; but she will have to take the whole Bible for a lesson if she hits many of these verses.

Over the recitation of one verse the young teacher laughed.

"Kitty, you little witch!" she said, "I do believe you have recited that same verse to me fifty times; why *don't* you get a new one? Boys! why, the idea of fighting in Sunday-school! I'm shocked!"

"He begun it," said the smaller boy.

"Well, he said I had red hair, and my hair is brown, ain't it, teacher?"

"Why, I guess so, a little. Anyway, it is

very wicked to quarrel about it in Sunday-school. The idea of the little mouse being sensitive as to the color of his hair! Did you ever *hear* of such a thing?" This to the patient visitor.

"He is a perfect little mischief; always in a scrape of one kind or another; his temper is as fiery as his hair."

"That largest boy in the corner troubles him," Rebecca ventured to say. "I think he would behave better if it were not for that boy."

"Oh, I haven't a doubt of it; *he's* a horrid boy; one of the worst in the class. Some of them act like torments all the time. I don't know what to do with them. There's no use in their coming to Sunday-school, anyway. They ought to be at home in the nursery taking naps. Well, children, our lesson to-day is about — Where is it, Rebecca?"

"It's about Stephen," said Rebecca, wondering in her heart how Almina was ever going to manage *that* lesson without having studied it.

"Stephen! How can such little tots be expected to know anything about such old patriarchs, or whatever they were? Who *was*

Stephen, anyhow? I can't recall a single thing about him."

"Give me the lesson paper. What is the first verse? 'Then said the high-priest, are these things so?' What things, I wonder! Oh, dear me! This lesson is all about the whole history of the children of Israel. Now what can I be expected to get out of this for the children? It is just *history*; nothing else in the world."

"Well, children, our lesson is about Stephen."

"What was his other name?" queried Neddie White.

Whereupon Miss Wardwell laughed merrily.

"Why, child, he had none."

"Why not?" said Neddie, looking both abashed and amazed.

But his teacher gave him no reply; she was bending with knit brows and perplexed face over the lesson paper.

"I'll read the lesson to you," she said at last, "and you may tell me about it afterward: 'And he said, Men, brethren, and fathers, hearken; the God of glory appeared unto our father Abraham when he was in Mesopotamia (Tommy you mustn't whisper while I am reading; that is very naughty), before he dwelt in Charran, and said unto him (Kitty, I don't believe you hear a word of what I am reading), get thee out of thy country, and from thy kindred, and come into the land (Fred, how many times have I told you not to kick your heels against the seat?) which I shall show thee (Rebecca, what *can* be the sense in trying to teach such a lesson as this?); and he gave him none inheritance in it.' "

"What's that?" interrupted Neddie.

"What is what?"

"Why, that that he gave him."

"He didn't give him anything, Neddie; it says he didn't."

"Why, yes, Miss Wardwell, you read about his giving something; that last long word."

Miss Wardwell turned a triumphant look on her guest.

"You see how well they understand this," she said; "see if they have a single idea about it. Children, what have I been reading?"

"About a man named Stephen," shouted two or three little fellows who remembered that the lesson was to have been about Stephen.

"Oh, what an idea! Well, what have I read about him?"

"That he was a good man," said Lucy Jones.

"No; he was a bad man," Willie Norton said.

"There!" said their teacher in triumph, "that shows how well you have listened. I haven't read a word about Stephen; it has all been about what he said.

"I know what he said," interrupted Neddie; "he said 'get out' to all the folks."

This answer raised a general giggle.

"Oh, dear! what nonsense!" Miss Wardwell said, when her laugh was over; "I don't know what to do. It is a positive desecration of the Sabbath to try to teach this lesson to babies."

Just here the sliding-door creaked a little on its hinges, and a gentleman peeped his head in. Miss Almina looked around quickly.

"Oh, come in, Gilbert; I was afraid you were Dr. Nellis. Mr. Snowdon, Miss Harlow. He is our secretary, Rebecca, and has come to receive my interesting report. Gilbert, don't you think, I have three new ones! Just *babies*, and I am expected to enlighten them concerning Stephen's defense."

"Do you know what he was defending?" queried the amused Gilbert.

"I haven't the least idea. Do you know the lesson?"

"Not I. What difference does it make to me or the babies what the old fellow did?" He has got done with it all."

"That is precisely what *I* think; but we must teach the International Lesson, you know. I am just sick of that word! I hope I shall never meet any of the stupid committee who chose the lessons. (Tommy, if you pull Charlie's hair again I shall send you out to the superintendent.) It would puzzle any one to know what to teach to grown up people out of this lesson, *I* think. Just a long list of hard names, and that is about all. (Clara and Annie, how often must I speak to you about talking so loud? You ought to know better than to set such an example as that, and you among the oldest in the class.) Gilbert, are you going to hear Bishop Vandermeer to-night?"

"Is *he* to be here? Oh, yes, we must go; but how will they get along without you in the choir?"

"The best way they can.   I am not a salaried singer; I'm under no sort of obligation to be there.   I go when I please."

"Then I'll call for you, shall I, at half-past seven?"

"Come down earlier, Gilbert, and we will try some new anthems.   Rebecca sings alto."

"Miss Wardwell, Trudie says she is going to see her Aunt Annie this afternoon; she says it isn't wicked to go visiting on Sunday. It is, isn't it?"

"Of *course* it is; don't you know the fourth commandment, 'Remember the Sabbath day, to keep it holy!'"

"Oh, Gilbert, you must be sure and go to the social to-morrow evening; we are going to do something new by way of entertainment. I'll tell you about it this evening. I really must go on with that stupid lesson now."

"Well, how many midgets are here to-day? *I* must go on, or Dr. Nellis will be looking at me over his spectacles."

"Oh, I'm sure *I* haven't counted them; enough are here, I assure you. Neddie, stop kicking your heels against the seat: they drive me half distracted."

"There are forty-one here," said the grave and watchful Rebecca, and she received the thanks of the secretary as he bowed himself out.

The teacher turned to her class and addressed them on this wise:

"Children, this lesson is not one that you can understand; we hope that some day Dr. Nellis will let us have such lessons as we like. But now we will have something that we *can* understand; you may all answer together, 'Who was the first man?'"

Of course they all shouted "Adam," and of course that was an indication that they were interested and benefited, no matter if they had known it, some of them, for four years. You know the list of questions, embodying proper and valuable historic information, certainly, only it becomes a question how much time shall be consumed in the endless repetition of it after it has once been thoroughly learned. But Miss Almina had "thoroughly learned" it too, and therefore she liked it. So they ran through the list: "Who was the oldest man, the wisest man,

the strongest man, the most patient man,"
etc., etc.

"Don't you use a blackboard?" questioned
Rebecca when the list had been gone through
with, and Miss Almina looked at her watch and
wondered why the bell didn't ring.

"No, I don't; I hate a blackboard; they are
such horrid dusty things. You get yourself all
covered with chalk, and just ruin your clothes.
I can hardly wear anything decent here as it is.
If I had a blackboard I should give up in
despair."

"I should think it would be a great help in
teaching children."

"Well, I don't know. It is quite the fashion
to rave over them. Dr. Nellis has been at me
for two months, but I won't have one. What
could I do with it? I don't know how to draw,
and as for making lines and marks and dots, such
as Dr. Nellis is always talking about, I am not
going to make an idiot of myself. What's the
use? Just as if one couldn't tell all those things
just as well as to chalk them down. Chalk is
dirty stuff, and I'm not going to muss in it. I
had enough of that when I went to school."

"There are pictures that some primary teachers use, aren't there?"

"Oh, yes. There's a leaf cluster. We have one here, but the pictures are horrid — great red and yellow daubs. Nothing artistic about them. I can't endure the sight of them. I never touch mine."

"But wouldn't the children get some idea of the lesson from them?" persisted the troublesome visitor.

"I don't know, I am sure. I think there is such a thing as having too many pictures and blackboards, and all that, just like a day-school. It doesn't seem like Sunday work to go to making chalk pictures."

Miss Almina had got back to the blackboard without knowing that she was away from her subject.

"*I* don't mean to do it, anyway. Let those people who have a taste for such things daub in them *I* say. I don't like them."

It was evidently a sore subject with her. She waxed indignant as she talked.

"That is another of Dr. Nellis' hobbies," she said. "He would like it if I would dawdle over impossible looking men, and trees, and houses, made out of chalk. It isn't my *forte*, I can assure him, and the sooner he gets a teacher who will be more to his mind, the better I shall like it. It is making altogether too gross a matter of Sabbath-school, I think, to play pictures with the children."

"Did you attend the State Convention when it met here?" questioned the visitor, thinking of certain very different ideas that she had heard advanced on this subject.

Miss Almina's lip curled so high as to almost retire under her nose.

"The State Convention!" she repeated in ineffable scorn. "No, indeed! Such a set as came to be entertained! I wish you could have seen them. More than half of them from the country, and such queer, common-looking people! I think conventions are nothing but humbugs; just a company of people banded together to see how long they can get entertained by strangers. Such impudence!"

"What a formidable undertaking!" Rebecca said, her eyes flashing. "How the leaders have to work, day and night, and spend their money and time, all for the sake of getting entertained for two days! It seems to me it costs more than it returns."

" Oh, well, you needn't go to being sharp. Plenty of people besides me think so. All the first families are of that opinion."

" I dare say. It sounds precisely like the first families. They generally have just such advanced and sensible ideas."

" See what sort of people they send," retorted Almina; " common looking set!"

" Do people have to be aristocratic looking before they are allowed to visit a city as delegates to a Sunday-school Convention? I never heard that argument advanced before. So far as the logic is concerned, every one knows that superintendents try hard to get the class of teachers who need benefiting most to be sent as delegates, though I admit it doesn't work that way, because the teachers who are almost failures *won't go*, and those who would do very well without the help of conventions are the ones who are eager and interested to be there. But, Almina, only look at your class. What a confusion they are in, while we are discussing conventions.

This isn't according to convention teaching, I assure you."

"I don't know anything about convention teaching. I never attended one, and I don't want to."

"So I supposed. No person of common sense could be familiar with them and their work, and then say such absurd things as you have been guilty of."

Almina laughed carelessly.

"How fiery you are!" she said. "One would think you were president of all the associations," and she turned languidly away.

The door creaked again. This time it was Dr. Nellis. Every little restless mouse resolved itself into instant quiet the moment his head appeared.

He shook hands cordially with the teacher.

"Have you had a pleasant time?" he said, genially.

"Oh, I don't know; we have had a warm time," the young teacher said, fanning herself vehemently. "I think babies ought to be at home on such enervating days as these."

Dr. Nellis seemed not to desire to enter into an argument concerning the babies.

"Is your lesson concluded?" he asked.

"Oh, yes, long ago. Why doesn't the bell ring?"

Dr. Nellis drew his watch.

"It is not quite the usual time yet," he said. Then he turned to the children.

"How many kinds of people have you heard about to-day?"

Now the simple truth, of course, was, that they had heard about no kinds of people, but, fortunately for their teacher, they were too innocent to say so. Therefore they said nothing. The pastor tried again.

"Give me the name of one person of whom you have learned to-day."

"Stephen!" shouted sharp-witted Neddie, and his teacher blessed him in her heart for remembering the name which she had already forgotten.

"Stephen! What kind of a man was he?" Silence. "Was he good or bad?"

There was a division of opinion. Some thought

one way; some another.   Their pastor tried
again :

"If we only had a blackboard here, we would
make something to stand for that land of Charran, where that old man used to live of whom
Stephen was talking.   God sent him word, you
know, to leave that land and take a journey
toward one that he would give him.   He promised that land to him and his children forever.
Now how long was it before they got what had
been promised them ?"

Of course the children didn't know.   They
took to guessing.

"Two weeks," said one.   "Forty years," said
another.   "They never got it," said still a third,
and interest and attention were fixed.

How deftly the good man told his story, letting their little tongues help him wherever it was
possible.   How skillfully he led their thoughts
presently toward *their own* "land of promise,"
promised by the self-same God, who had been
so faithful, whom Stephen by his history was
proving had been true to every detail.

"What is the name of this lesson ?" he asked,
suddenly.

The poor little aroused people did not know. When he had taught them he asked:

" Who was he defending ? "

" Himself," said they all.

"Ah, no indeed ! He did not take the trouble to defend himself. He was really defending Jesus. What does it mean to defend any one ? "

Here followed a succession of opinions and an animated discussion, and when it was settled Dr. Nellis set the little eager brains to work to give him a list of the wonderful things that they could say in defense of Jesus, he engaging to keep count on his fingers. When the list had swelled beyond their highest expectations he asked them:

" How many things does Jesus ask you to give him in return for *all* these ? "

Very skillfully he led the answers and the thoughts up to the one word " love." That is what Jesus asks in return. And when this little lesson was concluded, and their pastor turned from them, there thrilled in many a softened heart the desire and the determination to love this dear Jesus, and to defend his name forever.

They would not have put it in those words, but the dear Lord understood it.

Then the pastor turned back to the teacher, who during this lesson, finding Rebecca too much interested to whisper, had been reading a Sabbath-school book.

"It is a peculiarly happy lesson for the little ones to-day," he said. "Miss Wardwell, do you think any of the little ones here have given their hearts to Jesus?"

Miss Wardwell flushed as deeply as if the question was one of a personal and horribly embarrassing nature.

"Why, dear me!" she said at last. "Dr. Nellis, do you really think they are old enough to understand about any such thing? Little babies they are; nothing else. I try to teach them to be good children, of course, but as for them understanding theology, why, that seems to me too much to expect."

"Suffer the little children to come unto me; forbid them not," quoted Dr. Nellis, and added: "It is the Saviour's own direction, you know."

Then he went out of that sqeaking door again, and in a moment the long-looked for bell sound-

ed, and Miss Wardwell's martyrdom was at an
end.

Late in the afternoon of that same holy day
she lay, in becoming wrapper, on the bed in her
room, still trying to recover from the fatigue of
the morning. Rebecca sat in the low chair at
the window, two pink spots glowing on her
cheeks. They had been discussing the primary
class, and the visitor had become considerably
stirred.

"Dr. Nellis and I don't agree at all in our
views," Miss Wardwell remarked, complacently.

"He is a very grand preacher and a great
scholar, and all that, and the consequence is,
when he turns his thoughts to children he is in
a sphere that he knows nothing about. I told
him one day that he better take my class, and
he said he should enjoy it above all things.
Fancy the theological dissertations he would
give them."

"I thought he gave them a remarkably clear
and simple lesson to-day, based on the lesson
that you said could not be taught to children."

"Oh, well, you are a fanatic, Rebecca, we all
know; but I confess to talk about the conversion

of such little mites as these are in my class, in
my opinion is all nonsense. But don't let us
discuss it; I hate discussions. Don't you want
to read aloud? I'm just in the midst of 'We
and Our Neighbors,' but I can tell you the plot
of the story."

"It never occurred to me that 'We and Our
Neighbors' was a book exactly fitted for the Sabbath. Do you think it is?"

"Why not? I'm sure I don't know anything
bad about it. If Mrs. Stowe isn't a safe person
to read, I'm sure I don't know who is. I'm not
afraid that she will contaminate *me*. But if you
don't feel like reading never mind." -And Miss
Wardwell adjusted her pillows and gave herself
up to the fascinations of "We and Our Neighbors."

"Feed my lambs" was the direction of the
great Shepherd himself. And it is lambs of his
own pasture who are the victims of just such
miserable trash as this, and the under-shepherds
thereof imagine that they are actually *feeding*.
"Inasmuch as ye did it unto the *least* of these,
ye did it unto me."

CHAPTER X.

"BREATHING OUT THREATENINGS."

T was November, and a drizzly rain was falling, being blown in gusts against the window pane every now and then by the snarliest of east winds. Rebecca awoke late; she had passed a restless night, not awake enough to know what was the matter; not asleep enough to escape the sense of discomfort. When she finally awoke, she knew not what was the matter; there was a miserable crawling pain in one side of her head and nose, and the water oozed in an exasperating manner from one eye and one nostril.

"A horrid cold in my head," she murmured,

145

in a vexed and disheartened tone. No one
knew better than herself what those miserable
words meant, and the suspicion lurking in her
heart that her imprudence of the day before was
the sole cause of her affliction did not serve to
comfort her.

The blinds had been tightly closed, and the
darkness of the morning, combining with the
sound nap that had come to her late in the night,
had caused her to be very late. Dismayed at
this, and remembering certain breakfast duties
of hers that must have been long waiting, she
made a very hurried toilet, and without so much
as a glance at her closed Bible, and with a muttered excuse that there was no time for anything
this morning, she hurried down stairs.

Had the kitchen stove a cold in the head, accompanied by a throbbing neuralgia? The
smoke issuing from its throat would indicate that
something was awry. The small form bending
over this monster, and enveloped in the smoke,
was none other than Rebecca's mother.

This sight was shocking. Rebecca's mother
had been, during the dismal fall, almost an invalid, and it was Rebecca's work to be very care-

ful of her. At the same time she had all those
tiresome traits, so common to mothers, making
it almost impossible to spare her, as she knew
how to plan for every one's comfort save her
own. She looked around now with a wan face,
and shivered as she spoke.

"Something must be the matter with the
chimney, Rebecca; this fire won't burn; I've
been at it for nearly half an hour."

"And you haven't even a shawl over your
shoulders," said Rebecca, with a half groan.
"Where on earth is Sally, and what is the need
of *your* being at the fire at all?"

"Why, I forgot to tell you last night that
Sally was sent for to go home; her sister is bad
again."

"Her sister is always getting bad, and at the
most inconvenient times, too; we shall just have
to give her up, and look for other help. I've
thought so all the time."

"The poor thing can't help being sick, I
s'pose," Mother Harlow said, with a mild little
sigh, as she stepped back to let her energetic
daughter whisk in between her and the stove;
and for the next five minutes the rattle of damp-

ers shoved in, and dampers pulled out, and the clatter of covers lifted and slammed back, effectually prevented all remark. At the end of that time the daughter remarked, sharply, that "Some people had to work whether they were sick or not."

"She hated badly enough to go," Mrs. Harlow said. "She said she was afraid it would put us out dreadfully, Thanksgiving coming, and all; and she told her brother that she would rather be sick a month than disappoint us."

That word "Thanksgiving" was an unlucky one. It suggested to Rebecca all the horrors of getting ready for that time of feasting with no Sally at the helm. You do not know the Rebecca of this morning. If the sun had been shining, or if, despite the sun, those horrible crawling twinges of pain about her face had been away, our Rebecca would have been apt to answer, cheerily, "Oh, well, perhaps her sister will be better before that time; anyhow, we won't borrow trouble." And the probabilities are that the next thing would have been a cheery note of song. But it was just at this point that Mother Harlow opened the kitchen door to see what the prospect might be for a pail of water, and a gust of east wind and rain rushed in right across the offending cheek, and every exasperating tooth set up a special growl. "Do please shut that door! It is very imprudent in you to let that damp wind blow on you, and besides, you have got all wet with the rain."

Now, the "please" in this sentence was all that redeemed it from positive rudeness; as it was, the tone being one in which Mrs. Harlow was unaccustomed to hear herself addressed, was too much for her nerves; she answered quickly:

"For pity's sake, don't be crusty! I would rather get wet to my skin than be scolded. You got up too early this morning, I guess, though the land knows it is late enough; but it won't mend matters to be so cross." Which reply did not, of course, sooth the aching teeth or nerves, and the most ominous, not to say sullen, silence prevailed from that time until breakfast was steaming on the table. There are mornings trying to the souls of cooks, when it is well known that the kettle will not boil until it is waited for, and coaxed with special chips, and then it chooses an unexpected moment and boils over into the potatoes, and steak smokes instead of broils, and everything everywhere is totally depraved.

All these things and more occurred to Rebecca; and the alternations of hot and cold air in her transits from kitchen to dining-room and pantry, roused the throbbing nerves to a pain that was almost beyond endurance. So her face was still as dark as the morning when the family gathered at the late breakfast.

"I shall be late at the store this morning." was Father Harlow's first remark, as he looked up at the clock.

"It is well Sally isn't away very often; I hate of all things to be late. I meant to have breakfast at the usual time," Mrs. Harlow said: "but I don't know what got into the stove; I never saw it act so. I suppose it is the east wind; I worked at it for half an hour before Rebecca got down."

There was no reproach intended in this sentence. Mrs. Harlow was not one of those miserable women who hint at things; what she had to say she said plainly, but Rebecca *felt* it, and her father looked it, as he said, hastily:

"I wonder if *you* were working out in that

damp kitchen! You may have got your death; why didn't you call me? I could have left the chores till after breakfast, rather than have that. Rebecca, I wonder at you."

Now, all this was very disagreeable, but Rebecca's " nerves " made it more so. If, at that point, she had said: " Why, the truth is, I overslept; I had the neuralgia in the night, and I've got it yet, dreadfully," both father and mother would have exclaimed — " Poor child! " or some kindred word of sympathy, and the miserable cheek would have been toasted and cuddled, till from very shame it would have had to succumb. But she said nothing of the kind; instead, she looked down at her plate, and answered, pertly:

"I seem to be expected to know by instinct when Sally happens to take herself away. The first I knew about it was when I came down this morning; if I had been told over night I would have made the fire earlier."

" Well, I wouldn't be rude about it; you are too old for that." It was Mr. Harlow's coldest and most unfatherly tone. I wonder at these people. Why did they, on this miserable rainy morning, try so hard to make each other miserable? Why did not father and mother see that whatever happened to their daughter, there must be some explanation for it? So unlike was she to her sunny self. Why did not the daughter see how much harder she was making her own lot by sharp and ill-chosen words? In short, why do we, any of us, allow temper, and neuralgia, and colds in the head, to get the better of us? I'm sure I don't know; but haven't you done it?

Well, the breakfast was uncomfortable. The steak tasted as smoky again as it would if they had known its history, and father remarked upon it in a tone which he would not have used for the world.

And Rebecca maintained the most obstinate silence. What a morning that was! I don't know what *didn't* happen to try the nerves.

Then there is something in getting started the wrong way. It almost seemed as if Rebecca *could* not get back to anything like decency of tone and manner, especially as the snapping and snarling inside her cheek kept on without mercy. The milk boy was late, and he doubtless remembers yet the merciless scolding he received from Rebecca's lips.

"It rained so," he muttered, between chattering teeth; "and I hadn't any umbrella."

"That makes no difference; if your mother undertakes to sell milk, she should see that her customers get it in time. Boys shouldn't be such babies as to be afraid of rain."

"Come in and warm," said Mother Harlow; "it is real cold out, Rebecca," she added; "and the child has a cough."

"Well, sit around out of my way; you must not get into the oven if you are cold. I want that for bread."

This last, I am thankful to say, was addressed to the boy, and not to the mother.

He warmed in haste, and with sundry dismayed and astonished looks bestowed on Rebecca, that would, perhaps, have made her ashamed had she seen them; then he went out in the rain again, notwithstanding Mother Harlow's advice to wait till the shower was over a little.

The next knock was from a wet and draggled girl, who, with miserable drawl and hungry face, asked for "cold pieces." Rebecca cut her short in the midst of her pitiful story: "I haven't anything for you," and she slammed the door, shutting out the rain and the girl together.

"There is that cold pudding that was left yesterday, and the half loaf of bread that isn't wanted; she might have had them as well as not," said Mrs. Harlow, in regretful tone. "I've a mind to call her back yet, poor thing! She looked awful hungry; I dare say they are suffering."

"I dare say she is a humbug!" Rebecca said, disdainfully; "the most of those beggars are. I don't believe in giving to them, anyway; I think very likely it does more harm than good."

"Humbug!" said her mother, "why, didn't you know the child? She belongs to that Coon family, who moved down Ring Lane in the spring. They are dreadful poor, and the mother has the consumption. I never turn one of them away; they are decent people, and they need all they can get.

"Well, it's too late now," Rebecca answered, a trifle conscience-stricken, in spite of her nerves.

"She is out of sight and hearing by this time; she will find something to eat, it's likely."

By three o'clock, in spite of the absence of the skillful Sally, the Harlow kitchen was reduced to a state of perfect order and quiet. The stove shone, and the fire within it cracked, and the hearth around it was spotless. Rebecca had omitted no touch of order or neatness that could be bestowed; she had even savagely added some extra touches to the day's work, in the shape of polished glass and tin, that might well have been left for sunnier times. Meantime, the face and teeth relinquished not one whit of their fury, but growled and snapped in a way that was almost unendurable.

As Rebecca shut the door of her own room, all the work being done, it was with the intention of yielding to their importunity for a little while and retiring behind folds of hot flannel and laudanum, but as she passed the window she caught a glimpse of swift flying hind feet and drooping tail that belonged of a surety to Frank Edwards' brown pony. He was on his way up town, and he would surely call on his return; he always did. So instead of bed, she made a rapid toilet; perhaps you know how rapid it must have been, when you remember that her poor skinned nose had to be attended to between every snarl of hair that was drawn spitefully out. And when, at last, the pretty brown dress and cardinal ribbons were in place, there was no denying that the said nose was very red and swollen, and the bright brown eyes unmistakably dull and watery.

"He will know that I am sick, anyway," she murmured, "even if mother and father don't." There was comfort in that, if she did look horribly; and she descended to answer his ring.

How horrid that east wind was! And how damp the said caller was. It made her shiver to touch his arm, and she felt as if she could not stand in the hall while he threw off his wraps.

"Horrid weather, isn't it?" he said. "Why, what is the matter? Have you a cold? Oh, that is too bad; I meant to smuggle you out with me to-night to hear Beecher, in spite of the rain. He is to be at the lower hall, don't you think! A lucky blunder of trains — he missed his connection and can get no farther than here, and the Lecture Committee, of which you may

remember your humble servant is chairman, had
the sharpness to nab him and issue extras.
Haven't I been busy, though! Can't you go in
spite of cold? No, of course you can't; it would
be imprudent. How badly you look! Why,
dear child, who would have supposed that your
little nose could grow so big in twenty-four
hours!"

How was this stupid man to know that his
lady had "nerves?" The Rebecca of yesterday
would have laughed merrily even over the dis-
figurement of her own nose; this Rebecca wanted to box his ears, or to cry, or something. She
finally concluded to be belligerent — she ignored
Beecher and the lecture, and everything connected with it.

There was no other way, unless she gave up
and cried, for if there was one man more than
another that she desired with all her soul to
hear, it was Beecher. And now to be disappointed in this ignominious way, it wouldn't bear
thinking of. She jumped away over to Thanksgiving, and her tone was as cold and constrained
as icicles.

"I hope, Frank, you don't think that I am

going to your mother's Thanksgiving entertainment without an invitation? They have been out, I hear, for two days, and I seem to be the only one overlooked."

Frank stared.

"Why, bless your heart, Rebecca, haven't *I* invited you?"

"Oh, of course, but you are not your mother; and, Frank, I assure you if you expect me to go in any such way, you will be disappointed. I have borne a great deal from your mother, but I cannot bear everything." And Rebecca wiped one eye, and then her nose, and sneezed three times by way of emphasis.

This was a sore subject, even when she did not have a cold in her head, and the presence of that monster didn't lessen the magnitude of the subject. Be it known that Mrs. Alanson Edwards, widowed mother of Frank, stood, in her own estimation, on a higher social plane than Rebecca Harlow, and would have liked to ignore her entirely, had she dared.

Usually Rebecca was patient, and gentle even, with this state of things, but to-day was an exception. Frank essayed to comfort.

"My dear Rebecca, mother doesn't mean anything; she is old and we must humor her little fancies. As for this party, which is to be a regular bore, she expects you, as a matter of course; and has even spoken of it. I assure you she doesn't think a formal invitation necessary, under the circumstances."

Rebecca interrupted him, drawing herself up proudly, and looking as dignified as her skinned nose would admit.

"There is no use in talking, Frank; I shall have an invitation from your mother to the Thanksgiving party, or I shall not attend; that is all. I shall never enter her house without a a direct invitation from her, and you need not expect it."

Frank Edwards' astonishment was giving way to annoyance.

"You surely know," he said, speaking coldly, "that I cannot command my mother; she is not under my control."

"Neither can you command me; I do not ask you to do either. I simply say that I will not go to your mother's house without a direct invitation from her, and I mean it."

Frank Edwards started up suddenly.

"Well, I must go," he said; "my horse is very restive in the storm. I am sorry you are not able to be out to-night; take care of yourself. As for that other matter, we won't talk any more about it; it will be all right, I dare say." Which was the most that this man, who also had "nerves," and many of them, could make himself say. And then he went.

Perhaps you think that Rebecca went to her room and cried, or wrapped herself in that hot flannel and went to sleep. She didn't; she went directly to the kitchen and got twice as elaborate a supper as she need; she even went so far as to go twice to the pump in the rain, without so much as a handkerchief around her shoulders.

By the time the day was done she was at liberty to rest. The pain in her face, astonished at her obstinacy and endurance, had calmed into a dull ache, and stiff and sore in every joint, tired of heart and brain, she crept up to her room.

There lay the Bible. It was Saturday evening, and the last work for that day was always to look over the Sabbath-school lesson. Mentally

Rebecca declared that she would do no such thing that night ; the aches and pains said plainly that some one besides herself would teach her class on the morrow.   She did not want to think ; she wanted a word, something with which she was familiar, it made little difference what.   The Bible opened of its own accord to the previous lesson ; that was familiar enough, and as good as anything.   She began the words: "And Saul yet breathing out threatenings," through the familiar story until she came to the words : "And suddenly there shined round about him a light from heaven."   A great longing came over her to feel the radiance of that light.   If she could have been Saul !   And yet, what was said to him ?   And then she read that solemn message ; " Saul, Saul, why persecutest thou me ? "   The words were familiar, it is true, but they struck her with a force that she had never felt before. " Why persecutest thou *me ?* "   What had Saul done ?   He went " breathing out threatenings " against the children of the Lord, and the Lord accounted it as done to him.   Yes, he had said so before: " Inasmuch as ye did it unto one of the least of these, ye did it unto me."   How wonderful that it was reckoned as done to him!

It was strange! There was certainly no similarity between her life and that of the persecuting Saul, and yet she suddenly felt as if the voice of the Lord himself was speaking to her, and asking her why she had dishonored him? Wearily she went through the record of that day; from first to last she had spread discomfort. She had threatened to discharge poor Sally, she had been sharp and unkind to the milk boy, she had turned away one of Christ's poor from her door; she had been cold, and rude, and sharp, to both mother and father, she had been impatient with everything and everybody; and, finally, she had threatened, in a most unladylike manner, to Frank Edwards as to what she would and would not do. What a record of a day! What an example for a follower of Him who endured in such humility and patience!

It is well that you and I can not enter with our poor friend into that hour of self-communing; "every heart knoweth its own bitterness;" Rebecca went down into the very depths of hers. But, so wonderful is the light still shining, as certainly as it shone around Saul of old, that as Rebecca went in humility and bitterness of soul before the Lord, he came with tender words of love, and pity, and forgiveness. He called her by name, he gave her to feel in all her weary soul that she was his very own, and though Satan had tried to sift her that day, he himself had followed close, and held her from utter failure.

The Lord met Saul and gave him wonderful salvation, but he didn't save him from many a future trial and pain. He never promised to do so.

That fierce, and obstinate, and unnecessary fight with physical suffering, which Rebecca persisted in carrying out that day, met with its physical reward. She had her petting, plenty of it; mother, father, and friend ministered day and night during the weary time that followed when she tossed in fever, and among her waking hours there were bitter reflections that *if* she had not done thus and so, on that well remembered day, the inevitable results of her folly would not have followed.

CHAPTER XI.

REBECCA BEING LED.

REBECCA Harlow shut the door of her room with a very determined air, slipped the strong little bolt, and then, as if that were not enough, she pushed down the little catch over the lock. Someway, she wanted to be very much alone; there was a quick sigh of relief breathed as she thus doubly shut out the outer world, or tried to; but it must be confessed that very much of the outside world came in with her, despite all that locking. From first to last this had been one of her hard days; I know you will be amazed at this when I tell you that it

164

was the last day in which she ever expected to
have anything to do with Rebecca Harlow.

That young lady, with all her faults and vir-
tues, was about to end her career. Being
merged into Mrs. Frank Edwards, of course she
ought to have been supremely happy. In books
prospective brides are always in a state of high
and restful bliss, but in real life they seem to be
subject to like passions and disturbances with
every-day people. Rebecca was not one who
could close her doors on the outside world, and
sweetly reflect on the duties and joys before
her; instead she had to make every bit of the
cake herself, and see to preparing the turkey
and look after the jellies. She had been hard at
work all day long, with her head in the oven
enough of the time to give her a flushed and
wearied look. The endless last things that had
needed attention that day had hurried and
worried and bewildered her. Mother Harlow
was patient, and kind, and helpful; but she was
almost an invalid, you will remember, and the
fear, lest in this unusual strain upon her, she
would get sick added not a little to Rebecca's
worries; also be it known that the frightful

amount of eggs, and sugar, and raisins, and butter, that were being consumed in preparation for this wedding breakfast tried Rebecca's soul, or conscience. Her father's purse was none of the fullest; careful economy in family expenditure had been a lesson taught Rebecca years ago; and although the father was liberal with his last penny, and eager that his daughter should have the best that he could give, this very liberality had made it harder for that daughter to see the money swallowed up in this useless way, for she was unconventional enough to consider it useless. I am not sure but she was strong-minded: she considered wedding cake a humbug, a suggestion of Satan to beguile people into eating all manner of incongruous sweets, at all manner of improper hours. She would have voted for no cake at all; indeed, her taste would have been the quietest of breakfasts with her father and mother, and the friends coming in afterwards from their usual home breakfasts to witness the pretty ceremony. Left to herself, she would have inaugurated this new and pleasant fashion, thereby saving her nerves and strength, as well as her father's purse. But who ever heard of anybody doing so! This was the argument to which she had to listen, and by which she had to allow herself to be convinced both her mother and her mother's near neighbor and adviser, Mrs. Jonas Smith, considering it a most unanswerable reason why the prescribed track should be walked in. Rebecca, too busy with other thoughts and plans to enter into a vigorous protest, had succumbed and plunged her hands into the usual masses of cake, only awakening to the unwisdom of it all when she saw the astounding bills coming in. Her mother had not greatly comforted her heart.

"Never mind, child," she had said, "we will make it up; it won't cost us much to live when we are all alone." And then would come a suspicious sniff, and a surreptitious application of one corner of her cooking apron to her eyes, and Rebecca would know that she was thinking of the days when they *would* be all alone, and she would be sitting in Mrs. Edwards' elegant parlor. This also was a sore subject. Rebecca had desired to board at home, and had earnestly urged that view of the matter; but Frank, while he did not absolutely refuse, looked so astonished and puzzled, and so thoroughly uncomfortable over it, that she yielded in a quiet way that he did not even realize **was** yielding; and then when his mother in her positive fashion seemed to settle the point for them without any reference to her feelings, she was sorry that she *had* yielded, and meditated an outright rebellion.

"Of course you will board at home," Mrs. Edwards had said; "it would be absurd for Frank to keep up a separate establishment, and as for staying with your people, that is not to be thought of. It is too far away, for one thing; besides, Frank couldn't get along without his mother; he isn't used to it."

This last sentence was spoken laughingly, and, mother and son exchanged fond looks that ought to have been charming to see; but it only made Rebecca feel that she was a fly and there was a spider's web in alarming proximity. It isn't pleasant to be ignored, however gracefully it may be done; not that Frank Edwards had the least idea of any turmoil; on the contrary, he thought he was carrying out his bride's plans in almost every particular. There is no more perfect way of giving up one's own wishes than to do it without letting others know that it is being done. But Rebecca, as I say, had been tempted of Satan to be miserably sorry that she had not stoutly insisted on her own way. The last conversation about the matter had been held that very afternoon, and was so unnecessary, since it had all been decided, at least for the present. There was another small matter that had chafed her much that day. With her own hands she had swept, and dusted, and arranged the little parlor till it was a marvel of neatness and taste. John Milton, looking in as the finishing touches were being added, had said :

" This room looks like you, Rebecca, in every corner of it, and to look like you is to look like a piece of one's home." And then he had sighed, and she knew he was thinking that the room would miss her, and it had been hard to keep back a sudden rush of tears; not, certainly, that she was sorry that she had been called to make a new home for just the one whom she had chosen, but she was tired and nervous, and it would be hard for John to have the brightness of this home taken out of his humdrum life. She felt sorry for him. It was half an hour afterwards that Frank Edwards had called about some item of business, and standing in that very room with all its fresh touches on it, had apparently ignored them all, until at last she said:

"Frank, how do you like the new arrangement of the furniture, or haven't you noticed it?"

"Yes, I noticed it," he said; "did you do it yourself? You shouldn't tire yourself, Rebecca, with such heavy work; you will look all worn out to-morrow. When you belong to me I shall not let you indulge such tastes. Your strength will be too precious."

He did not mean this for a tacit rebuke to her father and mother for having been unable to keep her from such work; in fact he did not think of that at all. It was all because of Rebecca's weary nerves. But she felt it, and it jarred on her. She turned abruptly from him, and would have changed the subject. But he continued it:

"Why did you change the sofa to that corner? Do you like it better?"

"Don't you?"

"Why, not so well, I think. What was the object?"

"The object is a secret," she said, trying to speak gayly. "I'm sorry you don't like the arrangement; I quite fancy it for a change."

He laughed lightly.

"It is of extremely little consequence," he said, "except in view of to-morrow. Are we not to stand in front of it, and won't it be just a trifle awkward to approach our destination from just that angle?"

"Now, on the contrary, that seemed to me one of the advantages; I felt it would be a relief not to have so far to walk."

Frank laughed again.

"As you please," he said, gayly; "so that we get there together, it matters little to me from what angle. In fact I believe I was not thinking of my own tastes at all; but I can almost hear my mother saying, 'Why in the world do you have the sofa there? It will be extremely awkward to turn in that direction!' and my mother thinks the worst sin in the calendar is awkwardness."

"She must be willing to let us judge for ourselves in these matters at least," Rebecca said, and despite a struggle to be gentle, she could not help speaking coldly.

"Of course," Frank said and laughed; it was such a very little matter. "But she will be sure to express her opinion."

And when he called with her in the evening to make her first real call on Rebecca's mother, it proved to be the very first thing that she noticed in the neat little parlor. At least it was the first thing on which she commented.

"I don't like the position of the sofa; you are to stand before it, are you not? Well, that will be an extremely awkward turn. Why don't you have it in that niche between the window and the side table?"

Now, that was the very niche from which Rebecca's deft hands had removed it but a little while before. Frank Edwards looked slightly annoyed. He could question as to Rebecca's taste himself, but it was not pleasant to hear any one else do it.

"What does it signify?" he asked, speaking with the least possible shade of annoyance in his voice. "Never mind the sofa, mother; let it stand wherever it happens to be pushed; it is of no consequence."

"Yes, but it is of consequence; everything is of consequence that contributes to the comfort and elegance of a room where people live. We have to judge of each other's tastes and fancies by just such trifles as these. It is a small matter, to be sure, but there is no reason why the sofa should not be in its appropriate place. Rebecca, now that you look at it you surely see that it would look better at the other end, especially for to-morrow.

"Yes," said Rebecca, speaking with a little laugh in her voice, but with a heightened color spreading all over her face; "I know it would look better over there, and I knew it when I moved it here, but you are mistaken about there being no reason for its present position. The reason for it is that there is a hole in the carpet just at this identical and awkward spot, and the sofa is the only movable article of furniture in the room that will consent to cover it; I have watched that hole with anxious eyes for some weeks; I mean I have watched the thread-bare condition of things, but it didn't break into

a deliberate hole until yesterday, so there is no
help for it.   You see, Mrs. Edwards, there are
uses for sofas of which you never even
dreamed."

Now, was all this rapidly-uttered and somewhat flippant speech an entire mistake?   Did
Mrs. Edwards, in her perfect propriety and
dignity, dislike it exceedingly?   Would she
always remember it as an improper treatment
of herself and her suggestions?

Rebecca thought just then that she did not
care whether it was approved or not; but as she
thought it over later she would have been glad
to have recalled the whole sentence.   She could
hardly understand how she came to say it; she
had shrunk from telling Frank the real reason
for the sofa's removal, why should she have
been vexed into telling his mother?   What did
that mother think?   It was impossible to tell.
She lifted her handsome eyebrows slightly; she
laughed a well-bred little laugh that might
mean a dozen things, pleasant or otherwise,
according as you knew her, and then she said:

"So there are reasons for things, it seems, that
one didn't suspect.   Well, as Frank says, it is of

very little consequence; I'm sure it conceals the
break nicely." And then she had turned away,
and asked of Frank some question about the
new furniture for his rooms. *Was* the question
intended to remind Rebecca of the marked difference there would be between her new rooms
and this old home that she was leaving — this
home with an absolute hole even in the parlor
carpet? Rebecca did not know whether her prospective mother thought of such a thing or not;
but the whole talk thereafter was distasteful to
her, and bristled, so it seemed to her, with
insinuations as to contrasts and positions.

There was no mistaking the sudden gleam of
mischief and satisfaction in Frank Edwards' face
as the story of the carpet was revealed to him.
That spice of daring and freedom from conven-
tionalities that occasionally possessed Rebecca
was always a refreshment to him; possibly because his mother rarely indulged him in that way.

But this episode is just a touch of Rebecca's
day. It was made up of just such mosquito
bites; not a real poison sting or venomous
thrust from beginning to end. But who
wouldn't rather endure the sting of a wasp

than be bitten by a million mosquitos? You know now somewhat of how she felt when she slipped that bolt on the outer world and all its vexations. There was an unutterable longing to get away from everything. She was too tired to look forward to the new life with anything like comfort or joy. She had not seen Frank Edwards alone for a moment that day; in fact she had hardly seen him alone for weeks; it had been all dresses and wedding cake. She felt utterly weary of it; also, she felt vexed with her prospective mother. Instead of putting the finishing touches to her well-filled trunks, as she had designed to do, she dropped wearily into the first chair, and indulged in a look into the future that was neither wise nor profitable. The subject thereof was Mrs. Edwards, not herself; she felt instinctively that she would be simply Mrs. Frank and that everybody, even Frank himself would mean his mother when he spoke that name.

"That was all right, of course; but she needn't think that she was going to command me as she would a kitten; she will find that I am no pink and white doll, to shut my eyes or open them as she wills. I don't believe the same house will contain us for any length of time; I don't believe in commencing that way. If it were *my* mother it would be different; she isn't an atom like my mother, and never will be. I am almost sure I shall dislike her, if she *is* Frank's mother. If I should grow to absolutely hating her wouldn't it be dreadful!" And yet she thought this thought with a half feeling that it would probably come to pass, and a grim idea that it wouldn't be her fault; but would be due to relentless fate and Mrs. Alanson Edwards' capacity for awakening hatred.

Then she went over the events of the day in which the said Mrs. Edwards had been connected. She went farther than that, and looked back over the record of her acquaintance with the lady, and dwelt on each particular little slight, or what had looked like a slight, that she could call to mind. There were many of them, and she had treasured them well; so, long before she had reached the end, she felt as if she were doomed to be a martyr to the petty persecutions of Mrs. Edwards, and she was fully resolved to be a very belligerent and indignant martyr; to dispute every foot of the way; to yield not an inch of dignity or position that should fall rightfully to her, to show from the first that she had a will and ways of her own, and that they must not be interfered with.

"It will make trouble," she said, rising with a heavy sigh, as the striking of the kitchen clock reminded her that the hour was late, and that the morrow was to be an eventful and fatiguing day. "I feel certain it will make trouble, but I can't help it; it was foolish in Frank to insist on putting us into the same house to live; he ought to have known better. But he would stay with his mother, and if it has got to come to a choice between her and me, why he must make the choice; that is all." And at the same time she had lurking within her wicked little heart a sense of satisfaction that Frank Edwards *had* chosen *her* before all the world, even before his mother. Then she went about the task of arranging the heavy braids of hair for the night, and disposing of the numberless things that crowded her bed. Among them was her Bible, and she suddenly remembered that she had left it out of her trunk that she might have a last

reading of it alone in her room. Instead, she
had spent the time in fruitless thought. "It is
so late now," she murmured, a little conscience-
striken that the last hour of solitude should
have been so spent. "I really ought to go to
bed, I suppose; Frank will think that I look
jaded out, to-morrow." And yet from force of
habit, she took up the book. Was it chance
that she opened, or that it opened of its own
accord, to the story of those who, being "scat-
tered abroad by the persecution of Stephen,
went every where 'preaching the Lord Jesus,'
'and the hand of the Lord was with them?'"
Over this sentence Rebecca paused; she had
read it often before. With the aid of lesson
notes and comments she had made herself familiar with the meaning of the words; and yet
they came to her weary heart that evening with
a sense of spiritual meaning that they had not
brought her before. "The hand of the Lord
was with them!" She said the words aloud.
What a wonderful figure it was! Overshadowed
by the hand of the Lord; led by him in all their
turnings; sure to take the right path because of
that pointing hand. The book dropped from

her grasp and she sat still, going over and over
again in her heart all the sweetness and all the
blessed results of such leading. If one could be
sure that the hand of the Lord was really in
every phase of life, how greatly would it tone
and temper all the experiences thereof! If she
really felt that her Father in heaven led and
guided toward this new life of hers, not simply
permitting it to be, but actually familiar with
and interested in all the details, and knowing
what each arrangement was intended to work
out, what a different thing it would make of it
all! How petty the trials would seem! In fact,
would there really be any trials at all? Mrs.
Edwards, for instance, her " thorn in the flesh,"
and she was suddenly startled to realize that
she had actually arrived at a determination to
sow discord in that household, to set a mother
and son at variance! It sounded horribly, put
into words, but what else could her grim determination to yield no inch of the way, and to
exercise the power that she knew she possessed,
mean? Would such work be wrought if " the
hand of the Lord " were really " with " her? It
was a new view of the subject. Someway it led

her to remember that Frank was the "only son of his mother, and she a widow." How very desolate her life would be without Frank! How unreasonable it had been to think that he ought to desert her, and come home to Rebecca's father and mother! Could not a mother and father manage better without a daughter than a lonely mother could without her only son? It was strange that these thoughts had never come to her before. Then she found herself going over the supposed slights and discomforts that Mrs. Edwards had made her feel. They were remarkably small when one came to look at them separately and quietly; merely a matter of difference as to the position of a sofa, or the arrangement of one's hair; nothing definite, possibly nothing so very unpleasant intended. Could she not go into and make an atmosphere in that home that it did not now possess? Mrs. Edwards was a nominal Christian; she did not look like a very happy one; she was not certainly a spiritual one. Would not the hand of the Lord be with her, Rebecca, if she tried by her life, and her words, and her ways, to "preach Jesus?" Was this to what he was leading her? Surely he led his people now. Did he not say, "Lo, I am with you alway?" And there came to Rebecca such a longing to be thus led, to feel in every step of this new life that was opening before her, that the hand of the Lord had to do with it all, and that she was a vessel of his choosing, chosen to shadow forth his praise, that she dropped on her knees; and in the prayer that came from her heart's innermost hiding-place she gave herself again to the Lord Jesus who had called her, and chosen her, and she entreated that she might feel the hand, the powerful hand with her always. As she prayed for the mother who was to open her home to her son's wife every drop of bitterness went out of her heart, and in its place there budded and grew a desire and determination to go to that home and that mother with so much of the atmosphere of the Lord's garden about her, that the perfume thereof would freshen that conventional life and lead it, possibly, nearer to the Master. It was a time of heart searching and of repentance. She grew astonished over the secrets of her own wicked heart; she felt anew the need of pure, spotless blood to cover all the stains, a perfect righteousness under which to hide her rags.

Only resolves these were. They were yet to be put in practice; there was yet to be the grief and the mortification of many a failure. But how much nearer the Lord would she be than though she had never tried? Perhaps Frank Edwards will never know, until he reaches heaven, how much the atmosphere of his home was purified by that chance (?) contact with the word of God, on the last evening that Rebecca Harlow communed with her conscience, and sought help of God. It was in that same spirit that she went out on the next morning, the morning of Christmas-day, dressed for her bridal, and having in her heart no greater desire, no higher ambition than this: that the "hand of the Lord" should be with Frank and herself in that new life which they were about to commence together.

CHAPTER XII.

MRS. FRANK EDWARDS AT HOME.

IN her new home; the bridal tour over, the trunks unpacked and stored in the roomy attic, the pictures hung, every last little thing done, and now they were ready to settle down and begin life together.

It was just after breakfast; an elegant breakfast it had been. Silver and glass and china did their best at glitter and beauty. The napkins were those luxuriously large and delicately fine ones, that tell the story of a full purse, and no desire to scrimp. The table linen was faultlessly white, and in all the freshness of recent folds; and the breakfast, from the rich, hot, amber colored coffee, served in dainty cups that were first half filled with cream, down to the carefully broiled and steaming stake, was such a breakfast as Mrs. Alanson Edwards liked to see served, and she tolerated none but the nicest.

The lady in question had herself presided at the coffee urn, keeping, meanwhile, a careful eye on Frank, that he offended no sense of propriety in his somewhat hurried serving of steak and buckwheat cakes.

Several times she had quietly admonished him; " Frank, you are allowing the spoon to drip ; " or, " Frank, my dear son, if that is for me, remember that I am not an enormous eater; you are giving me a third of the steak ! "   Once she had a quiet word for her new daughter: " I wonder at you, Rebecca, for drinking your coffee so hot ; it is very bad for the teeth."

Rebecca laughed in her old gleeful way, and replied :

" I am like ' Fred and Maria and Me,' I like my coffee ' bilin'.'   Frank, did you ever read that delightful book ? "

" Never heard of it.   What an extraordinary title !   Is it good ? "

"It is capital," Rebecca had said, ignoring, as Frank did, his mother's question.

"Do you mean the book, or the title, my son?" Then she had turned to Rebecca: "Did you say that was the title? How very singular! One would suppose the editor would have corrected so remarkable a grammatical error as that!"

And Rebecca's eyes danced as she answered: "It is by Mrs. Dr. Prentice, you remember. She is one of our most popular authors; I suspect she wanted the grammatical part of it to appear just as it did."

After that, conversation had seemed to drag. Rebecca made several attempts, not seconded by Frank as heartily as she could have desired, the reason being that some items of business news, in the morning paper, absorbed a good deal of his attention. And his mother was either annoyed at her want of literary information, or vexed with Mrs. Dr. Prentice, for choosing to uphold grammatical errors. She answered as nearly in monosyllables as possible, every remark that was made to her. And at last Rebecca breathed

a little sigh of relief that the meal was concluded.

She could not help a smile at the thought of
the horror she might raise by at once setting to
work to gather up the dishes, and assist in their
washing, a duty which had always been hers in
the old home.

Many things here were different from the old
home ways. Some of the differences she enjoyed, and some cast a shade over her pretty
face. It was certainly a relief to escape from
that handsome dining-room, and be alone with
Frank up-stairs. All was in order there. The
deft and skillful second girl had been around
with carpet sweeper, whisk, brush and duster,
until the most exquisite and careful neatness
and order prevailed. Rebecca, in her pretty
morning wrapper of soft grey, with crimson fin-
ishings, sat down in the low rocker, put her
slippered foot on the fender of the open grate,
where the coals were glowing, and admired the
effect. This was very unlike her former occu-
pations. How she used to rush about her chilly
room, warmed only by a pipe from the sitting-
room below, and make her own bed, and do,

with rapid hand, her own dusting and arranging! It had never been a very great task to her. She remembered mornings when she had actually enjoyed it; the making of everything look fresh and neat again. At the same time, it was nice to sit there and survey the exquisitely tasteful appointments of that elegant suite of rooms, and feel that she was the mistress thereof.

Oh, there were a great many things about this new way of living that were decidedly pleasant. It was nice to receive calls from the girls, her old and intimate friends, and smuggle them off to her room for a few minutes, away from the stately propriety of the parlors, and hear their voluble tongues express delight, as their eager eyes took in all the appointments.

It was very pleasant to walk down town with Frank, in a becoming morning toilet, and meet old friends who had heretofore shared these attentions with herself, and realize that they were outside now, and she " belonged " forever. That was more than nice ; it was a joy for which she never forgot to express thanksgiving. "Until death us do part," she said that over in her room alone many a time; generally with a thrill of thanksgiving that it was for so long. Sometimes with a shiver of pain, that it was so short; that the inevitable "death" would surely come in and destroy all this.

But as I said, there were things that caused shadows. One of these haunted her this morning, as she sat with her feet on the fender, and watched Frank while he eagerly devoured the morning's telegraphic news, giving her bits now and then, which she did not understand, and over which she wondered much, as to why they should be interesting to any mortal. At last she broke in upon the reading.

"Frank, when are you going to have done with that dreadful paper? It will rob me of the whole morning, I think."

It dropped to the floor on the instant.

"I beg your pardon, my blessed little wife," he said, gayly. I have heard my mother say that wives were always jealous of newspapers; but the telegraphic information is more than usually valuable this morning in a business point of view. I declare! Is it possible it is so

late? Rebecca, did you know it was nearly
nine o'clock?"

"Of course I did, and I hinted a warning two
or three times. Now, must you go at once?"

"Well, very soon. Is there anything special?"

"Indeed there is; something very special. I
want to have a long talk with you."

"Begin it now," he said, sitting down beside
her; "and if we don't finish, it can be taken up
at noon."

"Oh, well, the beginning isn't so very long. I
just wanted to ask you one question about which
I have thought a great deal. Frank, do you never
have family worship here at home?"

"No," he said, at last; "we don't; that's a
fact. Of course, in my father's time it was
always observed, but since that we have never
been in the habit of it."

"But, Frank, why not? Why should you not
conduct family worship in your own home?"

"Well, I hardly know why," he said, musing a
little. "The fact is, my mother has never asked
it. I suppose she thought I was too young; and
lately, probably, she has never thought of it at

all. One soon gets used to a way of life, you know, and it becomes hard to make changes."

"I should have thought your mother would have missed it bitterly. I can't tell you how very strange it seems to me. I find myself lingering in the dining-room, as a matter of course; it doesn't seem as if the day were really begun without family prayers. I never was without that beginning before."

"Poor little bird," he said, softly; " now she isn't going to be homesick, and draw wicked little comparisons between the home from which I have stolen her, and this, where I have caged her."

"No, I am not homesick," she said, sitting up straight, and speaking cheerly. She was not going to allow herself to be petted away from the subject on which she had made up her mind to speak.

" And, Frank, you know, of course, that I am not drawing any comparisons between this home and my other one. That was very simple and plain, and this is elegant, and I like it better; you know I do. But for all that there are some things that I miss — some that ought not to be missed in a Christian home, and this is one of them. Now that we are a family, should we not have a family altar?"

"Well," he said, speaking again with hesitation; and seeming to be somewhat embarrassed; "that is one of the features of a home of *our* own, to which I have looked forward pleasantly, I will admit. But this is hardly a home of our own, you know; we have rather come into my mother's family, and we must be guided somewhat, by her rules and ways."

"But, surely, Frank, mother would like to have you read in the Bible, and pray with her every morning! What could be pleasanter to a mother than to have her son able to do this! What I wonder at is that you have so long let her miss this part of home life."

"I fancy her ideas of home may be a trifle different from yours and mine. Oh, of course she would have enjoyed it, but then we didn't do it, you see; and changes of this kind are especially hard to make. The ways of the house are established, and it would be extremely inconvenient for mother to change; in fact, it would be not a little difficult for us. It is nearly nine now, as you see; I am later this morning than I must often be. And then at night it would be a matter of endless inconvenience to us; I am often late, you know, and neither you nor my mother ought to be kept waiting for me."

I hope the young husband would not have felt too much grieved had he known just what this manner of reasoning brought to Rebecca's mind. The truth was, she had been reading and studying on her Sabbath lesson, during the hour that she had spent alone the day before, and despite all her efforts to put it away, there would flash back to her the specious reasoning of that graceless scamp, known as Jeroboam. Did not he say: "It is too much for you to go up to Jerusalem?" And as she thought of Mrs. Alanson Edwards, in her elegant home, and thought of the evident pride that she took in keeping up its appointments, and the time that she lavished on her household plans and improvements, it almost seemed impossible that the word would come to her: "Behold thy gods." If all these, and a hundred other kindred plans and ways, did not fill that lady's heart, what did? This train of thought had its startling side. What were the gods that she and Frank were to set up in this new home of theirs? If they were not to go up to their own altar to worship, was there to be a golden calf erected, around which they were to dance?

She shook off the remembrance of Jeroboam and his folly, and returned to the charge with renewed vigor, be it confessed, because of this moment spent with the sinner, of so long ago.

"Frank, do you really think it is right to have a home, and not recognize the Lord in it?"

"That is putting it in rather strong language," her husband said. "I am not ready to admit that we are a heathen household. Still, it would be pleasant, in many respects, to have worship together, if we could manage it. Would you like to have a quiet time together here in our room?"

"Just you and me alone?"

He nodded assent, whereupon she resolutely shook her head.

"I do not mean that I wouldn't like that of all things, and yet it wouldn't be my idea of family worship. Besides, I don't think it would be courteous to mother; it would necessitate endless embarrassing interruptions and inconveniences, or else we should have to explain to mother, and it would simply be leaving her out of the family. Frank, why wouldn't it be very pleasant for you, and mother, and me, to meet together, morning and evening, as other Christian households do ?"

This direct question seemed to need a direct answer, but Mr. Frank Edwards fidgeted and changed his position two or three times, before he said :

"To tell you the truth, Rebecca, I don't feel as though I could conduct family prayers with mother present ; besides I am not at all sure that it would be pleasant to her. It would bring up old memories and associations, and sadden her heart much more than it would help her."

There was certainly no connection between the ideas, and yet Rebecca could not help thinking of Jeroboam again, and the plea that he made to his heart for his wretched conduct. Did not *he* fear that the heart of his people would go out after the old associations? Meantime Frank went on musingly :

" My mother has had a good deal of sadness in her life ; I should be sorry to recall the past too vividly."

This sounded pathetic, and Rebecca surely ought not to have laughed, but she did.

"Frank," said she, "you remind me of Jeroboam."

" Not acquainted with the individual," he said, speaking somewhat coldly.   He would rather be struck than laughed at, especially when he was conscious of having made a foolish remark.

" There is no special similarity," Rebecca said ; " and yet the reasoning is a trifle like his."

" What about him ? "

" Why, it's the lesson," she said, and she spoke more soberly.

Frank was not a Sunday-school man ; he knew nothing about the lesson.   And the two Sabbath mornings that she had spent in her new home she had seemed to very much surprise the inmates by going to Sunday-school.   As a matter of course, Frank had accompanied her to the church door, and called for her when the service was over, but he had made good-natured comments on being unused to hurrying on Sunday

morning, calling it his lazy morning. And the
mother at the breakfast table had hinted that
sundry things were sadly awry because of the
need for haste, that Rebecca might have her
breakfast before going out. She had said that
she considered nine o'clock an absurd hour for
the service; and added that she thought matrons
were excused from duty. Rebecca foresaw that
the road to Sabbath-school would lead through
difficulties. So she was sober. "He was rather
fearful lest his people should over-exert themselves by going to Jerusalem to worship, so he
made a calf out of gold, and had them worship
it." Frank laughed.

"I should say that your ideas of family worship were not very helpful, if they remind you
of calves made of gold."

"It is the absence of the worship that reminds me," she said quickly, and added: Oh,
never mind that; it was a foolish comparison.
But, really, Frank, don't you think your reasoning about this matter will hardly bear looking
into?"

"It doesn't strike me as so very strange. My
mother is an elderly lady, of high culture, and

extremely fastidious in her tastes, and I am in her eyes only a boy. I should fully expect to offend her nice ideas of propriety, and give her more pain than pleasure."

It still seemed remarkably strange to Rebecca that a man should be afraid to pray in the presence of a Christian mother. But she said no more; indeed, there was no time, for her husband sprang up hastily: "I must really go," he said. "I have staid past the time. Well, good-by. I am sorry that I remind you of that old fellow, if the reminder isn't pleasant, and I should hardly think it could be. We musn't waste our mornings in arguing, after this; we might have had time for a walk to-gether."

And then he was gone, and the matter about which she had thought and prayed was farther away from accomplishment than she had supposed it was at first.

She felt very restless — unable to settle to anything. It was impossible to get away from a feeling of disappointment. It is dreadful to feel disappointed in the Christian character of the man whom you call your husband. Rebecca shrank from the acknowledgment of any such feeling.

Mrs. Edwards knocked, and left a message on the way to her room:

"Your friend, Mr. Milton, is in the parlor, Rebecca, and would like to see you. He has chosen an early hour for calls, hasn't he? As you are in your wrapper yet shall I excuse you?"

Now there was that in her tone which said what Rebecca had very well known before, that John Milton was not a favorite of the lady's; she considered his family rather "common." The lady in the wrapper resented the tone.

"Oh, no!" she said, springing up. "I am never ceremonious with John; he is too intimate a friend."

Then she went down to the great elegant parlor, whose exquisite beauty and propriety were almost too much for John. "How do you do?" he said, heartily, coming toward her and holding out both hands. "I am so glad you have got back again — I mean I am so glad to have got back to see you. They tell me you have been home for more than a week. No, I can't sit down. I ought not to have stopped. I

am out on an errand, and have hardly a moment; it is just an item of business. You were
not at the teachers' meeting? Well, they have
revived the plan of meeting from house to house,
and taking the houses of the teachers by streets.
It so happens that your house leads off, being
nearest to the church. And the question is, Do
you approve, and are you going to invite us to
meet with you?"

"Why, of course, I," Rebecca began. Then
she stopped in confusion. She was thinking of
the little parlor in Green Street. She had
for the moment forgotton that she had a new
home, and that she was not the mistress
thereof. For the moment I will not deny that
she longed with all her heart for a little bit of a
house belonging to her and Frank, to which she
could bid her friends a hearty welcome. How
surprised and vexed Frank would be if he
thought she felt other than that now. And yet
she tried to imagine the teachers gathering in
those elegant parlors. That certainly wouldn't
do. Well, then, the library. But that was
quite as elegant in its different way; and somehow she didn't know why, nor what was lack-

ing, but it seemed certain that there was not a spot in that house suited to a teachers' meeting.

"Well," she said at last, and her laugh had an embarrassed sound, "of course I shall have to consult my husband, you know."

"All right," said John. "You can talk it over together, and let us know. We want to get out slips for the season, with the names of the different places of meeting printed on. Just give us an answer in time for that, you know, and it will be all right."

Yet he knew, and she *knew* he knew, that things were very different from what they were in the little home on Green Street. She went up-stairs with a sigh. How manly John was growing, and how earnestly he was taking up church work of all sort! He said "we" as naturally as though he had been one of them all his life. Had he more Christian courage than her Frank? She put away that thought promptly, and gave herself heartily to the hating of Jeroboam and all his ways. How horrid it was that that odious comparison should ever have occured to her!

CHAPTER XIII.

HALTING BETWEEN TWO OPINIONS.

OST of the confidential communications in the Edwards household occurred at the breakfast table; that being the time when the family were together and inclined to loiter over the meal. It was on a certain Wednesday morning that Mrs. Edwards, senior, suddenly arrested the attention of her son and flushed the cheek of his wife, by saying:

"By the way, Frank, I am going to have a few friends to tea with us this evening; the Miltons and Falconers, and Judge Randall and his wife; don't make any engagement for the evening, and do try to hasten home in time to get a little rested before they come; I have observed that you are inclined to be so dull, if you come directly from the bank to the parlor."

"There is no telling, mother, whether I can be dutiful about that last request." It will depend on whether the day's accounts come out all right, or whether some bothering deficiency holds me a prisoner; however, I'll be as brilliant as the infliction will admit. You remember that I am not particularly fond of the Falconers."

"Oh, well, neither am I for that matter; but they are in our society, and among the first people, so of course we must do our duty by them. I haven't invited the Miltons in some time, and I couldn't have them and pass the Falconers; I am particularly anxious that you should be early at home to entertain them, because, of course, the main object in asking them is to introduce Rebecca to our friends."

Now, there were two items in the above conversation that made Rebecca's cheeks glow. In the first place, accustomed as she had been to the free and constant intimacy of true home life, it seemed very strange to her, that she, a daughter of the house, should hear at the breakfast table for the first time, that there was to be a tea party in the evening; even then she had not been told, but was simply permitted to overhear the words as addressed to her husband; then the manner in which Mrs. Edwards said: "Of course, the main object of asking them is to introduce Rebecca to our friends," was such a marked way of saying, that although she lived less than a dozen blocks from the house where she had spent her life, that she was in an entirely new world, socially, and needed an introduction to the choice circle in which she was now expected to move. She wondered what Mrs. Edwards would have thought if she had known how rebelliously her heart reached out after the old friends. But there was more than either of these thoughts that presently made her face grow thoughtful and troubled.

In the privacy of their own room the trouble came to the surface.

"Frank, isn't it strange for mother to have company to-night?"

"It is a perfect bore at any time," Frank said, stretching himself on the sofa and yawning. "I am actually tired now at the prospect; they are a wickedly stupid set that mother seems to think her duty to society involves having around her. Don't you go to having **any** duties to society, Rebecca, I hate them."

"But, I mean, isn't it strange in mother to choose Wednesday evening?"

Frank Edwards raised himself on his elbow and stared:

"What is the matter with Wednesday evening," he said, at last; "why isn't it as good as any other evening?"

The young wife made a little gesture of impatience:

"One would think, Frank, that you did not know there was such a thing as prayer-meeting, I am sure you used to go quite regularly."

"Well, upon my word, I had forgotten it; I don't suppose mother has thought of it either; she doesn't get out in the evening, very often you know. I don't believe she has been to prayer-meeting in five years."

Now it was a special gift of grace, just then, that quick-witted Rebecca was enabled to keep her tongue from saying:

"Why, she goes out to tea parties, and she

went to the lecture the other evening, when it was quite stormy, too." "Of what use to say it?" said her heart, so she kept still."

Her husband was still, too, evidently intending to say no more on the subject, so she went back to it.

"What shall we do about it Frank?"

"Why, as to that," he said with a little laugh, "there doesn't seem to be anything that we can do but endure the bore with the best grace we can summon."

"But, Frank, you don't understand what I mean. Is it right do you think for us to ignore the prayer-meeting because mother has company?"

"Why, Rebecca, you heard her expressly state that it was on your account that she invited company."

"I know, but she has never said anything to me about it; how could she know but that we had an engagement? I don't feel that it is right to stay at home from prayer-meeting for such a reason."

Mr. Edwards sat bolt upright at this point and

concluded to do no more resting. Presently he spoke in a half-injured tone:

"Rebecca, I hope you will not allow yourself to feel aggrieved at any little omission of etiquette on mother's part; she is an old lady, you know; she must not be expected to be so mindful of all those nice points; she remembers that you are one of the family now, and omits the exceeding proprieties where you are concerned."

"She does no such things," thought Rebecca; "she was never guilty of omitting a propriety in her life; she treats me as she would a stranger who was visiting some other member of her family and had nothing to do with *her;*" but put it to Rebecca's credit that she still only *thought* these things, and did not say them.

"Frank," she said, going over to his side and speaking very earnestly, "you don't understand me; it is not because I am offended that I think the prayer-meeting should come first; I do honestly think that you and I have made an engagement to be at the prayer-meeting whenever absolute duty does not keep us away."

"Oh, well, I subscribe to that, and in general I should look out for such things; mother will bear it in mind for the future ; we are in for it this one time, though ; the company is not of our inviting, so in a sense we can't help it."

Mrs. Frank Edwards did not look greatly relieved ; she began again in a doubtful tone : "Frank, there are very special reasons why I want to be there to-night ; don't you remember Mr. Foster's request that we should all make the meeting a subject of special prayer this week and be present to help it along? I have tried to do that part, and I feel as though I needed the meeting ; couldn't we be excused for an hour after tea? We could be home at eight."

Frank Edwards shook his head, half laughingly : "You know nothing of my mother's high teas if you imagine such a thing possible ; if you are allowed to leave the table by eight o'clock you may be thankful ; no, my blessed little puritan, we are fully committed for this time ; I am sorry ; I meant that you should not be tried in this way ; if mother had mentioned it before, her plans might have been changed ; all we can do now, is to look out for the future."

"But, Frank, suppose you and I, not knowing of this company, had been invited out to tea to-night and had been expected; wouldn't you and mother and everybody consider that a sufficient excuse for being absent? especially when the persons invited are elderly people and will be able to visit with mother."

Frank Edwards shook his head with a very positive air: "If you knew my mother half as well as I do, you would know that is simply an impossible plan of yours;" he said, decidedly, rising as he spoke: "What a way we have of wasting our minutes in unprofitable discussions; it is time for me to go. I am really sorry for this thing, as I said; and we must see to it that it does not occur often."

"You didn't answer me," Rebecca said, trying to smile.

"I wanted to know if you didn't think an engagement out to tea would release us? If you had promised Dr. Freeman to bring me to meet company at his house to-night, wouldn't you go?"

"There's a fellow who comes to the bank to argue finance, and when he gets in a tight place he always says: 'That isn't a parellel case;' so I shall answer all your troublesome questions in that way. Take good care of yourself to-day and rest as much as you can; for the most of those people are perfect bores; I shall have to lunch down town to-day in order to get home earlier to-night. Good-by."

And this was all that the conversation had accomplished.

"Oh, dear me!" said Rebecca, feeling in ill-humor with herself and all the world; "I do wish people thought alike on any one thing; and I wish one troublesome subject after another were not constantly coming to drive me to distraction. Now I never used to think of going anywhere on prayer-meeting evening, and Frank knows I didn't. What is the use of having a church covenant if it doesen't mean anything? I wish Frank had said right out boldly and fearlessly to mother that he would visit with her company until church time and again after he came home; that is the way I should have done. Now I don't know what to do; it is just one perplexity after another. I can't go off to meeting alone; how dreadfully that would look! But I honestly don't think it is right to stay at home; suppose I meet Mr. Foster to-morrow, and when he asks why we were not there, as he is morally sure to do, how will it look to say: 'Why, we had a tea party and I couldn't leave!' The whole trouble is of mother's making; if she would condescend to hint a few hours before-hand what disposal she expects to make of Frank and me it would save ever so much trouble. What a way to live! She, a member of the church and hasn't been to prayer-meeting in five years, and she has been out at least three evenings since I have been here! I wonder what she says to Mr. Foster when he calls? One would think any one so pointed in asking questions as he, would confuse even her occasionally."

Just at this point Rebecca's storm of thought suddenly came to a halt; there flashed over her the questions, almost as if they were asked with mortal voice: "What will the Lord Jesus Christ say to you? How will you answer his questions in regard to unfulfilled vows, unkept covenants?" It is noticeable that when we get down to the root of the matter and question how the Lord himself views us, instead of what human eyes see and human hearts think, we are apt to forget the mote in our brother's eye and busy ourselves solemnly with the beam in our own eye. Then there was a verse, very familiar to her because of its association with the coming lesson: "How long halt ye between two opinions? If the Lord be God, follow him." She said these last words aloud, with a subdued and solemnized voice. Would he have her stay at home and do her share in entertaining the guests, or would he have her go to the house of prayer? *Was* there anything in the nature of religious covenants that differed from business covenants? Would she, if she were a teacher in the ward-school, be justified in remaining away from her post because there was to be company? No, that was not a parellel case, because in that instance she would throw the school machinery into confusion; but that other, suppose she had promised to go to a friend's house, it was a positive promise, and she was expected, could she stay away to receive invited company at her own home? Certainly it would be a discourtesy that would require a great amount of explanation; she tried to imagine herself writing an excuse and explaining the circumstances; suppose she

wrote to Mr. Foster: "Dear pastor, please say
to the friends that Mr. Edwards and I can not
be at the prayer-meeting to-night, as we have
invited company to tea!" How would that do?
Whereupon, again she was stopped by the same
solemn thought; suppose she tried to explain it
to the Lord himself! "How long halt ye?"
"How *can* I go?" she said growing almost angry
at the humble voice. "My husband refuses to
go, and I am a bride, and the company is made
for me; if I had known about the circumstances
it would have been different." But, then, was it
probable that the lookers-on at her consistent or
inconsistent life would know anything about the
circumstances? Would she not dishonor the
Lord in their eyes? "But if Baal, then follow
him." Not that she desired to stay among the
guests, but it would be very hard to go; hard
to risk her mother-in-law's vexation, hard to
answer the courteous stares of surprised guests,
hard above all the rest to incur her husband's
decided disapproval.

Thus in much bewilderment as to which way
to turn, and in much discomfort of mind she
spent the morning. Finally she was literally

driven by her discomfort to the refuge where
one would think she would have fled at the first.
Why not, since she honestly desired to please
the Lord, ask him which he would have her do?
She did not reach this point until she had par-
leyed with Satan till she was well-nigh van-
quished; the specious reasoner had brought to
her mind the importance of making her religion
beautiful, of shining in the home circle, of being
respectful to her mother, of having regard for
the opinions of her husband; all splendid argu-
ments, only he omitted to remind her that the
Lord did not expect her to be shining at home,
when he had expressly invited her to meet him
elsewhere, and had interposed no providence in
her way. It all culminated in a little note,
which she herself left at the bank when she
went down for her morning walk, a wee little
note, but one which made her heart beat as she
handed it through the little door to the smiling
husband who was very glad to see her, and very
proud of her appearance.   This was the note :

"DEAR FRANK :—You won't be vexed with
me, I know, for you promised to bear with me,
and to take me for better and worse; perhaps

you will feel that this is 'worse;' but I honestly
feel that I ought to go to the prayer-meeting
to-night. I almost promised Mr. Foster to be
there, and I solemnly promised my Saviour to
let nothing less than a plain duty keep me away;
I can not feel that this is a duty; I have been
almost startled by a verse in the lesson: 'How
long halt ye between two opinions?' I will
just slip quietly away after supper, and be back
before you have had time to miss me, and I feel
sure I shall be doing right. I will not mind
going alone, for you know, our next neighbors
always go.

"Lovingly,

"REBECCA."

Frank Edwards, contrary to his mother's
directions came home very late, too late to do
much toward the entertainment of the guests,
indeed, they were waiting tea for him. He
found his wife, dressed in her prettiest, at least
she looked so to him, being as bright, and kind,
and genial as she knew how to be, and charming
her new friends; very little did he say to her,
except in a general way; he was unusually

prompt in his attentions to his guests at the table, and finally, when, as they were rising, he heard the bell for evening service sounding, he glanced toward his wife as if to assure himself that she was still of the same mind, then he said in as composed a tone as though he never contemplated any other arrangement: "By the way, our friends will excuse us now for an hour, Rebecca; it is the evening for our usual prayer-meeting; so we will give mother the pleasure of a quiet chat with you until we return." Of course they were courteous, and expressed the hope that he would not allow them to detain him, and at least three of them remembered that it was *their* prayer-meeting evening, as well as his; thus quietly was the exit made; but who will undertake to describe Mrs. Alanson Edwards' surprise and annoyance; she had never known her son to be guilty of like rudeness! Of course it would be attributed to no other than the new element that had so lately come into the household. Very quiet was Mr. Frank Edwards during the walk to the prayer-meeting. He wrapped his wife's furs closely around her, and drew her hand closely under his protective sleeve, and questioned as to the rubbers and wrappings generally; but beyond that he made no attempt at conversation, either on the way thither, or during the walk home; and Mrs. Frank Edwards was returned to the elegant parlors and to the entertainment of guests without having been able to determine whether her husband was displeased or gratified by the result of her decision. Mrs. Alanson Edwards was more open in her demonstrations; poor Rebecca had the satisfaction of feeling sure her mother considered that she had been guilty of unpardonable rudeness.

CHAPTER XIV.

MRS. FRANK EDWARDS BEING ADVISED.

THEY were up-stairs in Mrs. Frank's pretty room, herself and Sallie Holland. It was still morning, and Mrs. Frank was in her wrapper. I do not say she kept it on because it was a remarkably rich and elegant wrapper, and extremely becoming to her; but it really was pleasant to meet Sallie Holland, and feel that one was dressed in a most becoming manner, and that it was, after all, only a wrapper. There were not many times when Mrs. Frank cared a great deal about her dress; but whenever Sallie Holland was near, that was one of the times when she did; for had not Sallie Holland almost ignored her at times in the days of her girlhood, because she was so very plain in her attire? And was she not able now to wear what Sallie Holland need not hope to aspire to? She was sewing on a necktie for Frank, hemming it with dainty little stitches such as she liked to take for no other being in the world but him. There was a bright spot glowing on either cheek, and her eyes flashed with a sort of light that betokened a great deal of inward commotion. Sallie had brought her unending crochet for an hour's chat.

"I haven't a minute to spare, because this is for Emeline's wedding present," she had explained. "It is such a nuisance to make wedding presents, especially when you have to do every bit of the work yourself. Now you, I suppose, can just go and select your silver or your gold fancy, and send the bill to your husband, without anymore thought about it. I declare that must be nice.

And Mrs. Frank laughed and looked her satisfaction, as she admitted that that was what she would probably do, though really she had not given the matter a thought as yet; and she

heartily enjoyed it all.   Time was, and that but
just a few days in the distance, when Sallie had
had three times the money to spend that had
ever been hers.   Matters were changed between
them.   Mrs. Frank liked it ; but, for all that, she
went back to the vexed and uncomfortable feelings that had possessed her when her caller came
in.

Another annoyance had loomed up in the Edwards   family.   They were   always   coming.
They came more frequently every day; at least
so it was beginning to seem to the young husband.   As he went down town that morning, he
stepped   hard   and   swift   on   the stones, and
wished as he ground his foot down heavily that
there was such a thing as peace.   Rebecca, conscious of certain irritating things that she had
said to him, made herself feel more unhappy and
annoyed by their very memory ; but she gave the
credit of them, not to herself, but to the one who
had been the producing cause of the trouble ;
and that one was, of course, Mrs. Alanson Edwards.   You can imagine to what a state of irri-
tation she was reduced when I tell you that she

actually descended to the impropriety of spreading this family matter before her caller.

"Yes, they are pleasant rooms enough," she said, with a smile of conscious pride, in answer to some of Sallie's praises; and then she sighed. "But you needn't think, Sallie, that life is made up of rose leaves here, any more than anywhere else."

"I am sure I can't see where the thorns come, in your case," Sallie answered. "I am sure you have everything that heart could wish; a lovely home, plenty of money, horses and carriage at your disposal, and a husband who idolizes you."

Sallie enumerated all these blessings in a tone which said, unconsciously, that she rated them according to their worth in her eyes. In quieter moments Rebecca would have been amused at the idea of putting her husband last on the list. Now she made a most unfortunate reply.

"You have forgotten one blessing," she said, looking down, and taking an exceedingly small stitch, while the color flashed over her face again at the remembrance of her vexation.

"What is that?"

" A mother-in-law."

Sallie laughed.

" Why, is she so very disagreeable? Well, to tell you the truth, I don't particularly envy you that acquisition. I think you were very foolish to consent to come into the same house with her."

" So do I," Rebecca said, and the color mounted to her forehead. " She has the reputation of being anything but an agreeable old lady to get along with; and, of course, Frank is not expected to see it, she being his mother. No one need think that I shall ever consent to live with a mother-in-law; I know too much about them."

" Is she so very trying, Rebecca ? "

" She is the most disagreeable woman I ever knew in my life."

You would not have known Rebecca's voice had you heard her say this, it was so full of suppressed anger. The subject once started, it seemed almost impossible to let it alone, especially since Sallie was the most sympathetic of listeners.

" She would make an excellent matron of an establishment for the education of servants, or something of that sort," Rebecca began again. "She hasn't the least idea that either Frank or I are grown up; we are simply children, to do as she tells us, or be punished for our naughtiness. Why, she pays no more attention to *my* plans than if I were a kitten!"

"How horrid!" said Sallie; complacently setting a row of purple stitches in her tidy.

"It is real queer in Frank to endure it, isn't it? Such an independent man as he always seemed to be! I shall have to confess to you that I was always afraid he would be a little bit of a tyrant."

Rebecca was not so angry that she forgot to draw herself up, somewhat haughtily, at this familiar mention of her husband. Sallie saw it, and hastened to explain, lest future confidences might be quenched: "Not to you of course; but I mean I had a half fear of him, he was so decided and determined about anything that he undertook. I suppose he inherits it from his mother. But one wouldn't think she could manage *him*."

"She manages him and everybody else with whom she comes in contact," said Rebecca in great heat. "Sometimes I get so vexed I think I am a real simpleton for allowing her to interfere with my plans as I do."

"I would never allow it in the world; as you commence you will have to continue, only she will grow worse and worse. I have noticed that she had a very arbitrary way with her, but I didn't know that she would show it to you."

"I am the one, unfortunately, to whom she is particularly fond of showing it. I don't suppose I ought to say so, but she does vex me wonderfully. Only this very morning I have been so tried that I had half a mind to go home and spend the day, leaving her to herself. I dare say I should, if you hadn't come in just as you did. The fact is, I haven't in a great many years, been treated like a child, and I find it hard to get accustomed to it."

"I should think so," Sallie said, and her voice was wonderfully sympathetic; "your mother was such a gentle little woman."

Now, Sallie knew nothing at all about Rebecca's mother, beyond the merest casual sight of her, and Rebecca knew it. In her calm moments this sentence would have amused and

at the same time disgusted her. She paid no
attention to it now.

"What happened, to disturb you this morning,
you poor little victim?"

Now, Rebecca was really longing to go over
the whole scene again, not for the purpose of
telling it to Sallie, so much as to assure herself
of its exasperating nature, and tell herself that
no one with a spark of spirit could be expected
to endure it.

"Nothing so very serious, I suppose," Rebecca
said struggling to be composed; "only she is
always doing the same sort of thing, and I am
nearly tired of it."

"But what does she do?"

In a more quiet time Rebecca would have
observed and resented this persistent determination to look into her affairs, and rewarded it
with haughty reticence. She did not even observe it now.

"Why, she treats Frank and myself precisely
as if we were children, I tell you. Now, this
morning, Frank and I, before we came down-
stairs, had been planning to go down to Milton's
and spend the evening. Frank said we would

get together a few friends who liked John, and who knew that poor little Carrie, and take something along for refreshments, and give them a pleasant evening. John had been hinting to us how nice it would be for us to happen in. You know the poor fellow never feels at liberty to invite company. Well, we had it all arranged, and at the breakfast table his mother calmly remarked, just before it was time for Frank to go: 'We are engaged at the Haddingtons to-night.' 'The dickens we are!' Frank said, 'when did that happen?' And instead of answering him, she proceeded to read him a lecture on the impropriety of using such words, precisely as if he had been fourteen, at the very oldest. By dint of patient questioning, he finally learned that the Haddingtons had sent invitations for us three days ago, and they had been accepted. 'You were not in, of course, when the note came, and it slipped my mind.' This, mother said to Frank, by way of apology. But mind you, I was in. I saw the Haddingtons' man when he came up the steps. He had his hand full of notes, and I wondered then what invitations were coming. Now, isn't that a remarkable way to be treated?"

"I should think it was," said Miss Sallie, with great emphasis. "Of course you are not going; I wouldn't go a step if I were you."

Precisely the thought which was hovering through Rebecca's mind, though her husband had said with a gloomy face: "I suppose we will have to give up our little plan, then, for the evening. It's a great nuisance. I don't want to go to the Haddingtons." She had wanted then and there to say: "*I* don't mean to go to the Haddingtons, I have another engagement." She wished now that she had said it.

"I suppose we shall have to go, since our acceptance was sent without our knowing anything about it."

"I wouldn't," said Miss Sallie, complacently. She was one of those natures that enjoyed a fuss, no matter of what material it was made. "I should just send my regrets, saying I had not heard of the invitation in time. I think that would serve her just right."

"I almost believe I *won't* go," Rebecca said, flushing as she thought of the insult to her matronhood. "I am not obliged to carry out all the engagements she forms for me, as if I were a child. I have almost a mind to go down to mother's and spend the evening. I told Frank when he went away that I didn't believe I should go; so he will not be surprised."

"You might as well begin right, in the first place," Sallie said. "If you let her think you are a chicken-hearted little goosie, that will do just as you are told, you won't be able to have any mind of your own after awhile. I wonder that Frank likes to have her treat you in that way."

"Frank doesn't think anything about it," said Rebecca, quickly, beginning to be annoyed that she had permitted any one to speak so freely of her husband.

A sudden summons from home sent Sallie Holland and her tidy away, and Rebecca had what she greatly needed just then—a little quiet thought. Do her the justice to understand, that in less than ten minutes after the door had closed on her caller, she would have given almost anything in the world for the power to take back every word that she had said to her. Not that she was sorry for feeling it—she still imagined that she had a right to be angry—but it was certainly very unlike her to parade her home affairs before the eyes of a third person. How had she allowed herself to do it? Then she tried to take into consideration the advice given about the evening. It accorded exactly with her preference, and the advice that so accords is very apt to be taken. Just let her once establish her intention to have a mind of her own, and to accept and decline invitations as she pleased, and the matter would be settled without any further trouble.

Suddenly, Mrs. Frank Edwards, who had half risen to go about some other work, sat down again, and gave a half-annoyed, half-amused, little laugh, while a sudden flush spread all over her face. Why should she happen, just at that moment, to think of the story which the last week of study had made so familiar to her—the story of Ahab being advised by his wife Jezebel. Was it possible that she had been playing the part of that despicable king, while Sallie took the role of Jezebel? Certainly her mode of comforting was somewhat in that line, a trifle less outspoken, perhaps, but she had plainly insinuated, more than once, that both Frank and his wife were cowards for permitting such a state of things. Rebecca had utterly despised the king when she read of him. Was her trouble really more important than his? He wanted a certain field that he could not get. She wanted—no, back of that, Ahab wanted his own way; so did she. On the whole, he had been less dishonorable than had she; for, at least, it was to his wife that he went to pour out his childish ill-humor, while she had gone not even to an intimate friend, but simply to a chance caller, whose character she disliked.

To what depths had she sunken! And she had dared to express the most utter and unqualified contempt for King Ahab, declaring to Frank that she despised him even more than she did his wife, for she, at least, was daringly wicked, while he was a whining coward. She realized *her* cowardice as she sat there thinking over the morning talk. How utterly mortified she would have been to have had Frank overhear all the sharp and foolish, not to say wicked words she had uttered that morning! This thought brought its own keen rebuke. How could she have so entirely forgotton the ear of God, always open to the words she said? The result of all this was, that Mrs. Frank Edwards went down deeper into the valley of humiliation that day than she had ever been before in her whole life. She recognized herself, as in some sense, at least on a level with the despised Ahab.

There were several people in that household who were surprised that day. Mrs. Alanson Edwards had been made to feel that what was really only a thoughtless omission on her part, resulting from Frank's habit of deferring all invitations to her, and following her fancies, was a serious matter now that there was a *Mrs.* Frank. She resented that lady's evident offense even while she acknowledged to herself that she ought to have told her.

"I suppose," she said, drawing a long sigh as she thought it all over in her room, while she was preparing for her afternoon nap, "I suppose she will stay at home and sulk. I might have told her before, but, dear me, I forgot it, and it never used to make any difference with Frank. I don't see why boys want to get married."

As for Frank, he had not the least idea that his lady would go to the tea-party. Her excited face when she talked the matter over with him led him to expect different plans. "It wasn't very courteous," he said, thinking it over. "Mother ought to have told us, but I suppose she forgot it, and she knows I don't care about such things, but it is evident that Rebecca does." Then he sighed a little, and wondered whether it would end with a fuss or without one.

I don't know which of them felt the most relieved when Mrs. Frank, dressed in exquisite taste, came down stairs to meet him, as he halted in the hall, to tell his mother that she must excuse them to the Haddingtons, on the plea of a previous engagement, and said: "Why, Frank, you are late! We were invited for six; were we not, mother?" And neither the relieved and mollified mother, nor the gratified husband, had the least idea that that worthless couple, Ahab and Jezebel, had anything to do with this sudden lull in the domestic sky.

But this compromise did not quiet Miss Sallie

Holland's tongue. She had much material, gathered from a reliable source, and she made busy use of it, to Rebecca's sorrow and indignation, before the winter was over.

CHAPTER XV.

THE CLEANSING BLOOD.

T was a sunny Sabbath afternoon, and they were together in their pretty room, Rebecca and her husband. Frank Edwards in his handsome dressing-gown, the product of Rebecca's taste, with his feet incased in bright slippers of her choosing, and luxuriously resting on the arm of the low-backed couch, looked the picture of comfort and satisfaction. There was a glow of pleasure on Rebecca's face, and a brightness in her eyes that was even more marked than usual. She could not help feeling that a step forward had been taken.

Sabbath afternoon, since her marriage, had been in one respect a trial. From the time Frank Edwards could remember, it had been his custom to eat a hearty dinner on the Sabbath, some two hours later than usual, and then to retire immediately to the depths of a great cushioned chair, or the old-fashioned lounge in his room, and take a nap. When he awakened, the Sabbath was nearly spent, only time to prepare somewhat hastily for evening meeting. Rebecca's coming had not broken in upon this time-honored custom, and she being one of those unfashionable young ladies, blessed with splendid health, and having always had a great deal to do, could not make herself sleepy or tired on Sabbath afternoon any more than at any other time. To spend the sacred hours of the day in this fashion was not in accordance with her ideas, and she set resolutely about breaking the chains that had held her husband. But I doubt if there are any chains harder to break than sleepy ones.

Frank resolutely undertook to keep her company, and allowed himself to be read to; but no

matter what book was selected, nor how ani-
matedly Rebecca read, it only required ten minutes to read him into a refreshing nap, from
which the first bell for evening service was the
sound likely to awaken him. But on this particular afternoon there had been a victory. Wily
Rebecca had beguiled her husband into helping
her with the Sabbath-school lesson, and had succeeded in getting him so interested that all
thought of sleep seemed at last to be banished
from his eyes. It was just at this point that his
wife said:

"Frank, I wish you had a class in Sunday-
school. It is such attractive work, and I think
you would make an interesting teacher.

"Thank you," he said, laughingly. "You
mean if you were the scholar, I suppose. In
that case I shouldn't mind being a teacher."

"Frank, honestly, why won't you try it? It
would be so much pleasanter for me; you don't
know how I hate to start off alone in the
morning."

"You shouldn't do it, then," he said lazily.
"You don't know how I hate to walk down to
church alone, after you are gone. Why don't

I? Well, I hardly know; force of habit, I suppose. I never taught a class in my life."

"Isn't that all the more reason why you should commence?"

"Oh, I don't know. There isn't a dearth among that sort of workers, is there?"

"Indeed there is; real earnest workers, such as you would be. Why, Frank, Mr. Seymour occupies fully one-third of his time in filling vacancies."

"Humph," said her husband, "I should like to see the superintendent of public schools consuming his time in that way."

"I know it; but, you see, rules on that subject don't apply. The superintendent of public schools would dismiss delinquents, and fill their places. But suppose the Sunday-school superintendents could do it, how would they fill their places? It is voluntary work, you see, and the church is full of members who stay at home just as you do."

"You are willing to admit that I am no worse than scores of others, are you?" her husband said, good-naturedly, as he crossed one handsome

foot over the other. "Well, now, that is encouraging, so far as it goes."

"No it isn't," she said, with sparkling eyes,
and a little quiver of the lip. "I can't like to
see you in the company of scores of others. I
should like my husband to be a beacon light,
that it would be safe for others to look to."

"Sorry I disappoint you," he said, with an attempt at a serio-comic tone, but with enough of
the serious in it to make his face flush.

"You do," she said, earnestly, and her face
glowed like fire. "I am honest, Frank; you
disappoint me in Christian energy. If you were
not naturally energetic it wouldn't seem so
strange; but you know you are a thorough, me-
thodical, even an intense business man. I can
not feel satisfied to see you doing nothing in the
church or at home, just being a drone in religion.

"You are frank," he said, and he laughed
slightly; but he took his feet down from the
sofa top and sat erect.

"I know it," she answered, quickly. "You
would not like me to be otherwise than frank.
It would give me the greatest possible joy if you

would bring the same degree of energy into the church that you give to 'the world. Why haven't I a right to expect it, and be disappointed because you don't do it? The work is surely as important. You can see for yourself that it is not being done. Why isn't it your duty to try to do some of it? And, Frank, are you trying at all? Perhaps I am being unjust to you; of course I don't know how many things you may be doing that you say nothing about; but, so far as I can see, it seems to me that in the direction of that which you and I profess to believe the most important work of all, you are doing nothing."

He did not correct her; he had no disposition to do so. The fact is, and it struck him strangely enough at that moment, he was doing just nothing at all. He lived a correct moral life — faultless, so far as outward appearance went — and his name was on the church roll, and that was the whole of it. Coming in daily contact with such Christian living as Rebecca was trying to make, it struck him as a strange contrast.

"I was never brought up to do Christian

work," he said, thoughtfully. "I suppose that makes a difference."

"Neither were you brought up to be a banker," Rebecca said, quickly. "Don't you know you told me how your mother struggled against your being confined to business; how she wanted you to be a gentleman of leisure, and attend to your rents and real estate generally, and how you insisted that you must go into business; that you did not believe in an American gentleman, with good health and youth on his side, being a man of leisure, however large his property."

"You would make an excellent lawyer," her husband answered, smiling faintly. Then they sat in silence. Presently he said:

"I would be willing to be a Sunday-school teacher for the sake of pleasing you, if I understood the art; but you are mistaken in supposing that I would make a good one. It requires a sort of talent that I don't possess. Take this very lesson, for instance, in which you are so much interested to-day. I couldn't teach it. Beyond the bare facts of the case, which can be gotten by reading it over together, I see nothing to say. I'll be hanged if I see how it is possible to consume half an hour in talking about it, to intelligent people who are able to grasp the account at first reading. And yet I know there are teachers who will consider half an hour too short a time to bring out all the points."

"But, Frank, you haven't studied it; how could you expect to be prepared to teach it without making the preparation?"

"I might study it for a week, and the bare facts of the case would be there just as they are now; and I don't see how they would be a bit clearer. There is no mystery about it; it is a plain, clear statement, as direct and as clear as a report of bank stock, and that is all there is about it. How would going over and over it make matters any better? Suppose I had that class of youngsters that they are all the time at me to take, what could I do with them in view of this lesson?"

"Oh, Frank! I see so many things that you could do. Don't you know Fred Nelson is in that class, and see how like the captive maid he is situated; away from home all the week, you

know, working in that shop, surrounded by all
sorts of young men, and, as nearly as I can discover when I talk with him, every one is as sick
with the leprosy of sin as ever Naaman was,
and Fred is the only Christian. I was thinking
of that class when I was studying this lesson,
and wishing I could have a chance to remind
Fred what a work the little maiden accomplished
by simply wishing that her master could know
the great prophet. I am almost afraid that
Fred never has any courage to say anything
about his powerful Friend to the boys, or the
master."

"Go on," said her husband, smiling. "The
more you say, the more you convince me that
you were intended for a Sunday-school teacher
and I wasn't. Now I might have taught Fred
Nelson a dozen years and I should never have
thought of any possible connection between him
and the little captive maid."

"I don't see how you are going to be sure
of that," Rebecca said earnestly, "until you are
willing to make the test, and see for yourself,
whether there is anything in these lessons that
fit individual needs. To be sure there are not

many of them so fruitful as this, but they all surprise me, because of the way in which they fit into present experiences."

"As fruitful as this," Frank said, incredulously. "I tell you I never read a story that seemed more barren; interesting to be sure; but just as much so to read over alone, as with a teacher. There is nothing that has anything to do with present experiences. There is no leprosy now, and if there were, there is no prophet to cure it; no Jordan to wash in to be healed of anything. It all belongs to a dispensation that is past, and while it proves the power of God, it proves it just as clearly, without a teacher saying a word."

She interrupted him. "Oh, Frank! no leprosy now! I wish there wasn't. Surely you see how wonderfully, in every respect, it fits as a type of sin. So slight in its beginnings, so inevitable in its results; so awfully hereditary, so hopeless of cure by any human means. Then you know there is a Jordan and a prophet to point thither, now as then. Oh, Frank! it seems to me the most wonderful lesson. That class ought to have it taught to them as few lessons are. Think how perfect a Naaman they have in it. I believe Randall Morse is ready to do anything earthly, except the simple one that is required, in order to be cured. He professes, you know, to desire to find the way—to be willing to do anything. He is willing to give his time and his father's money. He would go on a mission to Africa—a pilgrimage to China. I think he would do anything but the simple one—washing in the Jordan. He is just as proud as Naaman was, and that is all that stands in his way. The way of salvation is too simple and too humbling to one whose father is worth a million. I want him to have the story of the haughty leper pressed home on his conscience. Then, Frank, in that very same class is poor Harry Turner, groping along in the darkness, too humble to believe himself saved. Some one ought to show him how prompt and entire Naaman's cure was, the minute he obeyed. It took no time, it was so sweet and entire a cleansing. It will surely give Harry courage, if he is only reminded of the similarity between his sickness and that of Naaman. Then, there is Willard Barnes, half indignant, because his prayer for his father is not answered. I know that is his state of mind, though I don't think he realizes it. If I get a chance I want to remind him that Naaman's washing himself in the Jordan six times would have done no sort of good, if by that time he had concluded that he ought to be healed without any more bathing, and gone away. Frank, I think it is a wonderful lesson."

"It depends, I tell you, into whose hands it falls," her husband said, regarding her with a mixture of amusement and respect. "You have given me more ideas about Naaman than I ever had in my life before. I tell you I shouldn't have thought of these applications, though they are remarkably applicable to the boys in that class, I will admit."

"It is just for them. I do hope they will have the right kind of a teacher for next Sunday. Frank, I would risk you before any of the teachers in that school, if you would take hold of it with all your heart."

"It is well to have a good opinion of one's husband," he said, putting up his feet again, "even if that opinion is unmerited."

"There is another point to the lesson," Rebecca said, in a low tone; "more important, I think, to us as Christians than all others."

"Say on; I am getting decidedly interested in the old heathen, and all that pertains to him."

"It is not about the heathen. It is the wonderful prayer given to us, to use, in the golden text: 'Wash me, and I shall be whiter than snow.' Only think of it, Frank! whiter than snow! That is our privilege to stand before God so white that even the whitest thing we know is shadowed, in comparison; and yet how little we try for it; how little of the whiteness we are willing to accept. We seem rather anxious to have the soiled garments left about us."

Her husband regarded her with an interested, yet half-puzzled face. Presently he said: "I am not sure that I follow your thought. Do you mean that perfection of whiteness is attainable here?"

"That is what it says, Frank; and it says it in so many places, that He is able to make us pure."

"I don't know about that doctrine. It is

very nice, theoretically, but practically we do not seem to attain to it; that is, nobody does so far as I can see. It is a continued repetition of the story. Sinning and repenting, sinning and repenting, seems to be our lot this side the river. I am inclined to think we must keep at it till we get rid of our bodies."

"So we must, if we are to do it. But, Frank, that is the very blunder, I think. We are willing to be cleansed in the Jordan, but after that, we want to see to it ourselves that we do not get sick again, and because we fail, because we find that we can not attain to perfect health, any more than we could cure ourselves of leprosy, instead of resting in the strength of one who said His grace was sufficient, and that he was able to keep us from falling, we go right on sinning and repenting as you say, and assuring ourselves that such is the way and that with such living the Lord who redeemed us must be content. He musn't expect us to trust him entirely, until we get away from earth. Is that fair?"

"What are you trying to prove?" he asked, looking utterly bewildered.

"I am trying to prove that you and I and

most of the Christian world are trying to make ourselves good. We were willing to trust Christ for salvation from punishment, but as for trusting him to keep our feet from falling, we don't mean to do any such thing. We are going to look after our own feet, and teach them by gradual steps, by the law of progression, the law of growth, and any other natural law that we can bring to bear on it to attain to a state of goodness, not to be kept to-day, but to attain next year to a place where we can keep ourselves. Isn't that it?"

"That is queer talk," he said doubtfully.

"I know it. Isn't it queer living? I never realized, until a few days ago, that I was trusting myself instead of Christ. I have even felt a sort of complacency at night when thinking over the day. 'I have done wrong in that thing,' I said, 'and in that, but in that other matter I came off conqueror. I am stronger to-day than I was last week. Oh, well, that is encouraging; I can't, of course, expect to be perfect all in a minute. I can only keep pressing on.' Now, whose goodness is that, Frank, but mine? Who am I trusting? Whom do I mean can not make me free from my besetting sins in a minute?"

Mr. Frank Edwards arose suddenly and began a slow, steady walk, up and down the room, his hands pushed into the pockets of his dressing-gown, and his face wearing a thoughtful, not to say troubled look. At last he spoke: "Rebecca, your religion means a great deal more to you, I am inclined to think, than mine does to me. I have always thought so. I begin to feel sure of it. We must look into this matter; you have taken me a step beyond my bearings. I want to understand what you mean. Let us study this thing. In the meantime, if you think it will be best and — and right, I will take that class next Sunday and try to give them some of your ideas about Naaman and themselves."

Rebecca sprang up suddenly, and went over to him as he paused in his walk. Such a light in her eyes as he had not seen for many a day! and the words she spoke were surely enough for him that she thought his decision was best and right.

CHAPTER XVI.

MANAGING JONAH.

ER husband was home at lunch-time, an unusual circumstance with him, and, what was more unusual, he seemed to have a little leisure time, and followed Rebecca up to their room for a talk. Once there he did little talking, but instead stood looking out of the south window at the bursting buds on the trees, and whistling a soft air that some way had a note of perplexity in it as it came to Rebecca's ears. Something was disturbing his peace. His wife did not know whether to question or wait. At last he said:

" Rebecca, how do you suppose that old fellow, Jonah, felt when he found himself in close quarters after the whale swallowed him, you know ?"

" Really," Rebecca said, laughing, " I am afraid that question suggests a reach of imagination that is beyond me."

" It must have been a charming experience, anyhow. I wish I could have a chat with him. I should like to know whether it was when he was shut up there that he decided to hurry off to Nineveh as soon as ever he had an opportunity."

Light began to dawn on Rebecca's mind.

" Are you trying to decide whether to wait until a whale swallows you before you come to a similar decision ?" she asked, quietly.

Her husband turned and bestowed a glance on her that was half quizzical, half searching.

" He was trying to shirk a direct command," he said, at last, turning back to the window as he spoke.

" I know it," Rebecca answered, and her tone had a significant sound.

" And you think I am doing the same thing."

He spoke the words in a sort of discontented

way, as if it was very trying that she could not give him a bit of comfort.

"Frank, I never, even in thought, instituted a comparison between you and Jonah; but, now that you suggest it, there are points in it that are somewhat striking. It would be real pleasant to you, I know, if I should indignantly disclaim any similarity between your life and his; but you don't think it would be true, for all that."

Her husband laughed.

"A regular Job's comforter you are getting to be," he said, speaking with a sort of surface gayety.

"I don't think you stand in special need of comfort. I shouldn't compare your case with Job's at all. It seems to me, what you need is to reach a decision; or, if you have reached it, to act upon it, and not take refuge in flight."

For answer Mr. Edwards began a slow walk up and down the room, in which his wife presently joined. After watching his face for a few minutes, as she slipped her hand under his arm, he said:

"Rebecca, I don't suppose you have an idea

what a difficult thing it is for me to institute
family worship in our house at this late day. If
I had begun it at the beginning of my Christian
life, when I was making changes in other respects,
it would have been so different; or, if we had
even started as soon as we were married, it
would have been infinitely easier."

"I know it," she said, in that same quietly
significant tone. "And, Frank, if you should
wait till next year don't you think it would be
harder yet?"

"That is taking it for granted that the thing
has got to be done at some time."

"Yes; Jonah went to Nineveh at last you
know."

He looked sober and half annoyed, and then
he laughed.

"Do you suppose you are the whale in this
case?" he asked, looking down on her with a
half-amused air.

"No" she said, quickly. "I am one of the
men on board who feared lest the Lord was displeased and the ship would come to grief through
the disobedience of somebody. Frank, to him

who knew his duty and did it not, to him it was accounted sin."

To this he made no sort of answer. The walk up and down the room was continued in utter silence for some minutes. At last he said, speaking in an altered tone :

"I ought to go to the bank at once, and you might have been taking this walk in the open air, instead of being shut up here."

"Frank," his wife said, and there was marked anxiety in her voice, "isn't this matter of more importance than the business at the bank? Can't you let that wait until you decide this?"

"I have decided," he answered, speaking firmly. "You can think of me as making straight for Nineveh all the afternoon. We will ask mother to come to the library with us and have prayers directly after dinner."

For a full hour after he had departed his wife gave herself up to rejoicing over the signal victory of this second Jonah over himself. Then she took time to be relieved that Frank had not asked her to make the arrangements, and tell the formidable Mrs. Edwards of the new departure. No sooner was this thought presented to her than she began to wonder whether, after all there was not something left for her to do. Could she not smooth the way so that her husband's embarrassment might be lessened? There was no use in saying that it was a most plain and direct Christian duty that he, as the head of the house, ought to have been obeying all these years, and that it ought not to be hard to him. That would not remove the fact that he had not done it, and that it was hard to him. Moreover, she had little desire to question his lack of courage, when she confessed to herself that she shrank from saying a single word to his mother on the subject of personal religion that she could have sooner walked through the fire, so it almost seemed to her, than to attempt it. And yet wasn't there something for her to do? Had she no duty in this matter?

There was not by any means the best state of things existing in the household. Of late both mother and daughter-in-law had seemed to have decided to let each other alone as much as possible. They made formal calls together, whenever the necessity occurred; they went out to tea together; they received formal calls at the same

time, in the same parlor; and that was really
the extent of their intercourse. When there
came a blessed afternoon into which none of
these duties intruded, Rebecca spent it in her
room alone, if she did not go out alone to follow
the bent of her own tastes. She no more thought
of seeking her husband's mother for the purpose
of spending a little time with her than she sought
the veriest stranger in the city. This fact,
among others, came up for consideration during
the next hour. There was presented to Rebecca the formidable suggestion that perhaps
she, too, Jonah-like, had been shirking some
plain duties, and fleeing to the quiet comforts of
her own room when she ought to have been in
Nineveh. The conclusion of some earnest
thinking was, that about the usual hour for calls,
she went daintily dressed in a home dress for afternoon, and with a bit of sewing-work in hand,
and tapped softly at the door of her mother's
room.

"Are you awake?" she asked, "and are you
ready to receive calls, because I have come to
call on you?"

"Really," Mrs. Edwards said, half rising from

her rocker, and looking bewildered, "this is an unexpected pleasure! Am I to take you to the parlor, where I usually receive my calls?"

"No," Rebecca said, laughing, and trying to ignore the quick rush of color to her face. "I am to be a more privileged caller than that; I have brought my work, and intend to make a visit. I used to go to mother's room and make a call very often."

The elder Mrs. Edwards was almost embarrassed. It was very unusual for her to have any such feeling, and she did not know how to treat it. Rebecca, however, had determined to pretend, at least that she felt very much at home. She helped herself to a low chair and brought out her thimble, and challenged her mother-in-law at once to know whether her work was not pretty. As she did so it gave her a strange sense of her unfilial life, as she remembered that that same bit of work had been the resort of her half-idle moments for some weeks, and that yet she had never shown it to Mrs. Edwards before. It proved to be a lucky piece of work. It gave Mrs. Edwards an idea, and suggested a line of thought that was so natural to her that she forgot the embarrassment of the situation at once.

Now, Rebecca's nerves were of the sort that made it very disagreeable to her to be wondered at for doing a piece of work in a certain way, when she was perfectly convinced that she knew all about it, and was sure that her way was in every respect the best. Yesterday, had Mrs. Edwards chanced to see this work and made this remark, she would have answered stiffly; that she embroidered dozens of yards of that same pattern for the church fair, and that hers sold for several cents more on a yard than the others' did, because every one said it was so smooth and so superior; that mother taught her when she was a child, and mother learned at an embroidery school which was noted for its superior work. Whereupon Mrs. Edwards would have been morally certain to observe that she must remember that *she* had bought hundreds of yards of that embroidery, and of many other kinds — bought it in Paris from some of the most celebrated houses in that city, and that whatever else she might not know, she was certainly posted as to needle-work; there was no nation in the world that could possibly equal the French in their accomplishments. Then Rebecca would have been very likely to have said that she did not belong to that class of people who were always extolling everything that was *French,* and looking down on their own country; and, though this would have been anything but a relevant reply, it would have answered for the basis of an argument, and I don't like to think of all the sharp and sarcastic and really biting things that these two smart women would have said to each other. No such thing happened; Rebecca had a special object in view; if that desire of her heart, the establishing of a family altar, with her husband as its head, was to be attained, it must be preceded by smooth sailing; she must not let the apparent inconsistencies of things be uppermost in her mother's mind that day. And even though she felt her cheeks grow red, and said to herself that this was very disagreeable work; that Jonah's ringing, clear-cut speech, "Yet forty days and Nineveh shall be destroyed," was nothing to sitting there and hearing her mother's teaching pronounced wrong, and her handiwork awkward in the extreme, she

made the healthful discovery that with a sufficient end to be gained she could bridle her
tongue. She even essayed to change her manner
of putting the thread over the needle, and
brought the result for inspection, which so mollified Mrs. Edwards that she agreed that as the
work was so nearly done it would be a pity to
change now, especially as she did the other so
wretchedly. She even added that it certainly
looked better made in that way than she should
suppose it could. So Rebecca stitched on in
peace, putting the thread serenely in the way
she had always put it, and heroically refrained
from saying, " I think it is the only right way,
and the other always looks horrid."

Then there was actually some pleasant talk,
having spots in it to be sure that, but for
Jonah and the remembrance of that journey to
Nineveh which her husband was taking, would
have made shipwreck of the afternoon's comfort.
It was decidedly periled once by a spool of thread.
Mrs. Edwards had brought out her sewing, and
was taking very small stitches in a bit of cambric,
when she said:

" This is miserable thread. I thought I would

try Clark's once, as I heard you say that you always used it, but I shall never be so foolish again. It was very rough, and it costs a cent more a spool than Coates'."

Now, neither of these ladies cared a pin's worth whether thread was six or seven cents a spool, and yet Rebecca instantly said:

"Oh, no, you are mistaken in that. Clark's can be had for half a cent less on a spool than the other kind, and I think it is much less likely to be rough. I never had a bit of rough thread of Clark's in my life."

"Your life is not a very long one and I dare say you have not used a very large quantity of thread. Young ladies situated as you were are not apt to. I suppose your mother did your little sewing while you did housework. But as to the price, of course I convinced myself that I was correct before I said anything about it. Clark's costs one cent more a spool than Coates' does. I always get Coates' for six cents, and this was seven."

How exasperated Rebecca felt! She not use much thread! Had she not sewed by the hour, swift; even stitched many a time when Mrs.

Edwards was sleeping or riding in her carriage?
And didn't she buy all the thread that was used
in the family; and didn't she know perfectly
well that Clark's thread was but six cents a
spool? How was it possible for her to sit quietly
by and endure such dreadful provocation as this!
Talk about Jonah! His trials were nothing to
hers. But this very reference to Jonah calmed
her; it made her think of her husband; it made
her remember that she had thought him weak
because he could not pray before his mother.
What sort of weakness was it that could not
keep one's temper with that mother over a spool
of thread! Instantly she resolved to ignore the
whole subject of thread, and with rare tact asked,
suddenly:

"Oh, did you know how to make that lace-
work that they used to have on French embroidery? Then will you show me how to do it some
time? I always thought it was so pretty, and I
never had a chance to be with any one who
knew how to do it before."

In short, with constant care, and many refer-
ences to Jonah and his trials, Rebecca got
through with that afternoon, and heard the

dinner-bell ring, and heard her husband's step on the stair, and rolled up her embroidery, which she began to hate, with a little sigh of satisfaction. She was just a little nearer to feeling as if she might, *some time*, feel at home in her mother's presence. She had a little bit of comfort, too, in that lady's exclamation:

"Is it possible that it is dinner time? I hadn't an idea that it was so late."

"Mother," Frank said, the instant the chairs were pushed back from the table, "I have decided to have prayers in the study right after dinner, and to have the servants in, if they choose to come. Will you join us?"

There was something wonderfully out-spoken about Frank Edwards as soon as ever he made up his mind to speak at all.

"Really," his mother said, looking at him with a surprised, not altogether pleased, half-embarrassed air. "This is a new and sudden development, isn't it?"

"New, yes; but not sudden, mother. I have been thinking about it for a good many weeks; in fact ever since I knew that my wife missed it. I have concluded that it is one of the things that

should not be missed from a home. Will you
come in, mother ? "

"I! Oh, certainly! I am sure it is altogether proper. I am glad that you begin to feel
the responsibility. The child must have missed
it. I missed it sadly enough when your father
went away from his home."

And there were actually tears in the usually
calm, cold eyes. The reference to Rebecca
seemed to have softened instead of annoying her,
as that young lady had feared. Whether it was
the embroidery, or the thread, or the lace-work
that she was to teach, or what it was, there was
certainly a more tender feeling in her heart for
her young daughter-in-law than there had ever
been before.

So the family altar was set up, amid great
embarrassment on the part of the son and husband, happy tears shed in quiet by his wife as
she knelt beside him, and a look of satisfaction
over the fitness of things by the mother who
heard her son's voice in prayer for the first time
in her life. It is quite likely that she thought
more than her quiet face showed.

As for Frank Edwards, as he went up-stairs

with his wife to get ready for the evening meeting, he said:

"I tell you what it is, Rebecca, I always had a kind of contempt for Jonah and his cowardly effort to dodge his work, but I shall know how to sympathize with him from this time forth."

"Especially can you sympathize with the time when he marched boldly into Nineveh and proclaimed his message," Rebecca said, fondly and proudly. But she said nothing about how nearly a spool of thread had shipwrecked her efforts in another direction.

On the whole, the day closed leaving husband and wife with a deeper insight into the depths of their own hearts than they had had before; and by so much were they stronger, because, seeing their own weakness, they had fled from self and hidden behind the Rock of strength.

CHAPTER XVII.

TRYING TO WORK IN LOVE.

EXTRACT FROM HER PRIVATE DIARY.

JUNE 7, 18—. I have had a curious sort of day. It is a singular thing that days can never correspond with one's planning. One would almost think that making plans was wrong. I had been thinking a good deal about Mrs. Edwards ever since we began to have prayers in the family. She seems to enjoy it, and yet she never looks quite happy and at rest. I don't think she is a growing Christian. It is so strange that she never went to prayer-meeting. I decided to ask her this very day if she wouldn't like to go. I thought I would take my work and go and see her again this afternoon, and we would have a quiet little time together, and I would tell her a little about the wonderful verses we are studying this week, and how Frank takes part in the meeting now, and get her interested if I could.

I quite looked forward to it. I knew it would be a cross. It is a dreadful trial for me to say anything about religion to her, because she always seems so unsympathetic. But I had got myself to thinking that it was a cross I was willing to bear, and someway I was quite in a hurry to bear it. I even decided that I would take the ruffles for my new dress along for work, and I would plait them in the way she spoke of, though I don't like that way.

Well, I didn't have a chance to plait them in that way, or any other. I was down in the dining-room feeding the bird. I had just come in from mother's, and she gave me a fresh cabbage-leaf for him. Mrs. Edwards came in while I stood there, looking flushed and worried. It isn't usual for me to comment on her moods, but someway I felt tempted to ask her if anything had happened to annoy her.

"Annoyance enough!" she said. "I don't know what I am to do. Susan's impudence has been too much for me at last; I wonder that I have endured it so long. I just told her she could go at the end of the week, and the miserable creature flared in an instant, and told me she could go at once, and no thanks to me for a warning. So she has actually gone, and the dinner not even under way."

"And Frank is going to bring home that man from New York, who is connected with the bank!"

This was my exclamation. I'm sure I don't know why I said it; she certainly knew it, so it was not for information. Perhaps it is no wonder that it added to her vexation.

"Of course I am aware of that," she said, testily. "It doesn't relieve one's perplexity in the least to be reminded of it. If there were a decent intelligence office in town I might go out and supply her place, but I heard yesterday there wasn't a single applicant worth noticing."

To this I made no answer, but kept poking

bits of cabbage at the bird and watching him bite them off in his spiteful little way, thinking rapidly meantime. I knew what I ought to do as well before thinking as I did afterward, but it really seemed to me that I couldn't do it. The day was so perfect, and I wanted to go out that very morning and take mother to ride. Frank had already left his order at the livery for the horse that I drive. Many a June day as perfect as this have I spent in the hot kitchen getting dinner, and thought not much about it; but it takes such a very little bit of time to get used to a new order of things! It seemed to me for the time being that I knew nothing about kitchens or dinners, and that I could not be expected to do anything in this emergency but to express dismay and sympathy. As to that, I was not expected to do anything. I knew that Mrs. Edwards often takes occasion to hint at my former kitchen life, and yet at the same time seems to ignore the possibility of my knowing anything about work. She couldn't get a decent dinner herself to save her life, and I know she thought I couldn't. For about five minutes it seemed to me that I wouldn't. Why

should **I**? We are only boarders. Frank pays
his board and mine as regularly as he would
if we lived at a hotel, and I have as little to say
about anything in the house, outside of my own
room, as if we were strangers to the family.

But at last I gave Dickie the last bit and
turned away from him. Mrs. Edwards had
dropped into the arm-chair, and was fanning
herself and looking worried enough to suggest
pity for her.

"Never mind," I said, "let her go; there
are quite as good to be had, I presume."
Though that fact I doubt, for she was really an
unusually good girl; but she has several times
confided to me the fact that she couldn't stand
being interfered with all the time, and found
fault with whatever she did. I am afraid I
sympathized with her. However, I went on
with my heroic sentence.

"*I* can get dinner—as good a one as Mr.
Romaine gets at a New York boarding-house, I
dare say. Just install me in the kitchen for the
day, and see what I can do."

Mrs. Edwards bestowed a glance of astonishment on me, not unmixed with dismay. She

would rather have had her help come from any other source. There was quite an argument as to the probability of my being able to cook fish and lamb, and their numerous side dishes, fit to be seen. But when one is without any help at all, and the dinner-hour is approaching, and there is to be company, what can one do but accept aid, even if the acceptance is somewhat ungracious?

So I went up stairs and wrote a note to Frank to countermand the order at the livery, and got our next neighbor's kitchen-boy to carry it to the bank. Then I took off my pretty street dress, just as becoming as it can be, by the way, and trimmed in just the shade of blue that always took Frank's fancy, and got out a last year's calico that is entirely accustomed to kitchen life, and, with the addition of a big apron, I looked like Rebecca Harlow again. If mother had only been down in that roomy, convenient kitchen, and we could have worked together, what a nice time we could have had! Mrs. Edwards was there, looking distressed and perplexed over every single thing that I touched. It was in vain that I assured her that I was perfectly well acquainted with legs of lamb, and that I had cooked as many fishes as there were in the sea, and that the summer Mrs. Demarest, of Boston, boarded with us, she asked me for the recipe for our fish sauce, because it was the best she ever tasted. She kept saying that she wouldn't have had it happen for fifty dollars, and Frank so very particular about the entertainment of company!

Now, the truth is that Frank isn't particular at all; he is the most reasonable and patient of men about board. It vexed me to hear her lay the blame of her fretting on his shoulders.

With the question of dessert came up new trouble. It so happens that, not having had much time for studying the accomplishments common to girls, I gave much time and fuss to the getting up of especially dainty desserts. During the season we kept those dreadful Boston boarders I really became an adept at that sort of work.

But Mrs. Edwards didn't believe it. She hovered over those eggs and that butter and sugar, and was sure I had too little butter and too much powder, and not the right kind of

flavoring. I became almost distracted. Several
times my tongue fairly ached to drop egg-beater
and spoon, and say: "Well, now, Mrs. Edwards, if you understand this business better
than I do, please attend to it, and I will go and
take my ride." I am so glad I didn't do it.
We nearly quarreled over the merits of soda and
cream of tartar versus baking powder. Mrs.
Edwards is certain that powder is an out-growth
of this degenerate age; says the cake is neither
so nice-looking nor so delicate that is made of it;
that she always tastes the powder, and that she
would never use it, if she went without cake. I
was really obliged to be firm in that, for I understand the art of making cake with powder, and
I don't know how to make it with those other
vile articles that must be balanced just so or they
make a fuss. Still, I might have got along
without saying: "So far as that is concerned, I
can tell at the first mouthful whether there is
cream of tartar in cake. I always taste it."
Whenever I say anything of that sort Mrs. Edwards is sure to remind me of my youth.

"Young people are, and always have been,
remarkable for their discernment," she said, very

drily. "Their mothers managed to make very palatable cake with the despised stuff before they were born, and long afterward. But as soon as the daughters get so they can stir up a gingerbread they of course know more than their elders ever did."

Now, what had that to do with the subject under discussion? I am sure I can't see. The simple truth is, that Mrs. Edwards can't even stir up a gingerbread; she knows nothing about cake-making; she has never been obliged to know. And I confess myself unable to see why, because a person has lived sixty years, she should be deferred to by one who has only lived twenty years, on a subject of which she knows nothing, while the other has given six or eight of her twenty years to the learning of that subject. I wanted to tell my respected mother-in-law that such was my opinion, but I forbore, and meekly asked her if Jane, the second girl, could be trusted to set the table, or whether she would rather have me do it. It was over the finishing touches to that table-setting that we had our final discussion. It began about those little imps known as "universal salts." I said I never

used them without thinking of the remark that
Laura Watson once made. She said if she were
obliged to use one she should want her name
pasted on the side, that she might have the
pleasure of sticking her own knife into the same
one every time. Mrs. Edwards looked severely
dignified over this, and, after a minute of ominous
silence, said :

"I should suppose the knife of any respectable
person would not contaminate Laura Watson.
I am reminded by her name that you are doing
a strange thing in renewing your intimacy with
her. She has put herself quite outside of the
pale of society, and should be left there."

Now, this is a very sore subject with me. I
don't uphold poor Laura, of course, neither does
the poor creature uphold herself. If people
knew all the truth, as I do, they would find her
at least as much sinned against as sinning. And
yet that is no excuse for her ; neither am I in the
least intimate with her; I simply do not cross
the street to avoid passing her on the sidewalk,
nor do I hold my head high and ignore her existence when I have to meet her. How I wanted
to tell Mrs. Edwards this, and to remind her of

the church covenant which she and Laura have both received. I felt so indignant that I could hardly keep from flinging her elegant napkin-ring, which I was at that moment fitting onto a napkin, on the floor. If I had spoken at all then, I should certainly have said something wicked. So I kept still, and gave my attention to the napkins. Mrs. Edwards continued:

"If the girl had any sense of propriety left she would not so force herself on the public, and oblige them to see her."

This was too much.

"Why, she only goes to church and to Sunday-school," I said. Would you have her stay away from these?"

"I would have her do just as she chooses for all me," she said, coldly. "Only she must not expect any attention from me, and I could wish that no one who bears my name would allow themselves to be mixed up with her in the least. But each to his taste."

How could I help being angry? I burst forth with wrath:

"Laura's worst sin is in allowing herself to believe, in defiance to those who knew better, that a villain was a gentleman, and allowing her name to be coupled with his. No one can sorrow for this more bitterly than she does; no one can repent more entirely. Is she never to have friends or society again because she has made one mistake?

"I am not so unsuspicious as some," Mrs. Edwards said, as if a suspicious nature was a special gift to be duly thankful for. "I don't know anything about Laura Watson, and don't want to. She may be as innocent as she pretends; I never said she wasn't; but I doubt it for all that; and, as I said before, I want to have nothing to do with her."

Every word she said made me more angry. I don't know why it was that just then there floated through my mind, like a song, the wonderful words, "I will heal their backsliding, I will love them freely." I said it aloud, in a softened voice, I think, then I added:

"It is a blessed thing that the just God is more tender and pitiful than men and women."

I thought I had offended her hopelessly, she was so still and so white. At last she said:

"There is a condition to his love."

"Yes, there is," I said. "It is given in the same connection: 'Take with you words, and turn unto the Lord. Say unto him, Take away all iniquity, and receive us graciously.' And if Laura hasn't done that it isn't possible to do it."

"You can't see her heart," she answered, almost fiercely.

"No, ma'am," I said firmly. "Only the Lord can see that, and it is only the Lord who has, therefore, a right to judge her."

I certainly never spoke so boldly to Mrs. Edwards before, yet I think my voice was quiet and gentle. It stopped our argument, anyway, and that was one comfort. I didn't say another word, neither did she. I went back to the kitchen and took up the dinner. She followed me, and hovered around, but she let me do it in my own way, and only altered the position of the pickle dishes, and the gravy boats, and the vegetable dishes, and a few other trifles, after I had arranged them. It was a comfort to me that she had afterward to alter some of them back to their original position, on account of room.

My dinner was a real success. Frank ate

serenely, and Mrs. Edwards, after the first taste, seemed to lose her anxious face and regain her quiet composure that is so much admired in the fashionable world. She has discovered that at least I can cook a dinner, and present it to be eaten in good style. I wonder if she has discovered that I can keep my temper? I have certainly been on the edge of a volcano all day. I am glad it didn't burst. But, oh me! how tired I am! My head aches to-night, and my limbs ache. All the three hundred and sixty-five dinners of the year in my mother's kitchen I believe never tired me as this one has. It is a queer thing, but when I look back on the day it seems as if the repeatal of that Bible verse tired me more than anything else. It was such a strange thing for me to do — to fling a verse from the Bible right into the midst of Mrs. Edwards' salt dishes that she was stamping! I know she felt the unfitness of it. I wonder that she did not tell me so. I suppose her silence was intended to do that. I can't help it. The verse is wonderful, and if she could only know that it kept me from an open explosion of wrath, and a complete desertion of that dinner to-day, perhaps she would respect it.

I didn't ask her to go to prayer-meeting. How could I, when the previous preparation that I had planned had to be given up? I said to myself, she is too tired to-night, anyway. And if she weren't I wouldn't ask her — no, not for an interest in a gold mine! Laura Watson goes to prayer-meeting regularly. She would think it beneath her to go to the same place. Into the midst of this thought broke Frank's voice:

"Mother, it is lovely to-night. Wouldn't you like a ride? I am going to get the carriage to take Rebecca to prayer-meeting. Suppose you ride with us. Don't you feel like it?"

How came Frank to say that? His mother looked at him a moment in a bewildered sort of way, and said:

"Well, I don't care. It is pleasant and cool. If you are going to take your own horses, and won't drive too fast, I will go."

And there was my formidable work that I had planned for all night done without me. I had nothing whatever to do about it in any shape.

Well, never mind, she went, and heard her son speak — a blessed little talk on the very verse, too, that I had sent across the room at her. "I will love them freely," I couldn't help wondering if she really felt the power of that wonderful love in her heart.

Oh, dear me! how weary I am. Frank has gone to a meeting of bank directors, and I am trying to wait for him.

I have half a mind to put my ruffles on my new dress in any way that I please, without regard to cross-grained views. I don't feel like making even so much of a concession as that.

It is partly the influence of that baking powder, I think. She said she thought she "tasted it slightly, though really it was very good."

CHAPTER XVIII.

PLANNING WORK.

SHE followed her husband out to the hall from the breakfast-table. It was late, and there was no time for a confidential talk together in their own room. Since the custom of family worship before the breakfast had been established the little talk that the two had enjoyed after breakfast had been cut off.

"There is something special in your face. I see it," was Mr. Edwards' smiling comment as he waited. "What is it?"

"It is not on my face; it is on this piece of paper," she said, handing him a bit of note-paper folded into small compass.

282

"Don't you think I have found a communication for us! I have copied it, and you are to read it when you get a bit of leisure from figures and cash. Good-by."

It was curious how eager Frank Edwards was to see the contents of that folded paper. He would have looked at it on his way down town, but for the fact that Rebecca had so carefully stipulated that it should be looked at when he reached the bank; besides, at the corner, Dr. Ferry joined him, and there was no chance for it.

Half an hour before lunch-time there was a lull. For fully ten minutes no one came in and there was nothing pressing on his attention. Now for that note. He smiled to himself as he unfolded it, and caught a glimpse of the dainty writing. Rebecca's brain was so fertile in planning little special ways of bringing subjects to his notice. She had so many schemes, and she so delighted setting him to work them out.

"What now, I wonder," he said. And then he read the line, "The Holy Ghost said, Separate me Frank and Rebecca for the work whereunto I have called them." Was ever stranger sentence brought before the eyes and thoughts of a

busy banker? He recognized the words; he
even knew their connection. There was nothing
new about it that should make the message so
startling, only the Holy Ghost had said those
words about Barnabas and Saul, two men who
lived so long ago, that it almost seemed as if
they had not lived at all, but were creatures of
the fancy. Certainly it had never before occurred to Frank Edwards that the same experience of life might be had to-day; that the same
Holy Ghost was still separating his workmen,
calling them to special work. Yet, of course,
it was so. Intellectually, he believed it; practically, he had ignored it. He had considered
his work to lie among those figures and that safe
at the bank. Other things — things pertaining
to home, to his class in Sabbath-school, to the
prayer-meeting — had been gradually taking on
more importance, it is true, but not being considered in the light of an actual call to work.

He folded the paper slowly, almost reverent-
ly; he half felt as though a divine message had
just reached him, sent down by a passing angel,
and he was to be set apart for something very
unusual.

" What is Rebecca planning for now," he said, and then he put the paper away, and tried to be as interested as before in checks and notes.

A rare thing happened to this husband and wife that day. Mrs. Edwards, senior, lunched down town with a friend, and Frank and Rebecca sat down together at a little table that was spread solely for them. How very nice it was!

"I read your communication," her husband said, at last, looking at his wife with amused, and yet with inquiring eyes. "I am well enough trained to know that it is only the beginning of communications. What are you going to set me at now?"

"Frank, the word wasn't from me; I only reported it. Don't you suppose it really has been said?"

" According to our supposed belief, it has; but I confess I never thought of it before in that light. What have you in mind, wifie? I know there is some work, to which you think I have been called, that I am not attending to. Out with it."

" That isn't the way it started in my mind. I was thinking of those two men, Barnabas and

Saul, and thinking how nice it must have been
to feel that they were actually set apart to a
certain work to which the Lord himself called
them. I wished it were so now, and then I got
to wondering whether it wasn't; and the more
I looked up the texts about work and about
guidance, I thought it was just so now. Then
I read that verse with your and my name in it,
and it made me feel strangely, as though I was
actually to be set to work by the Holy Spirit;
though, of course, I have always prayed for just
that thing. Then I went to thinking what the
work could be. I saw a great many things that
you could do; there didn't seem to be much that
I was capable of; but my thoughts kept going
persistently back to Dr. Ferry, and I couldn't
help thinking that that was your work."

"Dr. Ferry!" Frank repeated, with a little
start and an ominous gravity. "What on earth
made you think of him? And how could you
think I could do any more in that direction?"

"Oh, Frank, why not? Just see what a
wonderful influence he might have! How
many sick people he is constantly with, and
what a power he is among the young men, and

how popular with everybody. He seems to need only one thing to make him a splendid man, and I don't believe Christians ever ask him to seek that one thing. Did you ever?"

"No," Frank Edwards said, bluntly. "But, then, Rebecca, what's the use? He knows where I stand as well as you do, and he has as intelligent a knowledge of the way as I have. Why should I undertake to convince him?"

"He doesn't need convincing; he needs to be urged to the *doing*. Why shouldn't you try to influence him in that, as well as to try to urge him to accept that offer of partnership which you so persistently pressed on him?"

"Well, that was another matter; I happened to know things about that which he didn't know."

"Oh, Frank, don't you know things about the Christian life that he doesn't know?"

Mr. Edwards didn't choose to make any answer to this, and after a minute Rebecca said:

"It looks inconsistent; he doesn't understand your silence, you may depend upon it. Don't you know people, after they are converted, often speak of the strange silence of their friends on the subject?"

"I never spoke of such a thing in connection with you," Frank said, with a significant laugh.

Rebecca's face flushed, as she said, with a vivid smile :

"I was too anxious to be silent; but I know so many people to whom I *am* silent on that subject; it never seemed so strange to me as it does now. Frank, won't you try to influence Dr. Ferry?"

"I really don't believe I am the one to influence him. He feels too familiar with me; he can change the subject in a second. Besides, I am not calculated for that sort of work. I believe I should do more harm than good."

"But you don't talk so about other things. You know that in business and social matters you have a great influence over him, and over ever so many people. That is just the way you talked about teaching a class in Sunday-school; but see what success you have, and how your boys like it."

"That is because you made me study the lesson from Monday morning till Saturday night," he said, laughing again.

But his wife, was not to be driven from her

subject. In one form or another she presented it constantly during the hour they were together; and when her husband left her she had gotten a reluctant promise that he would bear the matter in mind, and if he had opportunity, and it seemed best, he would try to speak a word to the young doctor. Even a consent so full of "ifs" as this, was most reluctantly given. It would have been given to no other person in the world but his wife.

Mr. Edwards was somewhat surprised to see with what vehemence he shrank from personal work of that sort. His religious life had been a short one, and it is to be feared had been entered upon with very little definite idea of his obligations to others; to him religion had hitherto been a matter between him and God, too sacred so his mother thought, to be intermeddled with or talked about; there is so much religion these days that wants to be done up in pink cotton and laid safely away from human sight and sound. A genuine germ was in this young man's heart, but having most imperfect development; perhaps had it not been brought side by side with the vigorous growth of his wife's Chris-

tian life it would have been satisfied without development. As it was, the new idea oppressed
him. His good sense told him it was the most
natural thing in the world that, believing as he
did, he should try to urge others to an acceptance of his views. Yet the more he thought
about it the more he shrank from attempting
anything like personal effort. He realized his
inability to hide behind any such reason as his
lack of influence, his want of tact for such work;
the clear eyes of his wife would see through
such filmy covering in a moment. Besides, they
sounded like folly even to himself. He knew
he was a man of influence; that in the business
world he was becoming more and more known,
and that older heads than his deferred respectfully to his opinions. Why should he not be
able to say to a friend, "Don't you think you
ought to give attention to this item of business?"
Still, he earnestly hoped that Dr. Ferry would
be so constantly employed that he should not
be able to see him for many a day : not at least
till his resolution to try to do something had had
time to grow strong. To this end he sent a mes-
senger to him that very afternoon, when neces-

sity occurred for consulting, instead of going himself, as at any other time he knew he would have
done; and when, an hour later, the doctor called
to ask some questions relative to business, Frank
Edwards promptly summoned one of the seniors
of the bank, though he was abundantly able to
answer all questions. He was ashamed and
amazed at his own weakness. But still, he
argued that during business hours was no time
for such matters.

It was while the Edwards family were seated
at their dinner-table that the sound of the bell
was followed by the announcement that Dr.
Ferry was waiting, and would like to see Mr.
Edwards just a moment.

"Just let me step right to the dining-room a
moment, and not take you from your dinner,"
the doctor said, following his name with the
familiarity allowable in a friend. "Don't rise,
Frank; I can talk while you are eating. Good-
evening, ladies; it is a lovely evening. Mrs.
Edwards, don't you feel the need of a ride in
the moonlight?"

This last to Rebecca, and while she looked up
amazed the doctor made laughing explanation.

" The fact is, Frank, I have come to suggest a very benevolent thing for you to do. I thought you might need being set at work. I've lamed my horse; that is the beginning of my trouble, and I have a very sick patient about four miles out whom it is my duty to visit. At the first livery there isn't an available horse, and on my grumbling way to the next one Providence led me by your door, and I saw your horse waiting. Now, said I, who knows but Frank is going to drive in just that direction, and will let me occupy the spare seat for the sake of old bachelor times together."

Under any other circumstances than those existing Frank Edwards' reply would have been prompt and cordial; as it was, his own heart knew why he was embarrassed and hesitating.

" I was going to take my wife out," he began, slowly, whereupon Rebecca interposed.

" Why, Frank, I forgot to tell you that Sallie Holland sent word she was coming to call. I can't go to-night. Doctor, I am sure Mr. Edwards will be glad to serve you and humanity at the same time."

Was there any way of escape for Frank Edwards now ?

In less than half an hour they were trundling over the smooth road, one of the gentlemen silent and confused by the remembrance of his wretched promise. How strange that Dr. Ferry should have appeared on that very evening, and that he should have been forced into a ride alone with him ! As for the doctor, he was in an unusually merry mood; he told pleasant stories, he whistled, he hummed bars of merry tunes, he laughed loudly at the fun which he succeeded in making, and at last provoked his companion to say:

"You feel unusually happy to-night, don't you ? Seems to me I never saw you in so gay a mood."

Sudden quiet followed that sentence, and presently Dr. Ferry said :

"The truth is, Frank, I am whistling to keep my courage up, as the boys do when they go through the woods in the dark. I have got a man at the end of this road who is going to die. His wife is just hanging on me and expecting me to save him, and I can't do it. When a doctor gets to that place he has got to whistle or break down."

"Is the man ready to die?"

"No, he isn't; and he won't believe he is going to die. I have been just as plain with him as I dared, but he clings like a drowning man. No, he is very far from ready. A good sort of man, you understand, and a very loving husband, and all that; but when it comes to dying, those things, someway, won't do."

"I wonder that a man who realizes that, and who in his profession has occasion to see how uncertain life is, has not been led to get ready for the certainty."

This was Frank Edwards' next sentence, spoken in a low, solemn tone. It was not at all what he had meant to say; indeed, two minutes before he had told himself that he would not say anything; that Dr. Ferry was in too gay a mood to broach such a subject to him that night; it would be casting pearls before swine. But when he so suddenly changed his manner and the current of thought, it seemed someway the most natural thing in the world to say those words, and, though his heart beat high with the sense of the strangeness of his position, he felt as though he had not chosen the words — rather as if he had opened his mouth and some other person had spoken the words, using him, simply for a mouthpiece.

They were received by the doctor in perfect silence, until, as they suddenly turned a curve in the road, he said:

"It is a remarkably strange thing, now that's a fact. But here's my house, and you may as well tie your horses and come in, for if that is your mood you are just the man for this place. I'm glad I brought you."

What Frank Edwards felt as he saw such appalling work opening before him can be better imagined than described. He longed to insist on remaining in the carriage while the doctor made his call; but, under the influence of those words he had spoken, how could he?

It was more than an hour afterward that the two gentlemen emerged from the same house, and in silence took their seats in the carriage.

"Doctor," Frank Edwards said, as the horses sped swiftly over the ground, "let me speak a plain word with you. After the scene which we have witnessed you will not be offended. Don't neglect this thing any longer. You see what an influence you have; how people in bitter sorrow hang on your words. For their sakes, if not for your own, be able to point them to a better Physician than you, who can cure souls."

Not a trace of embarrassment or hesitation was in his voice. He had come from the presence of death; he had just risen from his knees, where he had been for an hour, praying and pointing the dying man to that other Doctor on whom he could put his trust with a certainty of there being no failure. He was upborne by the solemn thought that the Spirit of God had separated him to that work that night; had planned the way and made all the apparently trivial and really strange chain of circumstances combine to lead him; that the prayer of that bedside had been heard, and that even now there was another new soul in heaven. It seemed to him that he had had his baptism of faith; that his lips would never tremble again; but it is very likely that he needed the very words that Dr. Ferry spoke.

"Upon my word, Frank Edwards, this is the first time I ever respected your religion; I

thought you amounted to a good deal in everything but that. But your way of managing that
had to make me think that either there was
nothing in it or else you hadn't it. I have many
such a scene as this to go through. I tell you it
takes nerve; it takes something that I haven't
got. As sure as I live I want it, and, God
helping me, I mean to have it. Frank, I shall
thank you all my life for opening your mouth
to-night. I tell you I have found out that you
can pray, and I want you to pray for me."

When Frank Edwards told his wife of the
circumstances of that remarkable evening she
quoted to him this verse: "Then the deputy,
when he saw what was done, believed, being
astonished at the doctrine of the Lord."

CHAPTER XIX.

SEEKING AN OPEN DOOR.

THE days that followed were not filled with brightness to Rebecca. She had developed a consuming desire for work; not the commonplaces of her embroidery, or the ruffles on her dress, but real, earnest, Christian work, such as would bring results for the beloved cause. Her husband's unexpected and blessed success with his friend Dr. Ferry, had not only roused him to a new sense of his privileges and duties, but had thrilled her heart anew. Still as she had told him, there really seemed to be nothing that she could do. Her class in Sabbath-school seemed to have a spell of indifference that she could not break; they were interested in the lessons, and faithful in their attendance, but further than that the more eager and anxious she grew for their development the more unconcerned grew they. There were times when she felt well-nigh discouraged with them. Then she had tried to interest her friend Sallie Holland; but Sallie was skilled in avoiding personalities when she chose to exert herself. She could change the current of conversation a dozen times in as many minutes; she could apparently misunderstand the plainest and most pointed questions, and maintain the most unperturbed good humor and unconcern at times when a show of feeling of any sort would have been a positive relief.

Rebecca at last came to the conclusion that for the present there was nothing she could do for Sallie but let her alone. Indeed, it is to be feared that this impression took such hold on her that she could not even pray for her friend with the earnestness and persistence that demands answer. She tried to turn her attention to missionary work, out in the neglected portions of the town; she went on three successive after-

noons in search of Sabbath-school children, the
only visible results being that she created a
furore in the Catholic element to such an extent
that several children of Irish parentage, who had
before this drifted quietly into the school, were
withdrawn in indignation, and two little heathen
left a school where they were well established,
and being well taught, and took up their line of
march for the church where the pretty lady
went — not at all at her request or by her desire,
but in the hope of getting some additional
clothing and attention from this new source.
One most uncomfortable feature of this attempt
was that the Sabbath-school which had thus been
invaded persisted in considering itself insulted
by the other school, and therefrom arose uncomfortable feelings from both parties. Is it any
wonder that poor Rebecca was almost in despair?
I mistake as to results — there was one little
waif, who had never been to Sabbath-school in
her life, gathered into a class near Rebecca's
own; but she was a little bit of a shy creature,
scarcely making noise enough to be heard at all,
and looking like so insignificant a morsel that
Rebecca, in wearily recounting to herself her

failures, actually overlooked poor little Nannie
entirely! Never mind, Nannie came to Sabbath-
school every Sabbath, and heard there wonderful
things. Frank Edwards was as sympathetic as
possible with his wife's eager mood. His own
zeal and faith had been wonderfully quickened.
How could he look at Dr. Ferry and hear him
talk, and others talk about him, without this
being the case? Dr. Ferry was a power in the
town. There was genuine exulting joy in Frank
Edwards' heart. No other person had ever said
to him: "Frank, under God I owe this blessed
experience to you." A Christian who has never
heard that need not try to imagine how it made
him feel.

At last there started up an enterprise which
promised good things for Rebecca. This same
Dr. Ferry was the foundation of it. It was
nothing less than a mission-school down in the
most neglected quarter of the large town, where
the doctor had many patients. Hitherto this
portion had entirely run to waste; it was surely
time for helping hands to be put forth. It
struck some of the older Christians as strange
that they should have waited for this new recruit

to set on foot such an obvious bit of work as that. There was to be not only a Sabbath-school, but an afternoon-school, to teach reading and writing and sewing to such of the older pupils as could be coaxed in, and those eager in the work saw what a door would open for the dropping in of precious seed among these daily lessons — chance to sow words of life in that crude soil. Nothing ever took hold of Rebecca with such consuming power as did this new idea. She worked at the plans day and night. It was her husband who furnished the room ; it was her pocket-money that cleaned it and put it in proper order. She was to take two afternoons a week ; the other volunteers had been content with one, but she eagerly answered her husband's protest with the reminder that she had been used to plenty of work, and that she had nothing in the world to do. Behold her at last, set forth on the high road to a work that was to bring harvests !

It was a certain August day, unusually warm even for August. People on the street and at their homes had a general air of feeling wilted. In the Edwards' mansion the family were gathered at the noon lunch, languidly toiling with fruit and cream, as if even those two delicious articles were not appetizing just then. Mrs. Edwards, senior, looked more than languid; she looked positively worried, not to say dismayed.

" Mother, you don't look at all well," her son said, at last, regarding her usually composed face with anxiety.

" I am well · enough," she answered, in an annoyed tone. " At least I should be if I were not harassed to death. I am sure I don't know what to do. I shall have to give up housekeeping and resort to boarding, if this sort of thing continues much longer. In all my experience as a housekeeper I never had such inefficient help before."

" Why don't you change?"

"Change! That is just like a foolish boy. Isn't this the third girl I have had in as many weeks? and she is worse than any of them! If that miserable Susan hadn't left me in a pet, after being trained to my ways for so long. It is as much gratitude as they ever show. That fruit, those peaches that I ordered, have come to-day, of all others, the warmest day we have had, and they will no more keep till to-morrow than anything; and my girl knows as much about canning peaches as she does about most other things, which is just nothing at all. I don't know what I am to do!"

"Isn't there some one you could get to come in?"

"Frank, you talk as though you had not lived with me in this house for twenty-six years! Who is there that I could get, who would be likely to know anything about canning peaches?"

Poor Rebecca, with her eager desire for work! How well she knew of some one, who, alas! was already "in," who knew every little detail about canning peaches. And miserable, warm, sticky work it was! Mother had managed so that peach-canning was always done in the early flush of a summer morning. Think of boiling over the stove on such an afternoon as this! Besides, wasn't her brown linen hanging even at this moment across the chair in her room waiting to be donned as soon as the fierce heat of the day was off, while she went down into those beloved mission regions and gave the last loving touches to those rooms, and prepared for the opening on the next day? How was it possible for her to can peaches? She made no comment on the state of things; she let her husband depart without going to the hall to say good-by; she gave little heed to his earnest, " Rebecca, I would not try to go down to the rooms this afternoon, it is so very warm," so absorbed was she in this new door which yawned before her, and whose threshold she did not want to cross.

"They assayed to go into Bithynia, but the Spirit suffered them not." Why should this word from her morning reading persist in crowding itself into her thoughts? What possible connection could there be between that and the subject in question? Could it be possible that she was to read it, "I assayed to go down to the mission-room, but the Spirit suffered me not?" Why not? Was the direction only for Paul? Then why need to write it for her to read hundreds of years after Paul had gone to the visible presence of that guiding Spirit? Could the Spirit actually guide in such matters as for instance the canning of peaches?

What more she thought can be gathered by her sudden words:

"I know all about canning peaches; if you will trust them to me I'll see that they come out whole and white and all that."

"You!"

Who shall describe Mrs. Edwards' surprise? Each new experience with her daughter-in-law seemed to have surprise in it. There was much talk, of course; but it ended in their going down to the fiery regions together. Rebecca would have much rather gone alone. After such a sacrifice of inclination surely she ought to have had a good time, and felt herself blessed by her sacrifice. But, dear me, she didn't! The afternoon was filled with vexation. Mrs. Edwards, senior, knew nothing about the new-fashioned method of fruit-canning, except certain wise information which she had read from her cook-book. Now, every practical housekeeper knows what a snare of Satan a cook-book is, with its high-sounding, impossible directions and oracular statements. Rebecca would have none of them, and Mrs. Edwards would; hence, friction. Not outright rupture; something held Rebecca's tongue in check; something kept her from one outspoken vexation. I think it was that singular verse that she had made, with its solemn ending: "But the Spirit suffered me not."

Still, Mrs. Edwards was unhappy; was sure the peaches would go to pieces, and when they refused to do that was sure they were not done, and that the sirup was scorched, and that it wouldn't be clear, and that the cans would break unless Rebecca did thus and so, according to that cook-book, which finally Rebecca meekly did, and had a sweet revenge in seeing and hearing the can crack promptly, and the sirup flow serenely out on the stove, on the floor, wherever its penetrative and sticky self *could* flow. It was so manifestly the fault of the cookbook that there was nothing to say.

Oh, how hot it was! Rebecca wiped great beads of perspiration from her heated face, and pushed wildly at her hair with her dress-sleeves, in the hope of getting it to retreat a little from her hot forehead; and the kitchen grew hotter as the day waned, for was not the inefficient girl getting up the family dinner, and doing what she could, by pushing peach-pans to one side and knocking off cans and spilling the sugar, to add to the exasperated nerves already quivering?

It only needed the presence of Frank in that horrible kitchen to make tribulation reach its height.   That being the case, of course he came. They heard his quick, firm step on the stairs, and a moment after his indignant voice :

" Rebecca, I wonder if you are here, sweltering over the stove in all this heat, looking ready to drop with fatigue !   Mother, I wonder at you for allowing this ! "

It was his mother's pet phrase ; he had heard it from her lips so many times that it is little wonder he used it.   But of course he could have no idea how it annoyed her.

" Really ! " she began, " I didn't order her to come.   I assure you I do not interfere with her plans.   She offered to attend to the peaches, and as they are to be eaten by you and her I thought there could be no harm in her directing the work."

" Frank, lift off that cover; and don't fret about me or the peaches ; we are both coming out all right.   Be quick, please ! "

"Hang the peaches!" said Frank, savagely, as he sprang to do her bidding. "I would rather have them all emptied into the drain than have you cooked in this way, such a hot day as this."

You are to remember that Mrs. Edwards had been very much tried; that she had never schooled herself to any marked degree of self-control; that she had been used to seeing this son think first of her, show consideration for her welfare, then you may possibly understand the state of mind in which she seized that last pan of delicate peaches, waiting to be skimmed into their separate cans, and deliberately flung them into the drain! Then she said, in a voice which quivered with anger:

"Now take your wife and go out of my kitchen. I hope you will neither of you ever have to come in it again!"

What was there to be said? Frank, appalled at this exhibition of anger, turned away in utter silence. As for Rebecca, she was just in the state to do what she did; that was to burst into a passion of tears and rush up stairs. Her first words to her husband were:

"Oh, Frank, how could you speak so to your

mother? What made you come down stairs?"

Then she laughed hysterically. It was so queer to be lecturing Frank for not being considerate to his own mother. What a miserable ending of her day!

But it did not end yet. Into the midnight quiet there came a knock at their door. Frank answered it promptly, and through the keyhole came the response, from the inefficient girl:

"Your mother is took sick. I heard her groaning and I went to see. She wants your wife to come down there right away."

Before that sentence was half concluded Rebecca was on her feet and dressing rapidly. It was a queer thing, but an almost jealous pang shot through Frank Edwards' heart at that moment; his mother had sent for his wife but not for him!

Those were queer days that followed. Mrs. Edwards' outburst over the peaches had been the result, in part, of really overwearied nerves; the last warning before the string snapped. For days and weeks thereafter she had time to lie quietly and rest, and think of all her cares. She was not very sick; that is, no one felt the pres-

ence of danger; but she was weak and nervous
and very hard to please. Rebecca, of course,
was her nurse. Who else could so naturally be
installed in the sick room? But what weary
days they were to Rebecca! Those fierce August days, in which she meant to have begun
good work, wasted! Well, no, not that, of
course; she waited on Frank's mother, bathed
her face, combed her hair, prepared her food,
read to her, sang to her, soothed her as best she
could; but then, perhaps, a hired nurse could
nave done all this as well, only that for some
reason Mrs. Edwards chose to prefer her to a
hired nurse. Then the kitchen arrangements
had to be planned and watched over. Rebecca
was at home in that; she knew just how things
should be done; she knew just the bit of soda or
flour or powder that was wanted to make sour
things sweet and heavy things light and thin
things thick enough. The inefficient girl developed a consuming desire to know how to do
things, and having suddenly discovered one who
knew how to teach her, was not slow to learn.

But what weary days these were! That was
the burden of Rebecca's heart. What were all

these things that she was doing compared with what she had wanted and planned to do? "I assayed to go to the mission-school but the Spirit suffered me not." That kept ringing its refrain. Why was it so? Why had the Spirit so hedged her work? Wasn't her motive pure? What did it all mean? So she queried and sighed. Her husband was not a help during these days; he was overwhelmed with anxiety for his mother. In vain Dr. Ferry assured him that this rest was just what she needed; that she would add ten years to her life while she lay there. He could not forget that scene in the kitchen and the memory of almost the only reproachable words he had ever spoken to her; so he hovered over her, forgetting, apparently, that Rebecca was weary or heavy-hearted; thinking only that perhaps they were all mistaken, and his mother was going away.

There came a day when some of Rebecca's questioning was answered. She, bending over her charge, carefully smoothing the silky gray hair, and trying to say, cheerily, "You are better this morning, I think," when she was startled by the form and manner of the answer:

"I ought to be, my daughter. Such tender care as yours ought to bring a return. Child, do you know what you have been doing during these weeks? You have given me a sight of my own heart. Your religion is the kind I ought to have to live by, and I know I shall need it to die by. I have been one of those who had only a name to live; very little more. You must help me; you are helping me, daughter. I'm going to try to live as a Christian."

Poor, startled, half-frightened, wholly thankful Rebecca! How could she answer her other than by a sudden rush of tears, which dropped on the white face on the pillow as she stooped over her and kissed her forehead, and murmured, "Dear mother." She had never used that name before. To herself, in the silence of her room that evening, she said, as her voice lingered smilingly over the wonderful words:

"I am sure I see it now. I came to this vineyard to preach Christ's gospel, and a door was opened unto me of the Lord!"

CHAPTER XX.

SHE FALLS IN WITH A NEW GOSPEL.

IT is one thing to resolve that for the future one will live the sort of life that is becoming in a Christian, and it is another thing to live that life. Many a Satan-tempted soul has realized the difference. The senior Mrs. Edwards was one of those who so realized it; also her daughter did. Those days of slow return to strength — rather those days when strength was expected to return, and did not — were very trying ones to the invalid. She was not used to invalidism, other than the graceful kind which expends itself in feeling languid when there is nothing special to arouse or inter-

est, and when it is rather a pleasure than otherwise to feel languid. But this sort that would
be languid despite any plans of hers, that persisted in making her too weak to do the things
that her soul longed to do, this was a trial. Old
habits also tormented her; held sway over her.
She was not by nature meek or gentle. It was a
very difficult thing to realize as the days passed
that she was not gaining in strength; that she
was not able to assume family cares and respon-
sibilities, which, however they had tried her, had
yet been the constant accompaniment of her life,
and could not be laid aside without a protest.
It was bitter to sit listlessly in a chair and know
that another voice than hers was directing and
guiding the household; that the dinner was
planned, not, indeed, without reference to her,
but without appeal to her wisdom. This chafed
her, even though she knew that the silence was
because she was too weak to be talked with
about these things. It was a trial to think that
the parlors were being swept and dusted just
when Rebecca directed, instead of according to
her plans. It was really wonderful what an ad-
vantage Satan had over her during this time of

physical weakness; and how adroitly he used these hundred little pin-pricks about her, till there were days when she chafed like a caged lion; nay, there were days when she actually roared, in a refined, somewhat fashionable way, of course. But the bitter sense of shame and defeat which followed such days only added to the weakness and weariness.

The reflex influence of all these things were telling on Rebecca. To keep house in a dear little home that should be planned according to her taste, and to be sole mistress thereof, with only Frank to please, with pleasant little teas, in which the dear father and mother Harlow, and the young brother, would be entertained in her home, this was a bright dream in her heart; but, to be the real mistress of a grand and solemn old house, stylish in all its appointments; to feel the necessity of keeping up certain stately and trying family customs; to remember that there was a housekeeper in the south room of forty years' standing to defer to and please; to do one's best to weariness of body and soul, and then to be rewarded by long-drawn sighs that said volumes about mistakes and failures; this was another matter.

So many plans, too, were unceremoniously laid aside, nobody seeming to know or think that such was the case. The journey with Frank to Philadelphia must be given up; his mother was, of course, too feeble to leave. The Sunday-school class must be given up; it would never do to trust the details of Mrs. Edwards' breakfast to servants. The mission-school was a thing of the past, so far as she was concerned; not that it did not live and flourish. There were times in which this but added to the bitterness, to think that all the work of the busy Christian world could go on without her. The combinations of a hundred of these and kindred petty things had served one day almost to crush the life or ambition of this young bird so lately in a new nest. It was a day when kitchen trials had been many. Servants seem to have their days of nervousness as well as their mistresses, and Rebecca's helpers were no exception. Things had also gone wrong in the south room. Mrs. Edwards' new cap was a failure; her toast was a trifle scorched, or she thought it was; Frank had failed to find any fresh eggs for her, and Rebecca had spilled the medicine on her new wrapper. She had roared some, and sighed tremendously, and said to Frank, in the presence of his weary wife, that if she did not gain strength soon they must give up all attempt at housekeeping and try boarding ; it was useless to think of living on in this haphazard way. Rebecca went to her room and threw herself wearily on the bed, feeling that if she were not too tired it would be a relief to indulge in a hearty cry. There came also to torment her a memory of the day when Frank had told her he should not allow her to so overtax her strength as she did at home, when once he got possession of her.

"Strength indeed!" she said, indignantly. "I was never so tired in my life at home, and to think that it is all for nothing ; that I can not please her!"

Then a few tears insisted on gathering to the entertainment. Her comforting solace was interrupted by a message. John Milton was in the library ; would like to know when he could see Frank, or if she could tell him where he was to be found.

She sprang up quickly; there were certain things that she wanted to ask John about; he had taken her class in school; so she went down to him.

"Frank is at Judge Denton's; something about a bank-note; it could not detain him long. Sit down, John, and wait for him. I want to talk to you."

"You look too tired to talk," John said, sympathetically.

The tone recalled her sense of discouragement.

"I am tired," she said, almost tremulously. "Tired of everything, principally of myself, I think. John, sometimes life seems wonderfully full of warfare, without many victories. I shall be real glad when the fighting is all over and the rest commences."

Instead of answering, John eyed her searchingly, when he asked what sounded like a very strange question:

"Suppose I were Paul, and should come to call on you this evening, and should say to you, 'Have you received the Holy Ghost since ye believed?" what would you answer?"

" Why," said Rebecca, smiling, " I couldn't say I had not so much as heard whether there be any Holy Ghost.   Why do you ask me that? "

" Well, you see, I don't agree with you," he said, briskly.   " I think life is full of victories, and so long as we have a sure Captain to carry on the warfare and *know* there will be victories, why should we be so disturbed about it?   I declare I can't help thinking that there are some people who have not received the Holy Ghost, even though they do believe; not that he hasn't come to them, you know, but that they won't receive him."

" I don't believe I understand you, John."

" Well, it's like this: I know I believed in the Lord, and in the fact that he was my Saviour from eternal punishment, for a number of weeks before I found out that there was any more of it than that.   I had fights of all sorts, such as you wouldn't know much about; bad habits, you know; smoking was one of them.   I decided to give it up; but, bless you, to decide was one thing and to do it was another.   You see smoking is a kind of disease, or passion, or something, gets to be; and, though I was so young, I had practiced it a great deal, and I wanted to keep at it. The fact is, it was almost impossible for me to let the cigars alone. I craved them, and a good many times I smoked them, though I had said that I wouldn't. It's really a long story; I had no idea of telling it, but I'll make it short. At last it dawned upon me one day that I needn't fight this battle alone. Oh, I hadn't been doing that, but I had been calling it help, asking the Captain to let me help do something. 'Now,' said I, 'I'll try a new way. Suppose I ask him to do it for me; he doesn't need my help; my part is to do as I'm told; not to help him make me willing to do it.' Fact is, I stumbled on that verse where it says, 'My strength is made perfect in weakness.' Now, some people may not be weak, but I knew I was. That was precisely the thing I wanted; somebody who was perfect to do what I had worked at, and failed in. So I just went to him and told him all about it, and, Rebecca, he was equal to it! He came forward with his perfection and just did the work."

" What do you mean ? "

" Why, 1 mean that one night I went to my

room, feeling pretty well used up, because the sight and smell of a cigar made me want one so, and because as sure as anybody urged me to smoke I did it. And I came out of my room the next morning just as indifferent to a cigar as a fellow could possibly be, and I can curl up my nose now as high over the smell of a cigar as anybody on earth; a real genuine curl, too. I hate it."

"How very strange!" said Rebecca, and John, seeing interest in her eyes, went on, eagerly:

"There's another thing. I had a great time making up my mind to take part in the prayer-meeting. I went through all the excuses that fellows do, and they didn't have the strength of straws, and I knew they didn't; but for all that it was awful hard work. I blundered and stumbled through it several times, but I tell you it was a cross! I prayed about it, and asked help again, as if I was to do part of the getting ready and the Lord was to do the other part. And I stuck to it and tried to get ready, and it didn't grow easy, nor seem a bit like anything but a cross. One night I got to reading: 'My yoke is easy and my burden is light.' 'Humph!' said I, 'It isn't meant to be a cross, it seems; nothing is. He says take up the cross, but once taken up it looks as though he meant to see that it didn't drag on us.' 'Rest to your souls.' Precious little rest was I getting on Wednesdays. I worried over that cross all day, and by night it was a regular sweat! Then I looked up that verse about being kept in perfect peace. I tell you I thought I had a right to that peace. I was trying to do my duty as well as I knew how, and I had a right to the wages, so I just said so. I went to Jesus and said to him : ' Now I have come to you and I want you to give me rest about this thing. I'll open my mouth; that is the part you have given me, and you fill it. I'll trust you; I can't do even this thing myself, and I mean to stop trying.' The fact is, I'm not worth a red cent; it's a complete case of bankruptcy. I've been thinking I had strength enough to get through with this life with a little help, provided he would take care of the next one. But I see that's a mistake. And it is, Rebecca, you may depend, it is the power of the Holy Spirit in the heart that is going to do the work, not the power of my strength or will."

"John," said Rebecca, her eyes large with the thought of her new discovery, "you are a perfectionist."

"A what?" said John, with a bewildered stare. It was impossible to avoid laughing at his puzzled face.

"Why, one of those people who insist that it is possible to be perfect in this world."

"Humph!" said John, with emphasis. "I should think I was the farthest possible remove from that. I tell you I ain't *anything*. There is no strength in me; nothing to build upon. My part is to do as I am told, and the mistake I made was in trying to help the Lord do his work. It is like my little sister; she persists in thinking that she can walk up stairs, so she puts her feet on the stair and I put my arm around her, and I give her a spring and up she goes. And she says she went up the steps, only I helped her some."

"But she gets to the top, after all," Rebecca said, thoughtfully, struck with something in the illustration.

"Yes, I look out for that, because I am her elder brother, you see. But, mind you, she would go swifter and safer if she would consent to be mounted on my shoulder, and just put her arms around me and hold on."

"But the Bible says, 'Grow in grace,'" Rebecca repeated, still looking thoughtful.

"Of course it does. Now what does grace mean. I just looked it up in the dictionary, and I got light. Just see what Webster says: 'Grace: The divine favor toward man; the mercy of God as distinguished from his sovereignty or justice, and also any benefits or blessings it imparts; the undeserved kindness or forgiveness of God; divine love or pardon; a state of acceptance with God; enjoyment of the divine favor.' I just copied that into my diary that I might not be tempted to forget again what I was to grow in; grow more and more into the knowledge of God's undeserved kindness, of his wonderful forgiveness, of his continual favor. I tell you, you just trust him to help do things for you that you have found out you can't do, and see how fast you will grow in the knowledge of his wonderful favor. I tell you I am all swallowed up in this thought, and life isn't a dread any more. 'He is faithful who promised,' and he says he has called us to 'peace.'"

"But, John, that would leave nothing for Christians to do."

"Do you think so? I can't see it in that light. Do you fancy a boy hasn't anything to do for his mother because he realizes that he is not going to buy her love and care for what work he does for her? That is a free gift. Do you think you have nothing to do for your husband because he has promised to support you and care for you in every way, and is bound by his word to do it?"

"Oh, I don't mean that exactly. We can't buy love or care, of course. But surely we ought to struggle to conquer our own sins."

"Well, I tried it with all my might. I tell you I struggled for dear life, and what did it amount to? I couldn't even conquer a puff or two of smoke. Others might have done it. There are people who are stronger than I; but the gospel is for weak people as well as strong ones. And, after all, people don't seem to me to make much headway with their conquering.

Now, my baby sister, when I am taking her to walk, and she comes to the brook, she is sure she can jump over it, and she struggles at it with all her might, and it just ends in my picking her up and carrying her over, after she is done struggling and is willing to hold on tight to me. It seems to me her part is just to hold on, to jump when I tell her to and to stand still when I tell her to, and to cling to my hand when I tell her to do that. It is the way she gets through danger. I can't see that she accomplishes anything by her struggles."

"But, John, she would never learn to walk if you carried her all the time."

"But you see I don't. When it is safe for her to walk I tell her to trot along, and she is to mind, don't you see?"

"She is a young teacher of theology," Rebecca said, with a smile.

"She's a capital one, though; I've learned ever so much from the little thing. You see it's the Lord's own method of teaching. 'Except ye be converted and become as little children.' Not little children who are determined to go alone, when their Father knows they will stumble. I think sometimes he does just as we do with the children. He lets us stumble in a place where it is not too hard, so that we will learn that our place is to *obey.* I'm sick of trying to make myself good. I can't do it. I've got to be carried over the dangerous places, and I've got to hide when Satan comes after me; no use in my trying to fight with him; he always comes out ahead. Now, so long as the Lord said there was a place by him, and promised to hide us, and promised to shield us, and promised to cover us with his hands, and promised to gather us under his wings, why should we be forever starting off alone, or at best only allowing him to push a little while we go ahead and climb?"

"Good-evening," he added, rising, as Frank came in. "I've been waiting for you. Frank, you must take hold of the Young Men's Christian Association. We want you for president."

Rebecca arose and held out her hand. "Good-night, John," she said. "I have heard enough to give me food for thought for the rest of the evening. I am going to look into this thing."

"Do," said John, with emphasis. "You will

find that if this life is a warfare we've got more
than a Captain — we've a Commander-in-chief,
and we have nothing to do with the fight other
than to obey orders and keep behind the shield."

CHAPTER XXI.

SHE HAS A CHANCE TO BE STRONG.

IT was much more than an ordinary matter that was clouding her face with such a look of anxiety and distress. She was leaning against the bureau in their room, watching her husband while he went hurriedly from drawer to table, busy with papers and packages, and preparations that looked like a move of some sort.

"I can't understand it, Frank," she said at last; "there is no use in talking with me; I shall never see it in the light that you do. Why should your life be put in peril for the bank any more than the others, who have ever so much larger interests there?"

"My dear child, I am the only young man in town who has interests there that he can help control. There are hundreds who have placed their money there for us to take care of, and we must be true to our trust, even if it should be at the peril of life, which I am not afraid of. I dare say it was an absurdly false alarm of that cowardly youngster who sleeps there. He is too young and too foolish to be trusted in such a place anyway."

"But why can't you place the whole thing in the hands of the police?"

"Well, there are grave reasons against that. In the first place, as I said, it is probably nothing at all, and to set the police at work at nothing will start talk—stories of all sorts. It is as likely to create a bank panic as not. People are fools when their pockets are at stake. And, besides, if there is a plan to rob the bank, and the police or the law takes it in hand too soon, it will simply quiet the whole thing, not arrest it, and we shall have the pleasure of being in

jeopardy all the time, and not know which way
to look for the villains."

"I don't care if all the money in the bank is
stolen, if you are safe at home," his wife said,
with a sort of persistent despair in her voice.
She had little hope of moving him, but she could
not help saying it.　He turned toward her,
speaking tenderly:

"That does not sound like my brave, con-
scientious wife.　I had an idea you would want
me to brave danger for the sake of duty."

"But I don't see the duty at all."

"You will when you think about it quietly.
My dear Rebecca, you have often come to me
with a strong word from the Bible that has
helped me forward.　Is it my turn now?　Do
you remember what we read at prayers this
morning?　'Then Paul answered, What mean
ye to weep and to break mine heart? for I am
ready not to be bound only, but also to die at
Jerusalem, for the name of the Lord Jesus.'"

"That is such a very different thing," she said,
wiping the hot tears from her face.　"The Lord
Jesus had given him directions to go to Jerusalem, and he knew his work was there."

"But, dear wife, you and I believe that the Lord Jesus still gives directions to his servants. I have asked him for mine, and I as firmly believe that my work, and hence my duty, lies at the bank to-night, as Paul could have believed it to be his duty to go to Jerusalem. It is a different place, and the work is different, but the Lord commands us both."

What could Rebecca say? Her heart beat hard and fast, and she felt her whole soul rising up in rebellion against this idea of duty; but she had reasoned in this same way many a time. She could not gainsay her husband.

"For all that," he said again, in an altered tone, "I think we are making quite too serious a business of this thing. I really do not expect any trouble at all. At the same time, I shall take every precaution, and incur no risks that are not necessary; and I shall expect to be ready for a hearty breakfast at the usual hour to-morrow morning, and prepared to laugh at you for your fears."

"But, Frank, you don't *know*."

"No," he said, changing back to the thoughtful and tender tone; "it is true I don't *know*;

neither do you and I know when we lie down at
night that we may not awaken in another world;
but I am fully persuaded that it is my duty to
guard the interests of the firm, and the interests
of those hundreds who have trusted us. Now,
Rebecca, that last verse this morning was, ' And
when he would not be persuaded, we ceased,
saying, The will of the Lord be done.' Can't
you give me that message? His will toward us
is a very tender one. We are always in the
midst of dangers, but he cares for us."

Notwithstanding all of which comforting
words, she sat down in a wilted heap on the foot
of the bed, and gave herself up to bitter weeping,
as soon as ever the door had closed after her
husband. All this trouble was born of an impression, rather than a belief, that there was a
bold-laid scheme to rifle the bank, and that the
plans were likely to be carried out that very
night. It could hardly be said that anybody
actually believed that such would be the case.
Indeed, the seniors smiled at the notion, and
ridiculed the supposed proofs, which were
certainly meager and poorly founded; but they,
nevertheless, admired and applauded the young

cashier's announcement that he would take the place of the youthful under-teller who slept in the bank, and that he would arm himself heavily, and be prepared for rough work, should there be occasion. It was hardly possible to do much more than this, without, as he had explained to his wife, putting the scamps on guard, if there were any scamps, or creating a panic in the minds of ignorant people, who should hear rumors that they did not understand. Every one admired Frank Edwards' determination except his wife. She had to bear the horrible burden of her fear and anxiety in secret. Her mother-in-law was still too feeble to be trusted with a knowledge of such a state of things, and only knew that business matters connected with the bank required his absence from home, and she thought from town, for the night. So Rebecca watched, and cried, and prayed through the long hours of that night in solitude. She had eagerly urged that at least her husband should not stay alone; and when he had represented to her that it so happened that none of those whose duty called them to peril their safety for the sake of the bank were in town, save old men, and the young teller, who was too frightened to be of service, she had suggested John Milton.

Her husband's surprise when he said, "Ought I to invite him into what may be danger, when he has no interests at stake, and is not bound by any possible sense of duty to be there?" made her cheeks flush as she answered, "But you could explain to him; I know he would not be afraid."

"But suppose harm should come to him, would you and I like the feeling that we were the cause? Would we like to meet his mother, knowing that?" So she was silenced, and could only cry and wait. People are less wise, and more in danger often in this life than they suppose. It turned out that the young teller, who was sure that he had heard whispers of what concerned the bank, was correct, and it turned out that Frank Edwards' bold, rapid pistol shots prevented a heavy loss, and arrested two of the villains who had planned so skillfully; and it also turned out that he was wounded himself, and came home before breakfast indeed, but came in a slow-moving carriage, with his unconscious head lying on John Milton's breast, while Dr. Ferry watched his pulse with keen, anxious eyes, and an older doctor shook his wise head with a solemn frown when his eyes rested on the deathly face. Oh, the awfulness of the days that followed! alternating between hope and fear, and settling at last into the dreadful certainty of coming death.

" The shot will not kill him, but the fever will," said the gray-headed doctor. " He can't be saved from brain fever." And he wasn't saved from it, though surely they worked as few other doctors ever had — Dr. Ferry never leaving him day or night, save to snatch a mouthful of food, or an hour of sleep that should help him to keep up and watch. As for Rebecca, she did hardly even that; and her strength did not fail her; instead, it seemed to increase as the days passed — her intense, feverish, determined strength to hold on to her husband; to save him; to cling so closely, so persistently, so fiercely that even death would be terrified and shrink away. But who can fight with death? Steadily his awful shadow crept, steadily his fierce grip tightened, until even the doctors failed to speak one encouraging word, or look one encouraging glance. Their hope was gone. Still Rebecca wrestled and groaned in spirit, and clung. "He must not die!" It was all she could say. She turned sharply away from the anxious, pitiful pastor, who tried, with trembling lips, to beg her to pray for strength to say, "The will of the Lord be done." She said, with fierce brevity of speech and manner: "You don't know what you are talking about; don't talk to me." She would have no help from any one; she made no complaint; she shed no tears; she uttered no moan. She just hung over her husband with that dreadful face of living death, and held on. And it did no good. He was slipping from her —going without a word of good-by, a glance of recognition. Yet, almost the last words she had ever heard him say, were: "The will of the Lord be done!"

One morning John Milton caught her as she was passing swiftly through the upper hall. He seized her hand and held it with an eager grasp.

"One minute, just one minute, Rebecca, for the sake of my pity for you. I am not going to torment you; I just have a word of blessing.

This is what you are privileged to say: 'None of these things move me; neither count I my life dear unto myself.'"

"This is more than life," she said, in a cold, hard tone.

"Yes, I know, but you don't want him to live for *his* sake; it is for yours, don't you see? Don't count your life dearer unto yourself than it is to the Lord Jesus. I tell you he has said of you: 'I will show her how great things she must suffer for my sake.' Rebecca, you have learned how to *do* things for his sake; aren't you willing for the higher honor?" There are those, true Christians, too, to whom these words would have been no help; but they came to Rebecca like a revelation. How had she panted for work! something by which she could honor her Lord. She knew that had been her motive; she had prayed for it in eagerness of soul; was this the answer? Oh, not this, not this; she was not strong enough for this; she could not honor him so; she should bring disgrace, she had already; she had begged for something to *do*, not for something to suffer; she had never wanted that.

She gave a low, pitiful cry, as of one who was wounded to the very depths. "I can't do it, John; I can't, I can't!"

"No, poor soul," he said, quickly; "of course you can't. Do you think he expects it of you to bear such a trial as this! It is awful; I know it is; he knows it is. Remember what he knows of human anguish. I tell you he will bear it for you; he stands waiting; you must *believe* me; take it to him."

How white and wan she was! She turned hollow, yet searching eyes on him, and spoke quickly: "John, I *don't* know what you mean; I wish I did. Oh, in my very soul I wish I did. How can I ask him any better than I have? He doesn't hear me." The wise-hearted young man attempted no shocked rebuttal of her pitiful statement; did not try to prove that he always hears, and that she must not speak such words. Instead he said: "I tell you, Rebecca, I wouldn't pray any more for his life; your prayers are before him, and he will give you that answer if, for Frank's sake and yours, he can. Now I would ask for grace, 'grow in grace,' you know; ask for grace to suffer so that his name may be honored. It is given to you to show what a Christian can bear from the hand that loves her; how she can trust still; the chance is yours; you can't do it, but he will do it through you, if you will let him; don't struggle any more; rest."

She stood for a full minute looking up at his earnest, eager face, then she said: "John, I believe you have helped me." Then she ran swiftly back to her husband.

As for John Milton, he turned off into an unoccupied room, and buried his head in the cushions, and cried like a child.

Do you think Rebecca did not get her help? I tell you she did. It will not do to sneer and scoff at such truths as these; you are in no danger of ever being able to test them so long as you sneer, it is true. But the old proof holds good still: "If any man will do his will, he shall know of the doctrine." Rebecca Edwards *knows* that the Lord came to her, and held her hand, and said to the storm in her heart, " Peace, be still." And the tempest stilled. The days went on just the same after that; only those watching around that sick man spoke lower, and with a touch of reverence when they addressed his wife; they saw the change; the pale face was calm, the voice low, gentle, steady; the fierceness was entirely gone from her manner. She was just as watchful, just as alert, twice as helpful, but she was even then at rest. There were those who could not see it without tears. There came an evening, when that peculiar solemn hush settled down on the house, that betokens the very presence of the King. The quick moving up and down, to and fro, to try this, or that, ceased; there was no more trying. Rebecca knelt by her husband's side and held his quiet, nerveless hand. His mother sobbed unrestrainedly at his other side. He did not hear her; Dr. Ferry, with white lips and whiter face, stood watching at the foot. Other of the friends held back in respectful silence, ready to do, unwilling to intrude on sorrow like this. There were still others less considerate. They whispered in the rooms outside; among them Sallie Holland. Sallie didn't know how to whisper; yet she essayed to do it. "She is wonderfully quiet, poor thing," she whispered, meaning his wife; "I didn't think she would bear it so. Some people thought she married him for his

money; I never did; but you can't tell. I'm
sure I'm glad she can take it so."

Rebecca shivered as if in an ague fit. The
fire was hot, the flames were fierce and scorch-
ing; if she was not to do it to show how *great*
things she could suffer for his sake, what *was* it
for? Must even this be denied her? Would they
dare to think that she did not love him next to
God? Dr. Ferry stepped forward and closed
the door, and Sallie Holland had a glimpse of
his stern face. She shuddered a little, and wondered if Dr. Ferry thought such an ugly scowl
was becoming. Then, even she was still. The
door opened again in a minute; it let in the
grey-haired doctor. He came softly to the bedside; he looked at the quiet face on the pillow;
he exchanged quick glances with Dr. Ferry.
He stepped one side and whispered to John Milton, "Get her out quietly." Rebecca heard it;
she heard everything. "I'll go," she said, moving; and John put his arm around her and
helped her out. At the door of the library where
he put her, she said: " John, help his mother."
So he went back. Five minutes afterward he

came softly; Rebecca was kneeling before her
husband's chair in the library.

"May I come?" he asked; "may I come?
Rebecca, I want to tell you something."

"I know what it is," she said, without looking
up, "don't speak."

"I don't know whether you can or not. Can
you be as still and as brave for his sake as you
have for the Lord's?"

Then she looked up. "What do you mean?"

"I mean that the crisis that has been so near
to death is passed. Dr. Grey says there is wonderful change. He says he will live."

Then, indeed, Rebecca lost her self-control
and her consciousness together.

"Joy doesn't kill," John Milton said, aloud
and joyfully, as he laid her on the couch and
bent over her. "It is a second miracle. The
Lord's hand has stayed the knife, just as faith
had triumphed, and said: 'The will of the Lord
be done.'"

CHAPTER XXII.

A CONSCIENCE NOT VOID OF OFFENSE.

CURIOUS thing is this life of ours. Rebecca, when she went back to her husband's bedside, her pulses throbbing with the thrill of new, glad hopes that John Milton's words had born in them, felt as though she had been lifted above the common affairs of life forever. Felt as though there was no experience possible to her in all the future that should have power to drag her down again to feelings of unrest or discomfort over trifles. She had gone with her husband to the very gates of death; she had almost seen them open to let him in, and to shut her out; she had felt all the

345

awful solemnities of the parting; she knew what
it was to say good-by!   And then, suddenly, all
unexpectedly, those gates had closed again noise-
lessly, and left them together outside.   Wonderful experience!   How could common-places
touch her again forever!   Much she knew about
it!   It was barely six weeks from that day of
life in death, — or life out of death, — and now
she sat in that pretty room of her's, her face all
in a flush, her eyes bright with unshed tears;
bright with a flash of something very like anger
that refused to let the tears fall.   She was
having a trying afternoon; just as trying for
the present moment as though she had not
but a few weeks ago, been almost widowed, and
as though her husband were not at this moment
rejoicing in the hourly increasing strength of
body and brain.   Strangely enough, too, it began
about a bonnet.   Suppose some prophet had
whispered to Rebecca at that sublime moment
when she raised her dry eyes and burning face
to John Milton's as she took in the words so
strange, so wonderful, that they were almost
awful in their solemnity, — "The doctor says
that the crisis is past and he will live."   Sup-

pose, I say, that just then some prophet had whispered, "Just six weeks from to-day, you and Sallie Holland will have as disagreeable an afternoon as you ever spent in your life ; in fact, it will amount to a downright quarrel, and it will begin with your winter bonnet." What would Rebecca Edwards have thought of that? Was it supposed that *she* could ever think of, care for, argue over bonnets again. But she did.

Sallie brought her work that afternoon, and came up to the pretty room to be friendly, and have a nice little gossip. Worsted work it was. It was drawing near to Christmas, and Sallie Holland was one of those who have many worsted cats, and dogs, and things of that sort, to finish about Christmas time. Rebecca's mood was none of the sunniest. She was worried over her husband. He had gone back to the bank again, as she thought, by many weeks too soon. To be sure he had promised to be very careful; to do no thinking; no counting; in fact, simply to look around him, and see what was going on, and get used, by degrees, to the sound of business again, and only an hour or two a day. Oh!

he wouldn't think of working so soon again; she needn't be afraid.

He meant all this, and yet Rebecca foresaw how it would be, and was not surprised when he was gone for two hours, and when he went out again in the afternoon, not to work — just to look on. She was nervous and troubled, and she was one of those to whom, in such moods, a crochet needle is a positive exasperation; so I don't know but, after all, the crochet needle was partly to blame. She watched Sallie make it go in and out, till it seemed to her she should shriek, if it made one more loop. But she didn't; and it kept on making loops, and Sallie's tongue kept on. At that unlucky moment she suggested the bonnet question.

"Rebecca, what in the world made you have crimson in your hat this winter? You don't know how unbecoming it is to you. I never saw you look so badly in a hat."

Now when one has spent a reasonable, possibly an unreasonable amount of thought over a winter hat, and paid a price that, to say the least, is entirely sufficient for all purposes of propriety, to be told that it is very unbecoming is not comfortable. Rebecca was not fond of having her taste questioned, at least in matters of dress; in truth, she was not used to it; she had been a very queen among the girls in her tastefulness, even in days of poverty. Why should she not be authority now, when she had plenty of money, for, say what you will, the question of taste is very much involved in the question of purse. Her face flushed, and she turned her eyes away from the crochet needle lest it should exasperate her too much as she answered:

"Do you, indeed. I am so devoid of taste as not to agree with you. I like the hat very well. As to why I chose red, it must have been because I wanted it, you know. I have no other guide."

Now this was, perhaps, a trifle wicked in Rebecca. I will not say that she forgot she was speaking to one who sometimes was obliged to wear a red garment when she preferred a blue one, simply because the garment that had been red the winter before positively refused to wear out, and give her purse the excuse for a new one. Rebecca in these days had no occasion to make excuses to her purse. Did she mean to remind her friend of this? I think myself that she was not so unladylike, but so Sallie took it.

"Of course," she said, "we all know you have plenty of money, and for that very reason it seemed strange to me that you should choose in such poor taste. It is just the shade of red that is not being worn at all, and the very shade that the least becomes you, anyway. I told Mattie that I felt sure you must have been thinking of something else, and the milliner just cheated you into believing that she had put you into the height of the fashion. I said I meant to tell you."

"I ought to be obliged, I'm sure," Rebecca said, trying to laugh, and to speak lightly, and yet feeling excessively annoyed. There was something so very disagreeable in the way that Sallie Holland appropriated not only all the taste, but all the knowledge in the fashionable world, leaving none for Rebecca, she could hardly help putting a sting in her voice.

"If it had been *your* taste I was obliged to consult instead of my own, it would have been a pity to have made such a mistake; but, you see,

I arranged the hat to suit *my* taste, and it suits it exactly."

"It wouldn't," said Sallie, positively, "if you knew how unbecoming it was to you. You see since Frank has been sick you have grown real sallow; you didn't take that into consideration I dare say; but I thought of it the moment you wore your hat. And the red gives such an ugly flush all over your face, exactly as if you had been cooking the steak before you started out. It is real brick color; I don't like that shade of red anyway."

Had Sallie Holland known Rebecca as well as she might have done after all these years, the absolute silence with which this was received would have warned her that she was treading on very unsafe ground; but there were many things in this world that Sallie did not know. She took up the same subject, or a worse one, as soon as she found that she was to receive no answer.

"Speaking of hats, did you not realize what a flat crown you were getting? You got it so early in the season, I dare say it didn't look strangely to you, but it really begins to now, and it is such a pity; I suppose it is an expensive velvet, isn't it? Those broad crowns are really last year's shape; it is abominable in Mrs. McBride to take you in so; I wouldn't stand it if I were you."

Rebecca sewed away with much energy at the bit of blue flannel she was fashioning, and essayed to speak without a tremble of voice; feeling in her heart that she was angry enough with little Sallie Holland to take her up and shake her.

"Why, Sallie, I can't imagine what gives you such overwhelming anxiety about my bonnet; it is all wasted sympathy too; really aud truly I like the hat very well indeed; it was Mr. Edwards' choice and he has some reputation for good taste I believe; it suits him perfectly, and therefore would me, if for no other reason."

When this young woman wanted to be especially dignified to any of her old friends who had known her husband from childhood, she was sure to speak of him as "Mr. Edwards." Sallie's answer was prefaced by an exasperating little laugh.

"Oh! Frank. We all know what his taste was as a young man; still, he doesn't take into consideration that of course you have faded some ; it is no wonder I am sure, sitting up night after night as you did with him ; you were certainly a pattern wife ; everybody said so, Rebecca. Just the one to be with a sick person, too ; so composed and self-reliant. I told mother you acted quite as if you were reconciled to the inevitable, and had made up your mind to bear it with as few scenes as possible ; did you really think he was going to die, Rebecca ? "

Rebecca shivered as if a cold blast had struck her. This was infinitely worse than the bonnet talk.

"Don't," she said ; so sharply that even the obtuse Sallie felt it. That lady regarded her with a curious stare.

"You are growing nervous, aren't you ; " she said at last in a sympathetic tone. "I have noticed it for some time, and it is a pity ; nervousness has such an effect on one's appearance ; but of course you don't care much for that, these days. It is not to be wondered at with all you have gone through. That dreadful ogre of a mother-in-law is enough to make you wild, I should think."

A few months before it would have been hard

for Rebecca to believe that such a sentence about
her mother-in-law would have stabbed her so;
rude, she would undoubtedly have thought it : unladylike in the extreme, but that it would strike
her with a positive pain it would have been hard
to realize.   But during those few months there
had been changes.   Had not that mother-in-law
on this very morning pressed on her cheek a
tender, motherly kiss as she said to the happy-
eyed husband looking on : " This daughter of
mine is a great comfort to me, Frank ! "   Could
she sit still and have her called " an old ogre,"
after that ?   What kept her still ?   Why didn't
she flash her indignant denial on Sallie Holland
and silence her mischievous tongue ?   What but
the memory of that miserable day when she had
so far forgotten her position of wifehood, her
dignity as a Christian woman introduced into a
new family, as to allow her tongue to speak to
that same Sallie, plain and sharp words concerning her husband's mother.   How could she have
done it !   It seemed almost incredible to her
now ; and yet she remembered but too vividly,
even the formation of the sentence.   What was
there for her to say ?   Sallie maundered on :

"Karl Watson was speaking of you only last evening. You know his Nettie has lost her mother with the same fever that Mrs. Edwards had, and Karl said: (you know what queer things he says sometimes — he was as gloomy as possible last night; I suppose Nettie's gloom reacts upon him); he said: 'It was a strange way to manage things; it looked wonderfully as though chance had it all in hand. It seemed to him as though an intelligent being, knowing what was going on in the world, would have left Nettie's mother, who was the very apple of her eye, and who just now particularly needed her help, and taken Mrs. Edwards, who of course, would not be missed very much by Frank, since he is married and settled in life, and it would have been a positive relief to you.' It is a queer way to put it, isn't it ?"

Could human nature endure that, and keep silence ? "Sallie !" said Rebecca, and the sharpness of her tone made Sallie start and drop the worsted dog, just as she was taking a stitch for his eye, "won't you have the goodness to remember that you are talking about my husband's mother ?"

"My patience!" said Sallie, "what have I
said. Nothing so very dreadful I am sure. In
fact Rebecca, I don't see what there is for you to
flame out about in this way; I haven't said any
more, indeed I haven't begun to say as much as
you told me yourself in this very room; I'm
sure it is not my fault that you told me she was
horrid."

And Sallie put on an air of injured innocence.
What a stab this was! That very room; her
pretty home; hers and Frank's, sacred to the experiences of wifehood, and she had desecrated
it, and insulted her husband by talking over the
faults and failings of his own mother with such a
creature as this! Sallie, finding that she was not
to be answered, took courage and continued:

"You needn't think, Rebecca, that I am telling any secrets. Everybody knows that you
don't live happily with your husband's relations.
And you have our sympathy, I do assure you.
You needn't think we have turned against you.
We haven't. All the girls say they wouldn't be
in your position for anything. Nettie Wheeler
says it is easy to be seen that you are just a
drudge to your mother-in-law. I told Frank

myself, just a few days before he was taken sick,
that I thought it was horrid in him to mew you
up here, and give you no society, when you had
been used to such a happy home and to having
your own way about everything."

If Rebecca did not answer this, it was because
she was so horrified that her tongue seemed to
refuse her bidding. What awful gossip was this!
The tongues of the neighborhood wagging about
her husband and herself, and the unhappy relations in the family, and herself the one who had
given the first impulse to the talk!

The dog's nose refused to curve in the right
way, and Sallie gave undivided attention to it
for a moment and then went on:

"He didn't answer a word; just laughed in the
most unconcerned manner as if he didn't take it
to heart at all; though I was real earnest in what
I said. Frank always *was* selfish; my brother,
Wayne, says he was the most selfish fellow in
the class; always would have his own way, and
his own pleasure, and found it hard to understand why other people shouldn't be suited because he was. Men are the most selfish beings
in the world, anyway. When I marry, my

husband shan't make a tool of me, to please his mother, you may be sure of that."

Rebecca's scissors slid to the floor with a sudden crash; she arose suddenly; she had gotten the use of her tongue, and of her eyes, they flashed.

"Sallie Holland, I think I have endured enough; certainly I have reached the very verge of patience. If you do not know that you are guilty of a gross and unpardonable impertinence in thus insulting my husband and my mother to my very face, it is quite time you were made aware of it. I am not accustomed to sitting quietly and listening to the retail of slanderous reports about my friends, especially about my own husband. You will have to excuse me from further attendance."

Whereupon she moved like a queen across her pretty parlor, swung open the door leading to the inner room, closed it with a slam, turned the key in the lock, noisily; and Sallie realized that she was deserted.

"My patience!" she said, "what a perfect little fury that woman is."

Then she rolled up her worsted dog, hastily donned wraps and rubbers and slipped down the velvet-covered stairs like a velvet-shod cat, and let herself out of the Edwards' mansion in a very excited state of mind.

Speaking of excitement, what shall be said of Rebecca's? She never remembered to have been so angry in her life. She paced her room like a caged animal, her eyes dry and flashing, and controlling herself from actual shrieks by the force of will. It quieted into a burst of tears presently, and then she dropped, in an agony of shame and remorse and doubt as to what to do, on her knees. Her powers of physical endurance had been very much taxed during the season just passed, and had rendered her, as Sallie had said, " very nervous " over some things. And this view of herself had burst upon her like an avalanche. The idea that the young ladies and gentlemen of their acquaintance were meeting together to gossip about her husband and herself; the idea that they had pronounced upon him as a household tryant and herself as a drudge, and his mother as an ogre. Could anything be more horrible? Yes, there was something back of it, more horrible still; that was, that she had actually started this herself. What was she to do? What should she tell Frank?

His eyes were very quick to discern trouble where she was concerned. He would be sure to see that she was flushed and excited, and had been crying. How was it possible to make him understand why Sallie Holland dared to sit in his house and coolly discuss his, and his mother's character, to his wife? Could she ever bring herself to admit that she had so lost sight of his honor as to discuss *his* mother before such a creature as Sallie? Another thought made the blood roll in crimson waves to her very forehead: What if he supposed her capable of discussing him, his faults, his mistakes, with Sallie; Horrible! He could never think that of her; and yet, why not, if his mother was not sacred, why should he suppose himself to be? Rebecca felt that there was a difference, but she couldn't bring herself to be sure that Frank would feel it. She thought of her own mother, and tried to fancy the extent of her indignation had Frank dared to complain of her, to his gentlemen friends; but then she told herself, " my mother was certainly different from his." That, however, didn't comfort her; could she expect that he should see the faults in his own mother, as plainly as she had seen them? Could she even want him to? Could she have loved him so well, if he had been capable of coolly tearing to pieces the nature of his mother who loved him as her life?

It was all confusion to poor Rebecca; only this, she had done a wicked, wicked thing, in forgetting her wifehood, and the family secrets into which it led her, and spreading them out before that queen among gossips, Sallie Holland. Another stab thrust her just then; how much of her share in this did Frank already know? Sallie had actually dared to talk to him plainly about the sin of keeping her, his honored and treasured wife, in the same house with his mother! What horrible insolence! He had laughed to be sure; what else would her Frank have done to such information as that, from such as she? Since he couldn't very well knock her down, what was there but to laugh; and yet, she could well imagine how it had stung him.

Had he thought over it, and wondered if it were possible that she, his wife could have said anything to justify such words from Sallie? "Just before he was sick," Sallie had said; perhaps on that very evening, before he went to the bank. Perhaps that was the thought which troubled and saddened him during those waiting hours, and that had so nearly been his last night! She shivered again over the fearful memory! Oh, if all this had been nothing but pitiful envy of herself and her position, such as she knew Sallie was capable of feeling. If she had always proudly kept her own counsel, never for once descending to the level of confidence with *her*, it would have been disagreeable enough certainly, yet with what a cool tone could she have checked that rude tongue this afternoon; with what surprised dignity could she have reminded her that she was talking of what she did not understand. How quiet her conscience would have been — with what clear eyes could she have looked into her husband's, as she told him somewhat of the silly story; or, indeed, would there have been any such story to tell? Would Sallie have ever dared to hint such things to her, had not her own tongue given permission! Truly, Rebecca had not lived in "good conscience" before either God or man in this matter, and sharply was it goading her now.

CHAPTER XXIII.

NEW VIEWS OF THINGS.

REBECCA, what has become of Sallie Holland?" This was the question that suddenly startled Rebecca out of a reverie one evening, nearly a week after the events which were given in the last chapter. The week had been one of trouble to Rebecca. Her conscience was by no means quiet in regard to the quarrel. She had succeeded in avoiding any allusion to it, when with her husband, and had decided that it certainly was not her duty to tell him about it, as it could do no sort of good to any one, and would undoubtedly cause him much pain. But she found it a very difficult thing to keep. She

364

was accustomed to talking over the daily affairs of her life with Frank, and to change this habit suddenly was not so easy to do. Now this question both startled and confused her; she knew very well what had become of Sallie, only how was she going to explain the sudden cessation of her frequent visits? She sought refuge in an evasion.

"Why?"

"Oh, nothing, only I happened to be thinking of her just then, and it suddenly occurred to me that I had not seen her with you lately, nor heard of her calls. I thought she used to visit you very often. You have not quarreled, have you?"

The question was most carelessly asked, and ended in a slight laugh, as if the suggestion was the most improbable one imaginable; but Rebecca's cheeks glowed, and she found that she could not control her voice to answer. What had Sallie been telling him? For the moment she felt sure that the lady had actually gone to her husband with a complaint against his wife.

"What story has she been telling you?" she asked at last, trying in vain to keep the tremulous excitement which she felt out of her voice. Her husband regarded her wonderingly.

"Nothing in the world," he answered, promptly. "I have not even seen her in several weeks, I believe ; in fact, I don't remember when I saw her last. What is the matter my dear?"

"What made you think of her just then, Frank?"

"I'm not sure that I know. I was thinking of the question of moral influence and the power that we had as Christians to influence those around us. Naturally enough I thought of my wife and the opportunities that she had of this sort, and I suppose it was that train of thought which brought me around to Sallie Holland. Do you think she has any special interest in religious matters, Rebecca?"

Now, what was there in this simple question to make Rebecca feel perfectly dumbfounded? What but that her conscience said to her that during all the numberless times she had of late seen Sallie Holland and talked with her, not once had the subject of personal religion been suggested. Indeed it seemed to her almost as if it would be casting pearls before swine to talk to Sallie Holland of religion.

"I'm sure she hasn't," she answered quickly, "neither in that subject, nor any other that is worth being interested about."

"Then she is certainly in need of help, and you, my dear, who seem to have so much influence over her, are the very one to help her. I suppose you often talk of these things; people often have more interest than they choose to allow to appear; perhaps she is one of them. She must *think*, you know, even though she doesn't want you to believe it."

What was Rebecca to say? Every word was a sting to her conscience. How often had she talked in this same way to her husband about some of his friends, how often they had talked together about friends of hers, how sure he was that she would meet him half way in this new interest, and yet, how could she? A miserable feeling that she was deceiving her husband suddenly took possession of her, and caused her to make a resolve.

"You asked me if we had quarreled," she said, speaking quickly. "Frank, that is just it, we have quarreled; had a horrid time. She was here — it will be a week to-morrow — and she was so rude and insulting, you can't think how rude, and I spoke to her in such very plain words, that I don't think she can ever come again. I haven't spoken to her since, and indeed I don't see how I can; she not only insulted me, but you."

" But, my dear, I do not understand ? What power has Sallie Holland to insult us ? The most that I should think she could do was to be somewhat insolent, and as that has always been a characteristic of hers, and is really a fault of the poor girl's unfortunate home-life, we ought to be patient with it; and indeed Rebecca, I thought you were remarkably patient with her. I have admired that very trait in your intercourse. Your patience almost used to vex me in those days when her interference was a positive trial to me ; but it is long since she has had power to annoy me. Rebecca, she has said things to me, which were certainly insolent enough, but I always considered the source, and laughed over it. So long as she has nothing to do with our affairs, and her remarks are only the product of her imagination, what harm is it? I can imagine, possibly, the nature of your trial, from some things that she has said to me, but you who know what folly it all is, can surely not be hurt by it."

He did not understand; how should he? The special sting, that which was wound up in Sallie's retort: "I'm sure I am not saying any more than you told me yourself," was unknown to him. There was no resource but to tell him the whole story. If there is any one reading this who has not a high moral sense, and a sensitive conscience, that one will not have the least idea how hard this was to do. But she did it; going over with morbid care the details of the talk; going back of that, and explaining what was worse, the hinge on which Sallie's talk hung, that miserable afternoon when she forgot her Christian dignity and descended to confidence. He was very quiet and very grave; he arose once, but it was to take a seat nearer to her, and when she hesitated the most, and flushed the most painfully, while she was rigidly telling him just the words she used to Sallie about his mother, he put out his hand and took hers and held it closely. Rebecca never forgot that handclasp. After the worst was told, she went on eagerly, explaining how entirely her feelings had changed, how good his mother was to her, how much she loved her, not only for his sake, but now for her own; but that she could not forget, nor get away from that horrid burst of confidence with Sallie, and that she could not get away from a feeling of absolute hatred of her now; to think that she had set the tongues of the neighborhood to wagging about *her* husband, with actually a shadow of foundation to build on, given by his wife!

"I understand it," he said, when at last she paused; I understand it better than you think I do; I have not been deaf and blind. I know my mother has in many respects made it hard for you, and I have kept silence often for the very reason that I felt if I spoke I should make it harder. It is working out much better than I had hoped; the ministry of sickness has had its effect; in the end it will all be right. My mother is changed, and I am changed, and it is your influence, Rebecca, over us both.

What wonderful payment was this for all her

shortcomings, and for this last flagrant mistake!

"Don't," she said at last. "Frank, don't; I do not deserve to have anything of the kind said to me. I cannot tell you how I hate myself for many things that I have said and done, but especially for this; how *could* I have so forgotten myself, and you, as to make in any sense a confidante of Sallie Holland?"

"It is something that you will not be likely to do again," he said, with a quiet smile; "and now Rebecca, 'forgetting the things that are behind,' you know; let us begin over again, and make greater effort. We have both learned some things."

"But how *can* I begin over again?" she asked, nervously; here is this quarrel, and I don't know how to get away from it; and yet you are saying to me that Sallie is the one whom I ought to try to influence. How can I influence her in any way now?"

"As to Sallie, I can tell you what I would certainly do if I were you," he said, speaking earnestly: "I would pray for her."

"Pray for her!" and Rebecca sat upright

and looked as though the suggestion were entirely new and unheard of before.

"*Pray* for her, with all my heart and soul; throwing an intensity into the prayer that demands answer."

Rebecca sat perfectly still, while her husband went to the door to answer a knock and came back to explain that he was summoned to the parlor with a business call. She sat and tried to think, for sometime after he left her; and the burden of her thought was, that it did not seem possible to her that she *could* pray for Sallie Holland !

Her thoughts were still full of this matter the next day; so full of it that she hardly attended to what her mother was saying to her during lunch, till roused by a question.

"Do you feel able, Rebecca, to make a few calls with me this afternoon, or have you other engagements ?"

"Calls !" repeated Rebecca; "why, are you able for that infliction ?"

"I don't mean to make it an infliction if I can help it," she answered with a smile. "The truth is, I have been thinking a good deal about something which has troubled me of late."

Whereupon Rebecca fell to wondering if everybody's conscience started up occasionally and gave them twinges of pain.

"I feel that I don't know some of the people in our church as well as I ought to; in fact I might say, I don't know them at all, some of them. I have made up my mind to get better acquainted with them if I can; and I'd like it very much if you would help me."

"Certainly, ma'am," Rebecca said; "I will call wherever you choose." But she didn't in the least get Mrs. Edwards meaning; she went on:

"There is your friend Mr. Milton; his mother is in our congregation, I believe, and yet I don't know her by sight; I thought I would call there if you had no objections, and on several others whom I have in mind."

Now indeed Rebecca was thoroughly roused and attentive. She was not sure that she could believe her ears. Did Mrs. Alanson Edwards suggest calling on the Miltons; people with whom she had never come in contact socially in her life, and was no more likely to, than though they lived at the Antipodes.

"Did I understand you to say that you meant to call there?" she asked, trying vainly to hide the wonder in her tone.

"I thought of it," said Mrs. Edwards, meekly. "And, Rebecca, I don't suppose you know the Collinses and the Pecks, and those people, but they are good worthy people, and are members of our church, and it does seem as though we ought to know them; don't you think so?"

Rebecca's answer was meek enough and with a tone of respect in it, not unmingled with something almost like awe. She went up-stairs to dress for calling, with some very new ideas, that afforded her subject for thought. She remembered among other matters which had been hobbies of hers, this one of the distinctions of society formed by wealth, or position; no tongue could have been more brilliant than hers, no logic have ridiculed more skilfully. Yet she stood transfixed this day before that inexorable conscience, while it arraigned her on this very point. She had been able to see how the Edwardses and those of their set made themselves ridiculous by not calling on the Harlows for instance, and the Miltons, and people of that clique. But not once had it occurred to her that she herself and those same Miltons in omitting to call on the Collinses and the Pecks, people a notch or two lower down in the social scale, were guilty of the same silly exhibition of aristocracy. It was a new revelation. Why had she never called on these people? Why, because; well, she had never thought of it. Nobody called on them. Well, but, why didn't they? Could it be possible that it was because Mrs. Peck did not only her own fine ironing, but some for other people, and Mr. Collins was a day-laborer on uncertain wages? If this really was the reason, then how was she any better than Mrs. Edwards, who had not called on her mother because she lived in a little house on an unfashionable street, and did her own work, ironing and all? Going down thus into the depths of things, she began to realize that in both cases it was not so much these reasons, as that the customs of society separated the classes; each grade simply forgot the existence of the other, or at least forgot that there could be a line of

sympathy between them, and went their different
ways, thoughtlessly and selfishly.   So thinking,
she took her first lesson in the charity that seeks
to find excuse for others' faults.   Nevertheless,
she arrayed herself for calling, in a very meek
state of mind, wondering much what Frank
would think of this new departure, whether his
mother had confided in him, and was acting
upon his advice.   Wondering much also, what
the people to whom they were going, would
think or say, and whether Mrs. Edwards had
the least idea how embarrassing it would be.
One thing was clear to her mind; both her
husband and mother-in-law were taking rapid
strides in their Christian life; if it really were
due in part to her influence, as Frank had
earnestly stated, were they leaving her in the
background? The question was a solemn one,
and afforded that troubled conscience a chance
for another twinge.

CHAPTER XXIV.

BEING "ALL THINGS TO ALL MEN."

THE carriage which Mrs. Alanson Edwards habitually made use of, when she did not ride with her son, was a very handsome one ; and the toilet which seemed to her absolutely necessary in order to be ready for calls, was entirely in keeping with the carriage. Altogether Rebecca felt, as she sat opposite her handsome mother-in-law and rolled through the pretty streets of the city that they were about to astonish the Collins and Peck neighborhood, to say nothing of that neat little house near her own mother's, where John Milton lived. She could

377

not rise above a sense of embarrassment, and an
eager wish that Frank were along to help them
through with his easy gaiety.

"Do you know the Pecks at all?" Mrs.
Edwards asked as the coachman followed his
directions, and turned into the narrow, quiet
street.

"Not at all," Rebecca answered, and she felt
a glow of shame; they had been members for
years of the same church with herself. What
right had she ever to have sneered at Mrs. Edwards' aristocratic notions.

"Well, never mind," the elder lady said, "I
dare say we can make ourselves known to them."

And Rebecca wondered how, and felt exceedingly uncomfortable. She had yet to learn all
the resources of her mother-in-law. Miss Fannie
Peck answered the ring, and it was the pleas-
antest voice in the world that said:

"How do you do my dear? Is your mother in,
and will you ask her if she will see Mrs. Edwards, and her daughter, for a few minutes?"

It transpired, too, that though Mrs. Peck did
fine ironing for several people, she knew how to
conduct herself in an entirely respectable manner,

and when she came into the neat rag-carpeted sitting-room with her neat calico dress, and plain linen collar, she looked every inch a lady. To be sure she supposed that it was something about fine ironing that had stopped the carriage at her door; so she bowed respectfully and waited. Rebecca, who knew she was a very nice ironer, wished in her secret heart that they had come for the purpose of getting twenty tucked skirts done up, to avoid the horrible sense of embarrassment that she felt. It appeared that Mrs. Edwards senior felt nothing of the kind; she arose with promptness and cordially held out her hand, and said:

" My daughter, Mrs. Frank Edwards, Mrs. Peck. We have concluded that it is time we knew each other. We are members of the same church and meet every Sunday; it is high time we shook hands and remembered that we are sisters. We have come to make a social call."

Then, indeed, was Mrs. Peck embarrassed; her sallow face flushed, and she looked in bewilderment from one well dressed lady to the other, and knew not what to say. Rebecca looked on, and gradually forgot her own embarrassment in listening to the mother-in-law, and realized that she only half knew her. How gracious and winning she was! Topics for conversation she found certainly, and by some instinct seemed to hit on those with which Mrs. Peck was familiar, and about which she could talk. It was really becoming an interesting conversation. Perfectly frank, Mrs. Edwards was also; she did not ignore the fact that she had been a resident of the same city and a member of the same church with Mrs. Peck for seventeen years. She frankly admitted that her views and feelings had changed in regard to many things during the last few months, and she had concluded that she wanted to know her sisters in the church.

"I shall be very glad to see you at any time," she said, earnestly, as they were making their adieus, and the heartiness with which she said it, and indeed her entire manner during the call, left its impression of sincerity. Rebecca began to realize that her mother knew how to make calls. They drove at once to Mr. Collins'. Rebecca remembered to have noticed his wife in the prayer-meeting, and remarked the heartiness with which she sang. She received them at

the door, herself; knew them both, and ushered
them into her neat kitchen with the simple explanation that they did not have any fire in the
sitting-room until after school, when the children
got home.   Here, too, Mrs. Edwards introduced
her daughter.

"I know her," Mrs. Collins said, holding her
hand in great, strong, motherly ones; "I saw her
young, pretty face as soon as it came into your
pew, Mrs. Edwards, and I couldn't help watching the young things playing at life. You
haven't got far enough along to know that it
isn't all play yet, maybe."

" Indeed I have," said Rebecca, earnestly ; relieved of her embarrassed feelings at once by having her mind called back to the solemn ordeal of
life through which she had so recently passed.
"I have come very close to the valley of death,
Mrs. Collins."

" Ah, yes," said Mrs. Collins, " I remember;
well, did his rod and staff comfort you? For I
take it that we need more comfort when it is
our dear one who is passing, rather than ourselves. Did you claim the promise my child?
And did he keep his word ? "

"I did," said Rebecca, with the tone of one who was signing a covenant. "I did, indeed, and his promise is sure."

"Thank the Lord," said Mrs. Collins; and then the talk went on, lifted above the common-places of foolish embarrassment. Indeed Mrs. Collins had no idea of such a feeling; she was one of the the Lord's children, and here were other children of the same father, come to see her, and it was a pleasure to her to talk with them. The senior Mrs. Edwards' manner was perfect. The slight perceptible touch of condescension that Rebecca had detected in her talk with Mrs. Peck entirely disappeared, and in its place there was respect, not unmingled with awe. She had climbed high enough herself to recognize the fact that here was one who had gotten among the very mountains of trust and love; the result was that she bowed before her.

"It is shameful never to have known her before," she said, almost in indignation, to Rebecca as they bade each other a cordial good-by, and drove away.

"Why, she is one of the saints. I really enjoyed her. And that is certainly what I am able to

say of very few of my friends. I mean to have
some friends after this whom I can enjoy."

And she sat back among the cushions with the
air of one who began to realize that there were
sources of enjoyment that she had not dreamed
of before. The call on Mrs. Milton bade fair to
be the least comfortable one of the afternoon,
and Rebecca, who had been taken along to lessen
the embarrassment, had an uncomfortable feeling that she was the producing cause of much of
it. She had such vivid memories of having sat
so often in that stuffy little sitting-room, that
smelled of buckwheat and sausage; sat there on
entirely a level with Mrs. Milton and her sur-
roundings, and Mrs. Milton at least was
now so uncomfortably aware of changes, and
felt the necessity for making so many apol-
ogies, and yet was so constantly lapsing
into forgetfulness and calling her " Rebecca,"
and then flushing into consciousness and begging
her pardon, that Rebecca was ready to fly, in her
confusion, over this unprepossessing appearance
of one of her old friends. Also, Mrs. Milton was
stiff; she fully realized the fact that Rebecca,
married, had not been the neighborly creature
that Rebecca Harlow used to be, and without

understanding in the least all the numberless
reasons why this would have been impossible,
she laid it all at the door of pride, and was disposed in a solemn kind of way to resent it.   She
was also not disposed to be condescended to, and
if I may be pardoned in the use of a very rough
and at the same time expressive word, she was
guilty of almost snubbing Mrs. Edwards.   However, a diversion to her thoughts occurred in the
shape of the invalid daughter, who was as fair as
a snowdrop, and as frail, and as pretty as ever.
Mrs. Edwards' sympathies were immediately en-
listed.   She devoted herself to the pretty invalid
in such a tender and sympathetic way, that the
mother sensibly thawed under it.

"Was she able to ride," she questioned.

"Oh yes," Mrs. Milton said; "but it wasn't
often she got a chance, John was so very busy;
hardly ever able to go with her in the daytime,
and of course it was out of the question that she
should go out at night, and as for her father, he
knew nothing about driving, and was not to
be thought of anyway.   Mrs. Edwards looked at
her daughter:

"Here is a chance for you to have company,
Rebecca; I'm sure she would not be afraid to

ride after our horses, and the driver is perfectly
reliable ; you could often come for her on a bright
day, couldn't you ? "

Rebecca, with shining eyes, declared with
heartiness that she could. Why had it not
occurred to Mrs. Alanson Edwards to offer to
her such a delicious bit of enjoyment as that
before ? Could it be it was because she had
never thought of it, or realized that *there* were
people who could not have a ride, by simply
ordering the carriage. Possibly it was because
Rebecca, taking it for granted that she was too
proud to make such use of her wealth, had never
asked the favor. Still, there was another reason ;
certainly Mrs. Edwards was changed. The
suggestion of the ride was a happy one; it
thawed every vestige of distrust or coldness out
of Mrs. Milton's motherly heart; she became
genial and communicative and sensible. And
Rebecca rode away from her door with visions
of pleasant hours in the future dancing before
her eyes. Mrs. Edwards' most masterly stroke
of genius was reserved to the last hours of that
eventful afternoon. Two more calls they made
upon those doubtful people who did not know

just what their position was, but who stood much better chances of finding out now that Mrs. Edwards' carriage had halted for fifteen minutes before their doors. Then that lady looked at her watch.

"It is almost time for us to drive around and take up Frank," she said. "Do you think, Rebecca, that we would have time to stop a minute at your mother's? Not for a formal call of course, but just to run in?"

Now was not that a graceful way to put it? Be it known to you that Mrs. Alanson Edwards had never yet taken her aristocratic self to the Harlow homestead since the time that she had partaken in a dignified manner of the wedding breakfast; even her former dulled conscience had reproached her in regard to this, and she had intended at some time to go in state and call, but the time had never come; and Rebecca, while she was indignant over it, yet rejoiced in the sense of freedom with which she went and came, and in the royal way in which her husband treated his relatives, and decided that Mrs. Edwards was at liberty to do as she pleased; still it was certainly very pleasant to hear her-

self asked that question in exactly the tone that
Mrs. Edwards would have used had she been in
the habit of running in familiarly at Mrs. Harlow's side-door all the days of her life.   Mother
Harlow bustled out eagerly to greet her
daughter; it was very nice to see her alight
from such a carriage as that; the mother enjoyed
it, even though she was ignored by the grand
relations.   She paused when she saw the elder
woman getting out, somewhat in doubt as to
what to do next; Mrs. Edwards didn't leave her
in doubt.   " We have just stopped for a minute,"
she said, holding out her hand cordially, "because I knew this child wouldn't want to go
home without a peep at mother; she has been
doing penance all the afternoon, making calls
with me; this is her reward."   And the mother-
in-law gave to her an unmistakably loving smile.
Rebecca's heart beat high, many blessings were
certainly being added to her lot.   Her mother
was a woman of strong, good sense and refine-
ment of heart and feeling, else she could hardly
have brought up such a daughter as Rebecca.
It was not difficult for Mrs. Edwards, bent on
being pleasant and cordial, to find subjects for

conversation, and Mrs. Harlow sustained her part very well indeed.

"Oh! I had a little business," Mrs. Edwards said, as they arose to leave. "I had almost forgotten; we are making Christmas plans. I like to be early. We want you to come to dinner. Very socially, you know; nothing formal about it. We want a family gathering. I will drop in again or send Rebecca to tell you more about it; but I don't want you to make any other arrangements. You mustn't disappoint us. I meant to keep it as a sort of surprise for Rebecca and Frank; but I have concluded that I cannot get ready without her help, and so have had to take her into confidence. I find I need her help about most things in these days."

"She is a helpful child," mother Harlow said, proudly, her face flushed all over in the excess of her warm mother love.

"That she is," Mrs. Edwards answered, heartily; and she is in a great flutter, I dare say, to go for her husband. Rebecca, we must hasten or we shall miss him."

"We have had the most remarkable afternoon that ever was known," Rebecca explained to her husband, when they were in the privacy of her own room. "I can't think what has happened to your mother. You certainly wouldn't have known her. We have been out calling on wonderful people — the Pecks, and the Collinses, and the Martins, and she had been as gracious as a queen. What do you suppose can have started her?"

"I am not sure that she would have appeared so strange to me as she did to you," he said with feeling. "I used to know her when she had more of that spirit; when I was a little boy, I have distinct memories of visits that she used to pay with my father. They were different from anything that she has done since he died. My father was a grand man, Rebecca. I think it may be the remembrance of his spirit that has helped her in these few efforts. The producing cause, however, is doubtless the quickening of her Christian life. Grace in the heart, makes great changes in the life, you know."

At the dinner table Mrs. Edwards herself spoke of their afternoon's employment.

"It is strange," she said, "how long one's influence may last. Last night I was reading over an old letter of your father's, Frank. It was a sort of journal-letter which he used to keep for me years ago when we were young. In it he speaks of feeling greatly disturbed because he realized that there were brethren and sisters of the church whom he didn't know by name. 'I wonder,' he said, 'how I should feel if I should go to heaven and meet one of those whom I ought to have known in the church on earth, and the Lord should see that we were strangers!' Isn't that a wonderful thought? It just haunted me all night. I resolved to try to know more people. I am old to begin, but I shall try for it."

Frank looked at his wife with a significant smile.

"You and I would do well to take lessons of mother, would we not? Did you know these people on whom you called to-day?"

"Never spoke to them in my life," answered Rebecca, promptly. "I am ashamed of it."

CHAPTER XXV.

TWO WAYS OF DOING THINGS.

EANTIME, there was that trouble with Sallie Holland to haunt Rebecca's days and nights. She had been trying to take her husband's advice, and never was advice harder to follow. It was not that she could not, on her knees, in an orthodox manner use solemn and proper words of petition concerning her, but by no stretch of conscience could she make herself believe that this was praying. She had been too well taught. She felt each time as she rose from her knees as though her prayer did not rise above the ceiling, and almost it seemed to her as if it were mockery, and yet she sincerely

391

did intend it for prayer. What was the matter? Surely she wanted Sallie Holland converted. She thought she was willing to do *anything* to bring about such a result as that. She prayed for grace, to forgive her. She struggled with the wicked feelings in her heart concerning her; and at times felt as though she had conquered; and yet in no sense did she reach a state of peace. Plunge into Christmas preparations as she would — and the preparations for that festival were neither few nor meager in the Edwards' household — no amount of work had power to make her lay aside the burden of Sallie for more than an hour or two. Since their conversation together, Frank had not mentioned her name; he seemed carefully to avoid any allusion to her, which in itself almost angered Rebecca; she felt as though it would be such a relief to go over all the aggravating circumstances with him. At last she determined to break the silence and ask his advice. They had gone to their room for the night, and Rebecca was slowly pulling the pins from her hair, and trying to overcome an unaccountable dislike to commencing that subject again.

"You don't ask me any more about Sallie?" she said at last, in a half inquiring tone.

"What is there for me to ask, my dear?" he said, smiling. "I am waiting for the development of your efforts in her behalf."

"I can't make any, Frank; I don't know what to do; I cannot even pray for her. You don't know what a strange feeling it is; I cannot think that it is because I am still angry with her; I try not to be, and I don't believe I am; but it is like praying to space, and I don't know in the least what is the trouble, or how to get away from it."

"Has not your praying inclined you to go to her and have a frank talk, letting her know your feeling of anxiety for her?"

His wife regarded him with a troubled air before she answered:

"I am not in the least inclined to do so, and indeed Frank, it is more than that; it does seem to me almost impossible to go to her. It seems to me that I would be willing to do anything but that."

"Anything but that, in order that she might be a Christian, do you mean?"

She bowed her head, and he said, speaking very gently, but yet solemnly:

"Rebecca, do you think we ought to have an 'anything but that,' between the Lord and our prayers?"

This question brought the tears. He came over to her, and touched his lips to the little spot of forehead visible above the hands that covered her face, but he made no further attempt to soothe her excitement or grief, whichever it was. Her first sentence after this was a question:

"Frank, do you really think I ought to go and see her?"

"As to that, dear wife, I cannot you know, undertake to be conscience for you; I hold you entirely capable of deciding for yourself what you ought to do; only I know I have to be careful of making conditions, when it comes to a matter of prayer. It is the Lord's right to make conditions if he will; but it is not mine."

"There is certainly nothing that I could say to her except that I thought she had insulted me, and that I was trying hard to forgive her."

Frank Edwards smiled slightly.

"I am not sure that such a statement would

do her any particular good," he said, "and indeed Rebecca, I did not mean to suggest your
doing that which your own heart does not dictate,
and your conscience approve; I was simply
thinking that personal contact had much power
sometimes over hearts."

After that there was a long silence; Rebecca
went on with her hair pins, and then slowly
braided her hair and settled it for the night, her
face all the time in deep thought; her husband
had retired behind a small bank entry book, while
he waited for her, and was apparently oblivious
to anything but the row of figures before him;
yet he was ready with his answer the moment
she spoke.

"Frank, do you think it is the same as going
to see a person, if one writes a note? or, is that a
way of shirking a duty?"

"I don't know why it should be; sometimes a
note, which can be read in the quiet of one's own
room and thought over, answers a better purpose
than speech. There are many times when I
prefer to write what I have to say, and think it
the wiser course."

Before Rebecca shut her eyes in sleep that

night she knew by the heavy sense of something disagreeable that pressed upon her, that she had decided to write a note to Sallie Holland.

The question once settled, being the lady that she was, it was entirely natural that she should sit down to her writing desk directly after her husband's departure for the bank the next morning, bent on having what was a trial to accomplish, out of the way as soon as possible. But it would not get out of the way very rapidly. Rebecca, ready penman as she was, had never had so much trouble before; three times she drew the pen across the lines and secured a fresh sheet, and finally, because the morning was gone, and she was bent on sending her note before she saw Frank again, rather than that she was satisfied with it, did she hurriedly close and seal it, and dispatch a servant to the nearest lamp-post. Before that, she read it through   This is as it read:

"DEAR SALLIE:— You will be surprised, perhaps, to hear that I have been thinking of you a great deal during the last few days, thinking of, and praying for you. I do not know that anything in my manner of late, has shown my

desire for you, but I do most earnestly want to
see you a Christian; it is to this end that I have
been praying, and I mean to continue. Sallie,
don't you pray for yourself? I need not tell
you what a thing to be desired the Christian's
hope is, nor how little it compares in value with
anything else; of course you know all this as
well as I do; yet I feel as though I must tell
you of my anxiety for your welfare in this
matter. I wonder that I have not talked about
it with you, during the many times that we have
been together, you must have thought me very
cold hearted and unconcerned. I think so myself, and feel as though I ought to ask you to
forgive my apparent indifference; believe me
I am very much in earnest now.

" Your friend,

"Rebecca."

As Rebecca read this she felt that it was cold
and stiff sounding, and was almost on the point
of putting it in the grate; but for the fact that
she felt her inability to write anything better,
she would have done so; she had judged it
wisest to ignore the disturbance they had had,
because, as her husband said, it could do no

good to remind Sallie that she felt herself insulted, and what else was there for her to say? It must be confessed that she felt a slight touch of complacency over the thought that she had so far overcome her wounded feelings as to write at all; certainly Sallie would see that she was of a forgiving disposition.

"I have something to show you," she said, following Frank up-stairs when he came home to lunch; and her cheeks were glowing. Without further explanation she handed him a dainty note on tinted paper, and written with many a graceful flourish. Enclosed in it was a paper on which he recognized his wife's hand-writing; the other was Sallie's.

"MRS. FRANK EDWARDS:—I return your epistle to you with thanks, I do not know that I have any special use for it. If that is all the apology you see fit to send me for the insulting way in which you treated me the last time I was in your house, I beg leave to say that I do not want it, nor your advice, nor prayers; I can get along I dare say, without them both, valuable as they are no doubt. If you have forgotten the insolent words you spoke, and the insolent man-

ner in which you locked me out of your presence,
I have not, nor am, I likely to have it salved over
in any such ingenious way as you have devised.
Until you can treat me with decency, pray do
not trouble yourself to think about me at all;
I dare say I can even survive if you should
forget me.

"Sallie."

"What does she mean?" Mr. Edwards asked
at last, without raising his eyes from the paper.
"She certainly wasn't locked out; to what does
she have reference?" The question did not
decrease the glow on his wife's cheeks, for she
recalled the circumstance of her naughty departure, and the fact that she locked the door
after her. As she told these things to her
husband, she felt for the first time something
like shame over her part of the affair. It
undoubtedly was rude; the question was, had
she a right to be insolent because Sallie chose to
be? Her husband made no sort of reply to her
statement, further than to ask after a moment's
silence:

"Am I to read this also?" And he held up
the paper in her writing.

"Certainly," said Rebecca, "read the whole, and see whether Sallie is justified in her conclusions; it is stiff, I know, and sounds unnatural, but I could not make it any better; I spent the morning over it."

This too, he returned without comment; and when she questioned, simply said:

"Of course nothing would justify the manner in which Sallie has received your attempt; think how very sore-hearted she must be, when she can allow herself to descend to such unladylike ways. But Rebecca, as you say, your note was not quite like you; not such a note as you would have written to me, for instance, before we were engaged."

"I should think not," said Rebecca, promptly; "it is not such a note as I could have written to any of my lady friends; how am I to write as though I loved and respected Sallie, when I don't?"

"Ah, but, my dear wife, we must feel some little measure of the same love for a soul, that the Lord Jesus does when he calls after it, else how can we hope to reach it?"

This silenced Rebecca, and they went down to

dinner with grave faces. Just one more question she asked him, as he was leaving the house after dinner:

"What do you think I ought to do about it? There isn't anything that I can do, is there?"

"Yes," he said, with tender, smiling eyes. "Oh, yes there is; you can pray." Then he went.

Shut up to this resource, Rebecca struggled hard with her heart, and felt its coldness and tried to soften it. Suddenly, as if a voice from an unseen presence had spoken the words, there sounded through her brain the sentence: "If thou bring thy gift to the altar, and there rememberest that thy brother hath aught against thee, leave there thy gift before the altar, and go thy way: first, be reconciled to thy brother, and then come and offer thy gift." She arose quickly from her knees and the flush on her cheek glowed all over her face. What did it mean? What should she do? Was it possible that she ought still to seek reconciliation with Sallie? How was it to be done? Had she not tried to overlook her gross insult, and take her into friendship again, and had Sallie not rudely refused to be forgiven? If only she were the one in fault, and an apology was all that was demanded, how easily and how promptly would she make it! Just at this point she, as it were, stopped thinking, that is, her heart gave one of those sudden bounds that indicated a new and startling thought, and then, for an instant seemed to cease to beat. What if, after all, she should be the one who ought to apologize! not the *only* one, mind you; Sallie was certainly in fault, but since she could not apologize for *her*, what business had she with that part of the question? Not Sallie's conscience, but her own was the one that demanded her attention. Were the words that she spoke to Sallie just the words that were entirely right and proper to come from the mouth of a follower of the meek and lowly Jesus? Was the manner that she showed calculated to impress Sallie with the beauty of the Christian religion, and the superiority of a mind under its control? Sharp questions these; how could Rebecca, in the silence and solemnity of her own soul-questionings, answer other than nay? Then had she really dishonored her profession, sullied the fair name of Christian, put the dear Lord to an open shame? And again in bitterness of spirit her truthful answer was:

"I have."

What then? Should she not simply, and heartily say, "I am sorry; forgive me for showing you such evil fruit from the grafted tree."

Then, indeed, she discovered that what had seemed such an easy and proper duty, so long as she deemed it belonging to another, became a hard, an almost impossible task to her. But, when one's soul has solemnly put questions, and one's conscience has solemnly answered "aye," there occurs either a step forward, or a long stride backward. The soul is not to be toyed with as a plaything. It ended as that first thud of her heart had told Rebecca that it would have to end, sooner or later. She got out those writing materials again, and the note was simpler than her last. She wrote rapidly, paying little attention to the wording, and sending it out of the house directly it was done. This was the note:

"DEAR SALLIE:—Forgive me for the rude words that I spoke to you in my own room that afternoon; I was very angry or I would not have spoken as I did, nor left you as I did; this of course is no excuse, as I should not have been angry. I see that I was chiefly to blame for having given you cause to think evil of my husband's mother; she is very different from what I once supposed her to be; she is all to me that a dear mother could or should be." (Over this sentence Rebecca's pen had paused a moment, and then moved on swiftly again, while into her face there stole a tender smile as she realized that that was not too much to say; how could a mother do more than this one was doing?) "Sallie, I ought never to have told you what I did, and I ought not to have said what I did the other day; I beg you will forgive me; and let me again ask you to think about that other question. There *is* a beauty in religion, though my life does not show it. There is beauty, and power, and purity in the Lord Jesus. I want you to know *Him.*

"Your friend,   REBECCA."

The reply to this did not follow so quickly as the other had. It was not until the next day that the little errand boy from the Hollands left for her a dainty perfumed note. It ran thus:

"DEAR REBECCA:—You are a good girl;
ever so much better than I am; I'm sure I wish
I were half as good. I didn't mean to hurt your
feelings that day; in fact I never thought of
such a thing; you are more sensitive than I am,
I dare say. Well, never mind, I am not one to
bear any ill will; I shall be just the same to you
as before. And I shall be real glad to get back
on the old footing again, for to tell you the truth,
I have missed you dreadfully. Have you seen
Gracie Dennis' new dress? It is just the shade of
your green one, but it isn't half so becoming to
her as it is to you.

" In haste,   SALLIE."

Over this characteristic note, Rebecca could
but smile before she sighed. She wondered if
Frank would see how plain the " surface " was.

"I tried again, Frank," she said to him in the
evening, "and this is the result."

She did not show him her part of the correspondence this time. Sallie had not sent it back,
and besides, she did not care to show it. He
read the note carefully, thoughtfully, taking
more time than its brevity demanded. Then he

handed it back with a smile, and yet with a grave face.

"I see," he said, "that there is not much material there to build upon. Rebecca, she is a strange friend for you, nevertheless I would hold to the friendship. One can never tell when natures of this sort may be stirred ; she has depth somewhere. One of these days something will reach it. Meantime, you feel differently, do you. not ? "

He knew perfectly well what her note must have been, and could imagine the struggle. Rebecca was not by nature gifted with humility.

"Yes," she said, answering his smile with heartiness, "I find that I can pray for her now, with all my heart. I did not know what was the matter before. "

CHAPTER XXVI.

"PEACE ON EARTH, GOOD WILL TO MEN."

PREPARATIONS for that Christmas dinner went forward with speed and skill. Never was there a Christmas dinner in which Rebecca Harlow Edwards was so interested. It developed in her, feelings and fancies that surprised herself, and about which she kept silence, but marvelled much. In the first place, she had had much to say in the privacy of her own mother's home about the "state dinners" of the Edwards' household: very unnecessary, and very foolish had she considered many of the forms and ceremonies which were then carried out. But now, to her own surprise, she found that she did

407

not want one of the least necessary of them
omitted. Since it was judged proper to do thus
and so for other guests, she desired the same proprieties to be observed for her father and mother.
Another feeling surprised and bewildered her;
she pondered over it in silence, feeling no desire
to communicate it, and ask advice as to its cause.
It was all very well to call on the Pecks, and
the Collinses. She was glad that Mrs. Edwards
had done so. She honored her for it. She
would admire her still more if she should invite
those people freely to her handsome house, and
make them feel at home. But the fact remained
that she did not want them asked with her
father and mother. Since *they* were to be wel-
comed for the first time, she wanted as their fellow guests those who would do them honor. So
she watched with jealous care to discover who
were to be included in the invitations. Though
both father and mother might be overwhelmed
by some of the people who were on Mrs. Edwards' visiting list, not knowing what to say, or
how to act, still they must be sacrificed to the
eager desire to honor them. When she finally
discovered who were invited, she smiled a satis-

fied smile, and retired from her anxiety, feeling
confident that her mother-in-law understood the
situation, and was wise enough to carry out her
plans triumphantly. It transpired that Mrs. Edwards always invited her pastor to her Christmas
feast. Now as her pastor was also the pastor of
the Harlows, of course it was eminently fitting
that he should be included at this time. Besides, he was unexceptionable. Knowing how
to get himself through all the bewildering ceremonies of dining without making any blunders,
in fact, with absolute credit. And his wife, besides being thoroughly posted in all these matters, was a sunny, cheery woman, who could talk
almost with a post, "and mother is no post,"
reflected Rebecca. "She can talk as well as any
of them, if people will only talk common sense."
Besides them were Senator Parker and his wife
and widowed daughter. Now Senator Parker's
family, besides being as high in the social scale
as one could get, had also that rare quality of
common sense. So when Mrs. Edwards said :

"I don't believe we had better give any
other invitations. Just have a quiet, sensible

time together with people who can enjoy each
other ; wouldn't that be the best ? "

" Rebecca assented heartily, and drew a little
sigh of relief, wondering meanwhile whether
Mrs. Alanson Edwards was sharp enough to
detect the true metal in her father and mother,
or whether this was simply tact. Whatever it
was, it was very gracefully done, and she felt
grateful. She came down to the pretty winter
kitchen and helped with the pies, and made the
cake entirely herself, her mother-in-law remark-
ing in a satisfied tone :

"It is so nice to know that I can trust you.
To be sure you don't make cake as I do, but then
yours tastes very good indeed, and I dare say
your mother will like to eat some of your making again."

When one considered that Mrs. Edwards did
not make cake at all, but only theorized about it,
and gave what she was pleased to consider directions, this remark of hers had its exasperating
side ; but people cannot be perfect in this world ;
at least they don't seem to succeed very well,
and Rebecca's mood on this particular morning
was so sunny that she hardly noticed the cake

question at all; and the cake, as if taking the reflection of her serene mind, was never lighter or flakier. Mrs. Edwards herself pronounced it a perfect success; and Rebecca, remembering her trials in that kitchen, so short a time ago moralized on the rapidity with which scenes could change in a household. She had other cares. Mrs. Harlow had hardly spent as much thought over her dress for a life time, as her daughter Rebecca bestowed upon it for that occasion. It was a plain black silk, that had seen years of service, and was guiltless of overskirt, or puff, or ruffle, or trimmings of any sort. She had so far conformed to recent fashion, or rather to her daughter's urging, as to have a new basque waist made, and Rebecca, as she surveyed it, was secretly grateful that she had coaxed mother to go to Mrs. McBride, to have it cut. The fit was perfect.

"Mother," she said, surveying it thoughtfully, "this dress would be very handsome indeed if you had an overskirt, and the basque matches my black silk very nicely. You know that overskirt is long and plain, and if I should take out the loops and make it fit you around the waist, wouldn't you wear it just this once ? "

Whereupon Mrs. Harlow resolutely shook her head.

" No, no, child," she said, in her most positive tone; " fine feathers do not make fine birds, the old adage to the contrary notwithstanding. I should just be the old fable stepped into life : a jack daw was it that put on the peacock's feathers ? An overskirt on me ! I wonder at you, child ! Why, I shouldn't know myself, let alone you knowing me. You must just take me as I am, and don't be ashamed of your old mother because she never learned how to fix up. It is too late to begin now."

" I am not in the least ashamed of you, and never was," Rebecca said, indignantly, and she put aside the question of overskirts. But she took care to see that her mother's cap was as immaculate as pure soft laces and plenty of them could make it, and that the ruche in her neck was as soft and white as down; ruffles for the wrist, she found herself unable to compass, by reason of her mother's determined spirit; but she knew the cuffs would be immaculate in their snowy smoothness. And when among the

Christmas-eve presents, was a set of delicate sleeve buttons, small and modest looking, but of the finest gold, and on the card, the words: " For mother, from her son, Frank," what could mother Harlow do but wear them on Christmas morning, even though she "poohed" a good deal as she fumbled over them? Christmas-day proved to be cold and somewhat stormy, but they sturdily got themselves ready, this father and mother, "because," said father, as he put himself into a clean shirt, " there is no kind of use in Rebecca's knowing that we would a great deal rather sit down in our own chimney corner, and eat our roast chicken and baked potato in quietness."

" I wouldn't," mother Harlow said, speaking cheerily, " I want to go; Rebecca has gone into that house, and without fussing or complaining, or having talk of any kind, has just wound things around till she is pretty much mistress, at least Mrs. Edwards is as proud of her as she need to be ; and I for one am glad of it, and I'm willing to go and look on at the life she lives."

Mother Harlow, you see, did not know as much about things as Sallie Holland did;

gossiping tongues had taken care to be very silent in her presence.

As for Rebecca, she worried a little over the snow, fearing that her mother's rheumatic ankles might be the worse for her walk, to and from a street car; and she meditated asking Frank as to the wisdom of getting up his ponies and going for her; she had not mentioned it yet however when Mrs. Edwards said at the late breakfast table:

"Frank, you will see that Lewis gets started in ample time for our guests, will you? and have him go for Rebecca's folks first, as they belong to the family; we shall want them to get nicely warmed, and feeling comfortable, before the others come."

Rebecca's anxieties suddenly left her, while she reflected that she had not yet learned all the privileges and comforts of being wealthy. Then there was a most loving side to that sentence; with what infinite ease and naturalness had she said: "as *they* belong to the family." It had taken Mrs. Alanson Edwards a good while to realize that they so belonged, but Rebecca, in her gratitude over the present gracious state of

things, resolved to ignore this, and all other
unpleasantnesses that had ever been, and give
herself up to the *pleasures* that surrounded her.

What a very nice dinner party it was! Of
course the dinner was perfect; there was absolutely nothing to mar the beauty and comfort of
the feast, and the guests had certainly been well
chosen.   Rebecca, as she helped her mother
emerge from the great cloak that had protected
her from the snow, and saw the effect of soft lace
and snowy cuffs, and placid face, and motherly
grey eyes, shining under her bands of hair that
were silvering fast, felt that she was every inch
a lady.   And behold, there was a thing occurred
to bring a heightened glow to her face, partly
the result of pleasure, and partly a tribute to the
better taste of her mother, for when Mrs. Senator
Parker arrived, and had shaken out her drapery,
and made her way into the parlors, she was
dressed in a long, plain black silk, without ruffle
or pleat, without overskirt or loop of any sort;
and Rebecca, glancing from her to her mother,
admitted that for old ladies it was certainly a
becoming way to dress.   Here is a question for
your deliberation.   Would she have felt certain

that this was the case, had Mrs. Senator Parker
been attired in the height of the fashion? For
her father, Rebecca had felt no anxiety; who
expected anything of old gentlemen in the way
of dress but to be in clean linen, and shining
boots, and with well brushed clothes? All
these were part of her father's daily life, and
there was nothing but satisfaction expressed in
the swift critical glance that she gave him.
What nice people they all were! They wel-
comed father and mother Harlow to the circle
exactly as though they had taken their Christmas
dinner in that house, or one equally well appointed, all their lives. Mrs. Alanson Edwards
was almost affectionate in her greeting, and
when Frank came, and in his gracious way,
made the rounds of the parlor, halting at her
mother's side and speaking the word "mother"
loud enough for everyone to hear, and when, as
a moment after, as her father drew away from the
fire, he wheeled out the great easy chair
from the corner with the words, "take this
chair, father," Rebecca felt that her sense of
comfort was complete. The feeling arose to the
realm of positive pride during the dinner-table

talk; it centred on a topic of public, and just
then, of absorbing interest; and Rebecca, who
had wondered whether her father would be
interested, and feel enough at home to join, was
both surprised and gratified to see the eager
way in which he threw himself into the discussion, and the gradual air of interest which
spread over the face of the Senator, as he
listened to her father's views; at last there was
almost deference in the way in which he was
appealed to, and his opinions sought. Not even
the Minister was so well posted.

"Your father is a capital talker," Frank took
occasion to say to her in the course of the day;
"I haven't met a man this season so thoroughly
posted in regard to this new movement. Senator Parker says he has a remarkably clear
brain."

"He has a remarkably good heart," said Rebecca, with pride, "and this subject appeals to
it." But she was very glad that Senator Parker
thought him clear brained.

As for mother Harlow, it transpired that both
the minister's wife and the Mrs. Senator, were
specially interested in a case of trial, and great

need, that had recently been brought to their notice, and in their kind attempt to explain the
subject of their conversation to her, it appeared
that she was thoroughly posted, much more so
indeed than they were themselves, having known
the woman for a long time, and having faithfully
ministered to her during the fall and early winter.   From trying to give information, they
turned listeners, and questioners.   Mother Harlow knew who the woman was in her girlhood,
and the pleasant country home from which she
had come, the peculiar and pitiful circumstances
connected with her early womanhood, the story
of her repeated attempts at earning a living for
herself and child, and her bitter failures.   There
was no question suggesting itself to these eager,
sympathetic hearts that mother Harlow, out of
the knowledge won by patient, sympathetic
ministering, could not answer.   And Rebecca,
listening, felt rather than heard the tone of respect with which Mrs. Parker presently said :

"Indeed, Mrs. Harlow, I think you have been
doing all alone, and quietly, a work of which an
angel might be proud."

"I," said Mrs. Harlow, brought suddenly

back to self. "Why, bless you, I haven't done anything but give the poor creature a trifle here and there as I could spare it, and a word of sympathy. Poor thing! Words don't cost much, you know. Oh, I haven't done anything; there is plenty to do."

"It is that very unconsciousness which might increase an angel's pride."

This, Mrs. Waterman, the widowed daughter, said in an undertone to Rebecca, and her eyes glistened as she spoke. Mother Harlow didn't understand what she meant, but Rebecca did, and felt that she should love Mrs. Waterman after this.

Altogether the day was a complete success. Each one forgot that he, or she, was in a sort of new atmosphere expected to assimilate forces that were not used to being assimilated. They just gave themselves up to the pleasures of a good, cheery, social time, closing the day with a hymn in which both father and mother Harlow joined, and with a prayer which brought tears to the eyes of old and young.

"Your father is just a splendid man!" Mrs. Edwards said when they were alone; Frank having accompanied the father and mother home in the carriage. "I wonder you haven't told me more about him."

Rebecca had never mentioned his name in her presence, and would not have thought of such a thing as interesting her by so doing. Mrs. Edwards continued:

"How wonderfully well preserved your mother is for a woman of her age. I think you will look like her when you are old. And be like her in some respects I dare say; she is worthy of being copied. She has done a great deal of good; and she tells me she has had little to do it with."

And then Mrs. Edwards sighed, a gentle little sigh; she was beginning to realize that she had been an unworthy steward. That there were those who, with one talent, had accomplished more than she with her ten.

Frank was jubilant over the day. They talked the whole thing over that evening together, he and Rebecca.

"I tell you, Rebecca," he said, "I always knew in a vague sort of way that my mother felt and thought above these fashionable ruts into which she had fallen; I was always wishing she could be gotten out; but I didn't know how to set about it. In fact, I was there myself, and not in a condition to help anybody out. But only see what an improvement this day has been! Look at the conversations we have had together, instead of the stuff that it is generally, though proper to talk on such occasions! Now I think of it; I don't believe we have ever .gotten two sensible people together in our house before, though we have generally managed to have one."

"Because you were generally here, do you mean?" Rebecca asked saucily, breaking in on his thoughtful mood.

"You understand me." he said, laughing. "I tell you, dear wife, there has been a great change in this house since you came to it; rather it has changed back to its normal atmosphere. It is coming nearer to what it was in my rather's time, and you darling are the cause of the change.

"How ignorant people are about themselves," Rebecca said, her eyes glistening the while. "Now you don't seem to know what is as clear to me as the sunlight: that both you and your mother have taken a great stride forward in the Christian life; and what you attribute to me, is just the grace of God in your own hearts."

"God forbid that I should doubt it," he said, with unusual emotion. "Indeed, the Christian life is more to me in every sense than I ever imagined it could be to any one; and the way grows clearer with each step; and I believe, as you say, that my mother has begun to drink of its fulness; but it is my precious wife, with her consistent, patient, pains-taking Christian life and Christian forgiveness that has shown us the heights; we will try to climb them now together, and to thank God for his gifts."

And then the mother came up, as had been her custom of late, to the pretty room, and together they sang the old Christmas anthem: "Glory to God in the highest, and on earth, peace, good will to men." And then they bowed in prayer together; thanking God for each other, and for home, and for *himself* revealed in Christ Jesus the Lord.

THE END,

Thirty-fifth Thousand. Crown 8vo, cloth, elegantly bound. 5s. With Steel Portrait.

FROM LOG CABIN
TO WHITE HOUSE.

The Story of President Garfield's Life.

By W. M. THAYER, Author of " The Pioneer Boy, and how he became President," " Tact, Push and Principle," etc.

CONTENTS.

First day at School—Before School Days—Getting on—Trials and Triumphs—Boy Farmer—Sunday in the Woods—Higher up—Boy Carpenter—Barn-building—A Black Salter—A Wood Chopper—A Canal Boy—Triumphs on the Tow-path—The Turning Point—Geauga Seminary—After Vacation —Keeping School—Third Year at School—The Eclectic Institute—Student and Teacher—In College —Return to Hiram—Top of the Ladder—Incidents of his Manhood—Maxims and Sayings—From the White House to the Grave.

"The Author has acquainted himself, evidently by dint of careful research, with the facts of Garfield's early life; he has collected a great number of incidents which throw light on the character of the President, and furnish the explanation of his success in everything he has attempted; and these materials Mr. Thayer has worked up into a most interesting volume. To most young people the book will be as attractive as any tale of adventure, while their seniors will find it contains a thoroughly trustworthy account of Garfield's career up to the time when he began to play an important part in public affairs."—*Scotsman.*

LONDON: HODDER & STOUGHTON, 27, PATERNOSTER ROW,

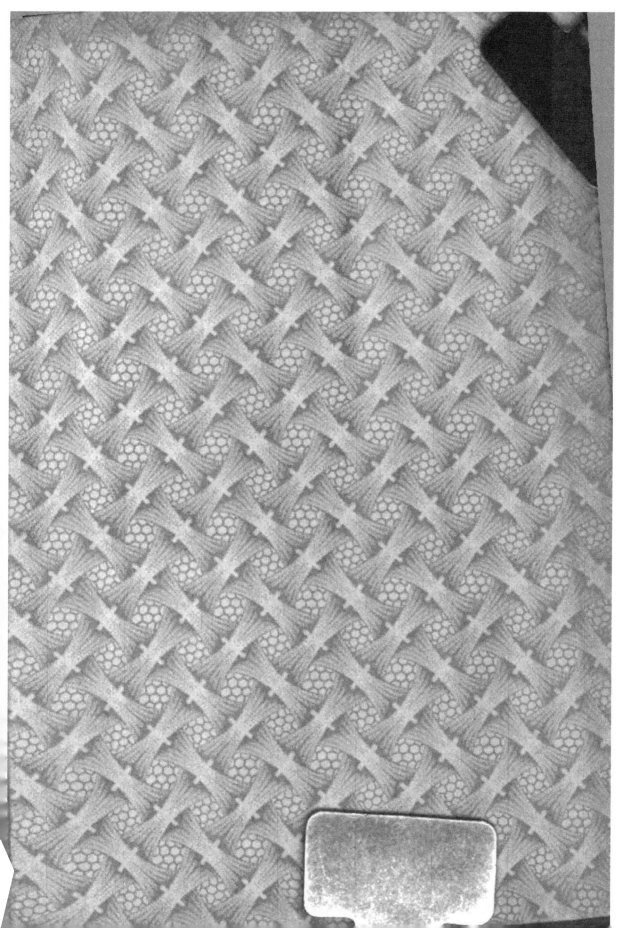

Lightning Source UK Ltd.
Milton Keynes UK
UKHW031545150822
407326UK00007B/1609